Subconscious Demons
And
Conscious Delights

iUniverse, Inc.
New York   Bloomington

Subconscious Demons and Conscious Delights

iUniverse books may be ordered through booksellers or by contacting:

iUniverse
1663 Liberty Drive
Bloomington, IN 47403
www.iuniverse.com
1-800-Authors (1-800-288-4677)

ISBN: 978-1-4401-5360-0 (soft)
ISBN: 978-1-4401-5361-7 (ebook)

Printed in the United States of America

iUniverse rev. date: 6/26/2009

Subconscious Demons

And

Conscious Delights

VOLUME V

BY: TODD ANDREW ROHRER

I dedicate this diary entry to Lily Allen, Cindy Lauper, Jill Bolte Taylor, Madonna, Sheryl Crow, Lisa Randall, Joan of Arc, Cleopatra, Helen of Troy, Marie Curie, and the lemur monkey.

The angel you fear is the angel that steers.

This is a reader note:

I perceive because of this accident I can write words that will enable one who is not subconscious dominate to become subconscious dominate. I am going to write sentences and some will anger or upset you. When that happens, feel that emotion and pause before reading again in order to let that emotion to dissipate. If you read something that makes you feel very good or arrogant, feel that emotion and stop reading for a moment until that emotion passes. If you read something that is funny or you understand it and you feel laugher that is okay to enjoy. So I am telling you up front, I am only writing what I write as a mental conditioning tool because I am in extreme subconscious dominate state of mind. When you finish the book the cycle in your mind will have been started and it will take perhaps 4 to 5 months for you to be fully aware of it. Good luck you will certainly need it.

I perceive:

I will start by labeling the volumes as I see them from what I recall in relation to the emotions and clarity contrast since the accident.

Volume 1 was very reserved and very careful.

Volume 2 was extremely long and the emotions were under control

Volume 3 the emotions were growing in relation to the clarity.

Volume 4 was a disaster and emotions were out of control.

Volume 5 the emotions are way out of control but the clarity is also stronger.

The emotions appear to be extremely deep seeded and thus very strong when they do arise. I could very easily censor them but that would simply defeat the whole purpose of keeping an accurate diary of my mental state on a daily basis. Think about all of your deep seeded secrets and dark secrets and imagine if they were all thrown to your conscious state. Where would you hide them then? They would no longer be deep seeded secrets they would be mentally out in open at all times. So one might suggest I am rather strange in my words and I am not shy or self conscious or worried about what I say. Much like a child says wise things beyond their years and if it is an improper thing to say they are not aware of it. Some in nirvana of no sense of time suggest one must have compassion on the ones who are not in nirvana but I am uncertain what compassion is. Perhaps they are suggesting I should lie but I am far too foolish to be able to achieve that at this stage of the accident. Perhaps I will be able to lie to you before to many more books.

The way I perceive the mental states at this stage is, when one is conscious dominate or emotional dominate their clarity is not very great and their emotions are not very great, so they are able to mask them both well. Then when one goes subconscious dominate the clarity is extreme and thus the emotions are extreme. The catch is subconscious dominate means one is strictly cerebral and not physically orientated, so my anger is strictly mental not physical based.

I am harmless on a physical level but I tend to go on some very dark mental journeys.

One might suggest my mental demons kick my ass on a regular basis at this point since the accident but I am pleased to announce I almost won once.

You do not have to try to be perfect you just have to get use to the fact you are.

Understanding you are perfect takes quite an imagination.

Conquering the universe with a word requires epic concentration.

It is okay to defend your honor, but understand you will lose your grace if you do.

Even the greatest lion must face its eventual isolation from his pride.

People keep secrets in an effort to wield leverage.

You are supposed to want to be like yourself.

"The term subconscious is used in many different contexts and has no single or precise definition. This greatly limits its significance as a meaning-bearing concept, and in consequence the word tends to be avoided in academic and scientific settings."

http://www.absoluteastronomy.com/topics/Subconscious

Subconscious is dominate when the mind has diminished some senses to enable other senses. The diminished senses include sense of time, sense of taste, sense of touch or pain and sense of hunger and thirst. The heightened senses are feeling through vision and extreme concentration. This dominate subconscious state is achieved through emotional conditioning, such as facing ones fears, conditioning away from attachments such as cravings and desires for a short periods of time. Some verbal emotional conditioning techniques are also effective, such as using the word perhaps and maybe, often, and putting one's self in humiliating situations to condition away from the emotions embarrassment and shyness.

The subconscious aspect of the mind is the part of the mind that tells a fireman to run back into a burning building to make sure there are no people he may have missed. The subconscious aspect of the mind is the part of the mind that tells a soldier to charge the enemy when the bullets are flying all around him because it is tired of watching his friends get mowed down. The subconscious aspect of the mind is the part of the mind that told the Chinese guy to stand in front of that tank in Tiananmen Square. The subconscious aspect of the mind told Washington he should fight the British even though he had no chance to win on paper. The subconscious aspect of the mind is the part of the mind that determines it is better to dive into the hottest coals of the unknown than rest on the shores of safety.

"People who rely more heavily on the right half of their brain tend to be more imaginative and intuitive. They see things as a whole and are interested in patterns, shapes and sizes. The right brain is associated with artistic ability like singing, painting, writing poetry, etc. Left-brain dominated people may find their thought processes vague and difficult to follow, for they are quite opposite in the way they think."

http://www.indiaparenting.com/raisingchild/data/raisingchild060.shtml

An easy way to look at it is a left brain dominate person is troubled when they are not safe. A right brain dominate person is not as troubled by loss of safety. These states of mind are not set in stone. One is able to condition their mind into either state. Facing fear such as fear of dying can enable one to leave the realm of safety of the left brain aspect and transform into a right brain dominate. Facing death is an extreme because there are many things people fear such as words or ideals or how they look that work just as well as conditioning factors. Ones who reach extreme right brain dominate reach what is known as nirvana. Some suggest they are enlightened but in reality they are just very different from ones who are left brain dominate or they are alien in contrast to ones that are left brain dominate.

Each state is typically the reverse of the other state. I prefer to suggest I am subconscious dominate because I am uneducated and never really amounted too much, and now I understand everything I read easily, since the accident, so to me, right brain dominate term does not cut the mustard for me.

To me it is not logical that I would have such a difficult time dealing with the world and information and understanding religion and science and politics and then take a handful of pills and believe I was going to die and not seek help and wake up the next day and within 9 months of that I understand everything about everything I read. To me it does not gel to suggest I just went right brain dominate and now everything makes perfect sense. So something is odd here, outside of me of course.

I fight with all of my might to stay in the realms of science and psychology. I try to avoid the religious and spiritual connotations because that kind of thinking may lead me to understand I made a promise I will regret forever. I may quote some religious texts but that is because I see wisdom in everything, or I see everything as one thing. One way to look at it is I lost my ability to label things. I try to keep everything under the heading of psychology.

"For instance, right brain dominated people are often poor spellers as they tend to rely more on their intuition rather than actually studying the order in which the letters in a word occur."

http://www.indiaparenting.com/raisingchild/data/raisingchild060.shtml

I am much better at spelling in this fifth book than I was in previous books but I am not able to use commas properly

2

and my sentences tend to be very messed up in relation to the order I put the words and I am unable to determine where to break paragraphs. From my perspective it does not really matter because two months after the accident I decided to write infinite books. I do not recall I have to write proper books or wise books or books that are accepted by the norms of society, I just have to write infinite books. This left brain and right brain ideal explains clearly how this "light and dark" concept in religion was brought about. Extreme right brained people become cerebral and in turn lose the physical or material focus. The left brain aspect is more physical based and less cerebral. The left brain physical dominate aspect is the majority simply because the no sense of time cerebral aspect is somewhat difficult to achieve. Thus the religious comment "they are like the grains of sand in the sea". This is in direction relation to why there are so many physical wars and physically violent people. It is not in relation to some spiritual hocus pocus, it is simply being left brain physical focused is the norm and the extreme right brain cerebral focus is perhaps a rarity. So there is simply this "us and them" or "good and bad" mentality. Ones who are left brained and physically based in contrast to ones who are extreme right brained dominate and strictly cerebral are evil. But this works both ways because the extreme right brain beings cannot communicate properly to the left brain beings simply because they are at opposite ends of perception. One perceives a very physical existence and one perceives a very cerebral or "spiritual" or intangible existence. One see's limits and labels, and one see's infinity and everything being one thing. "They see things as a whole". So there is this behind the scenes epic struggle that has been going on for thousands of years. So anyone who is religious and has a strong sense of time is what all the western religious texts call the "darkness". There is no question in my mind about that, but it is not in relation to demons or spirits it is in relation to the psychology which is left brain beings tend to be more physically or materialistically motivated and thus subscribe to labels and these labels cause the mental isolation. So the bottom line of this is one can use some basic psychological emotional conditioning techniques to enter this right brain extreme where they will perceive reality differently. But it is not a good or bad thing if they do not or they do. It is simply an option one has a choice to make. Both types of people left and right brain are required for a harmony in civilization. So if one is religious and they deem they understand what is evil or what is bad or good and they have a strong sense of time and strong hunger they perhaps should take a long look around before they start throwing stones. The struggle is the cerebral ones are not allowed or prone to ever use physical weapons to win this struggle in general so they can never win. This is their nature but that is not cut in stone but that is a generalization. My understanding since the accident is to attempt to do my part in the battle using infinite books but I also understand I will never achieve much. That is right up my alley because I prefer battles I can never win. So when you see words of anger and rage in this book or any of my books please be mindful I am writing infinite books with the understanding they will not do affect the outcome of the battle. Please be mindful every time I type a word I am reminded I am engaged in infinite vanity and it rips my being apart.

Right Brain Dominate = Near Subconscious dominate

Extreme Right Brain Dominate = Extreme Subconscious Dominate = Nirvana

Left Brain Dominate = Conscious Emotional Dominate

Extreme Left Brain Dominate = Extreme Conscious Emotional Dominate = Emotional Wreck

This book is written by a being that is in an extreme subconscious state of mind. That means this book is written in strictly random access thought patterns. Completing this book will start a mental cycle that will lead anyone who completes the book to go from sequential strong sense of time based thoughts to random access slight sense of time based thoughts.

Skip around because the book is not in sequential order.

"Psi (uppercase Ψ, lowercase ψ) is the 23rd letter of the Greek alphabet and has a numeric value of 700.The letter psi is commonly used in physics for representing a wavefunction in quantum mechanics Psi is also used as the symbol for the polygamma function, defined by where Γ(x) is the gamma function. The letters Ψ or ψ can also be a symbol for: psychology, psychiatry, and sometimes parapsychology" WIKIPEDIA.COM

In physics PSI represents wavefunction. In the polygamma function there is a gamma function numerical function.

"A gamma wave is a pattern of brain waves, associated with perception, consciousness and concentration on a particular object or activity." WIKIPEDIA.COM

On my EEG test two months after I lost my sense of time my gamma waves were just slightly elevated yet still within normal limits. That slight elevation in my gamma waves, caused me to have extreme concentration, perception, and a change in consciousness. One might suggest it is heightened awareness. I understand I went extreme subconscious dominate or extreme right brain dominate. I understand by conditioning away from desires and cravings as the result of playing a video game to an extreme but I understand that video game situation was 4 months after my final suicide attempt. I accidentally became "meek shall inherit the earth (subconscious)", "turned the other cheek (on emotions)", Submitted to blocking(Wrath) emotions, avoided attachments to avoid suffering to reached mental clarity.

Please make your own determinations in relations to what happened to me because I am extremely biased about what exactly happened. One might suggest I tripped over the fountain of youth and fell right into it.

Some do the right thing by going about it the wrong way.

You're something and you're never going to be something else,

5/1/2009 6:06:06 AM

Behind every tragic accident is a perfect understanding.

Having a mind is difficult enough; mastering it is out of the question.

Finding a mind is rare enough; controlling it is not possible.

The mind controls your thoughts; ones goal is to controls its thoughts.

Behind every patient is a psychologist attempting to work things out.

Fits of rage usually result from a moment of clarity.

It's easy to let go once you understand you cannot control.

The hardest part of anything is understanding it is simple.

Detecting truth takes a good eye; detecting lies takes a good ear.

Mastering life requires much questioning of what one is thinking of doing.

Every sentence in this book relates to psychology except this one.

Trained psychologists make difficult patients.

Saying what you meant to say takes extreme diligence and a touch of madness.

A sentence of hate creates a book full of regret.

An epic mental struggle cannot begin without a doubt.

When one loses a mental struggle they often win understanding.

4

Understanding men is much easier than understanding why women tolerate them.

A good psychologist can help everyone but their self.

Behind every safe bet is often a harsh reality.

I may never buy your argument but I would consider it.

My goal is to keep my diary in a format of how I progress from a mental perspective in adjusting to becoming subconscious dominate. I perceive everything I write may be of value further down the road.

 One way to look at Extreme Subconscious dominate is heightened awareness. Of course that is misleading also. It is more accurate to suggest they are conscious beings.

 A conscious being is not fooled as much by mental delusions such as hunger, hate, evil, love, enemies, fear, paranoia, cravings, desires and thirst. Evil is relative to the observer. Hate is relative to the observer. Love is relative to the observer. What this means is a being who perceives evil is unconscious because they are under the influence and manipulated by delusions created in their emotional mind to a point they are literally delusional and believing those delusions.

 A being who hates to the point they actually act out in reality in a physical manner is an insane being who is acting on their delusions. This being perceives an evil and then hates it in their mind, and then goes as far as acting in a physical manner to bring physical harm to that being they perceive is evil. So they are the textbook definition of one in full psychosis.

 The beings in psychosis perceive they must correct an evil they perceive, in a physical harmful way. It is healthy to suggest opinions with words and fight wars in your mind against things you perceive are evil, but no matter who you are, once you start acting in a physical harmful ways towards these perceived evil hallucinations created in your mind, you are officially considered an insane delusional being in full psychosis that is a threat to yourself and those around you.

 If you want to find out if you are unconscious mindfully and delusional mindfully, do not eat for one day and if you get hungry and feel weak from not eating, you pass that test. That is all one has to do to find out if they are under the influence of extreme emotions. All beings have emotions but the beings with silenced emotions are ones with subconscious dominate minds and are not as prone to delusions caused by the influence of extreme emotions. There are also many complex clarifications that need to be made about these emotions.

 I tend to not be able to stay on topic very well at this stage of the accident. I tend to repeat myself at times because my short term memory is altered drastically.

Two months after the accident I decided to see if I can write infinite books in my lifetime. I threw down a gauntlet and nothing else matters, even me.

Please do not attempt to acknowledge me or my books or suggest they are good books or bad books because that will only convince me I need to write the books faster. One might suggest that is a request from my blood soaked fingers.

I am trapped in some sort of mental progression. I simply cannot stop it, although I have tried. Do not assume at any time my writings are suggesting I am better than anyone else. I had an accident which denotes I did not ask for this to happen. Do not assume I am ever suggesting I am better than you because in reality I am cursed, or my fate has been sealed by this accident. I am cursed because the extreme clarity has one serious side effect, extreme mental anguish caused by the extreme understanding. I look at beings and only feel perfection caused by this telepathy aspect and then I read in the news they are killing each other for money and stupid reasons and it rips my being apart and I just want to escape this understanding. Then this subconscious aspect reminds me I decided to write infinite books two months after the accident and I should write about that in my book, and I am fully aware I will simply come to further understandings that will lead to further anguish and gnashing of teeth. Then I realize my fate has been sealed.

I am not worried about your fate because I am too busy attempting to deny mine. I cannot harm you because I am too focused on exterminating myself. I hate the clarity because it only leads to me loving the gnashing of teeth that follows it. All I know is I am only seven months into this accident and I cannot take any more mental torment. A stone can throw itself at others so try moving that stone with your mind and you will understand self control.

The trick about humanity is: Everyone learned everything from the ones who came before them, so the very first humans only knew nothingness.

I talk myself into awkward positions but always end up talking myself into a more awkward positions.

You have a subconscious and when it is dominate you will see, we are all very powerful mentally speaking. The mentally clarity is great and the telepathy is out of this world.

I am subconscious dominate so in order for one with a sense of time or one who has pronounced hunger to understand this diary they have to consider the opposite meanings to the sentences. Conscious or Emotional dominate beings have a strong sense of time so subconscious dominate beings have the reverse, altered sense of time. Conscious dominate beings have hunger or cravings to eat, subconscious dominate beings do not have this "I need to eat because I am feeling weak" aspect at all. So everything is nearly the reverse.

I will discuss my definition of infinite patience. Perhaps it is when a being writes a 100,000 plus word book and is unable to remember what they even wrote because they had an accident and it eliminated their short term memory in order to increased their long term memory and altered their gamma waves in their brain, which affect perception, so they are literally unable tell if the sentences are "right" or "wrong". And perhaps that being wants to just give up and stop writing but they are compelled to keep writing into infinity. I guess the lesson of the situation I am in is perhaps: Do the best you can and if people do not like it, ignore them. I am still mentally adjusting to the new mindset. So perhaps that leads up to the lesson: The problems one adapts to swiftly are perhaps not problems but only obstacles they swiftly overcame.

Perhaps the lessons one learns in life are not important if they are not applied diligently.

Perhaps my lack of literary mastery is made up for by the fact I can pump out a book of 100k words in 30 days or less.

This is a psychological look at democracy,

Perhaps the truth of democracy is every single person who is able to vote, should vote for their self in every single election and runoff election. Perhaps this way a government will never be elected. Perhaps any being who votes for another being is simply saying "I am not at a level of understanding my opinion is as valuable as any other beings."

Perhaps every being over 18 is allowed to vote but the moment they do not vote for their self they become a sheep because they give away their freedom to vote for their self and thus think for their self and thus decide for their self. Perhaps no matter who you are, I perhaps have full faith that you are able to make just as good of decisions as perhaps the ones in elected office can. I perhaps have full faith no matter who you are, you perhaps cannot possibly make worse decisions than the ones in elected office do. I perhaps have full faith that you being in elected office is as good as anyone who is in elected office. I also have full faith I can make just as good decisions as anyone in elected office can. I also have full faith I cannot make worse decisions than ones in elected office do. This way the ones who vote for others instead of their self would be only saying they have no faith in their own abilities. I do not vote at all because I already know who won my election.

Washington suggested everyone is equal which means everyone should vote for their self in any election unless they believe they are not equal, and in that case they have what is psychologically called, self doubt or a form of depression. They look at their self as less than others. They are in a sense a racist against their self, simply because Washington said you are equal to everyone else period. No one is more or less than anyone else. So why would you vote for anyone but yourself in an election, unless you have a low personal outlook about yourself. You vote for yourself and allow the ones with low self esteem to be lead like sheep. If Washington suggested you are as important as everyone else, you should take his advice because he was wise. It is wise to take the advice of one who is wise. An election is not about picking one who will herd the sheep next. An election is about voting for the one you think is wisest. If you do not think you are the wisest person you know, you have serious self esteem problems, serious self doubt and serious mental issues, period. Wisdom is strictly relative to the observer or each individual. You are the only one you will ever have, so you should like yourself enough to vote for yourself in any election. It is called a write in vote, and it is there for a reason. It is there to see who has emotional self doubt problems and who does not.

If I voted, I would vote for you if I didn't always vote for me.

"In 1862, in order to support the Civil War effort, Congress enacted the nation's first income tax law. It was a forerunner of our modern income tax in that it was based on the principles of graduated, or progressive, taxation and of withholding income at the source." http://www.infoplease.com

In 1862 voters who where were voted into congress passed a law based on loss of security. In relation to "Those who give up liberty for a little security deserve neither." So Congress in one way or another convinced voters, that is was best to pass a law to make people give their money to the government so they would be safe from the South. That is what terrorism is. A terrorist will make you do things based on a promise of fear or insecurity. So Congress said, "We will lose this war if you do not give us tax money and you will all die." That's a threat. That is a scare tactic. So in 1862 people voted to give your money to the government. Now in 2009 you are giving your money to the government based on a fear tactic used in 1862. The government is also voters. So the problem is the voters who are in government also hang their self. The voters in Congress voted to give their own offspring's money to the government apparently until the end of time. And they did it in 1862. So for the rest of eternity we have to give our money to the government in the form of taxes because of a single vote taken in 1862 based on fear and loss of security, to save liberty (life). We simply did exactly what Franklin warned against. We gave up tax money of our own hard earned money to save ourselves from this certain threat. We gave up liberty for a little security and now we are in a tyranny. And at least as far as taxes, it factually happened in 1862.

Now certainly some will argue they would die instantly if it wasn't for the government because they have given up on their freedom, and prefer to allow others to make their decisions for them because they do not trust their own ability to make decisions for their self. I find no argument with that and I do not blame them. But the point is, the government only makes it harder for people. Without a government then you keep all you tax money. If a road needs to be repaired ones who wish it to be repaired repair it. If an army needs to be raised the citizens will see to it, but it will not be raised unless there is a threat to the nation, not some far off colony or empire building scheme.

The army is raised after the country is invaded not before, because if it raised before, that standing army will simply look for a war to justify itself. I am certain people would say that sounds crazy and scary. What I understand is crazy and scary is a group of men that lived over 140 years ago signed away a good portion of my income for the rest of my life. That is much more scary and crazy. There are no governments in the world that would consider invading a land where people can grab guns and be armed in about 1 hour. The army they would need to invade America would have to at least be 600 million strong to stand a chance because we have home field advantage. This whole separation of the military from civilians is improper. The military are civilians first. Every weapon and gun the military owns is mine and yours first for foremost. We paid for it and it is ours. It is not the militaries. It never will be. Everything in the country is the voters property not the governments. The government is a byproduct of ignorant decisions and ignorant votes cast hundreds of years ago. The government is unable to make a good decision. They are biased. They are only thinking about making their self stronger and that means the voters have to get weaker. That is what the checks and balances are about.

The government's very nature leans towards a dictatorship over the voters. The government is supposed to tell the voters they should give the government more money. The voters are supposed to tell the government tough crap, we will take liberty over security every time. Of course apparently many voters today perceive Ben Franklin was an idiot because he lived 200 years ago and he certainly could not have been as intelligent as we are in our luxurious dictatorship.

So it will come down to a point in time when the government will come out and say if you give us your soul, and the soul of everyone who comes after you, we will make sure this being, we have determined is your enemy, will be kept at bay. And that is what happened in 1862. And there was one being who summed it up clearly, what he would do if such a thing happened. He said "Give me liberty or give me death." His comment to the government, if it ever tried to blackmail him with fake threats and stupid reasons to sign away his soul and his offspring's soul was to kill himself indirectly or directly. So his answer to "Pass the patriot act so we can be safe." was "I will take my chances with not being safe because I have a mind and can avoid danger without having some dictator watching my back."

The patriot act gave the government power to spy on the voters. The government does not care about the Taliban. The Taliban is not a threat to the government, the voters are. But the reality is, voters keep giving the government more money and more power while the voters lose more money and more power. Perhaps the founding fathers knew we would vote ourselves into a noose and we have.

We cannot get out of that noose now. The government is to strong and if you try to get out they will say you're are a terrorist and lock you up or kill you. And we did that, but more importantly you did that to me because I have never voted in my life ever. So no matter what you want to say. I am your fellow citizen and you screwed me over, to do the governments bidding, so you are a threat to my liberty and my freedom now.

No vote is going to get you out of it now. No vote is going to get me out of it now. We are in a tyranny and there is nothing left to do but pray for a swift death and hope to god the founding fathers are not awaiting us for ruining their country when we die. I certainly hope there is not an afterlife. Washington is going to ask you us thing. "Why did you vote away your freedom for a little security and ruin my creation." And those who voted are going to say "I didn't know." And that will be the last thing they will say in the afterlife.

The truth is, Washington sacrificed everything he had and put everything he worked for on the line to get this land of the free going. That might not mean much to you but I am certain it meant a lot to Washington. You took his beautiful painting and spit on it. The problem with that is, from what I hear, Washington was a bad ass. Ask the British how dangerous Washington was. He lost nearly every confrontation with the British and never blinked. Washington was outnumbered and outgunned in nearly every battle and he annihilated the British at the end of the day. I am certain you cannot do something like that but I am certain by voting your freedom away for "security" you pissed off the guy who gave you that freedom.

Maybe there is no afterlife and you have nothing to worry about, but the problem is, you do not know that for a fact. Maybe you better keep thinking everyone forgives and forgets, maybe you better pray to your god with all of your might there is no afterlife, and if there is an afterlife everyone is happy and nonviolent. My answer to Washington is "I never voted and one day I woke up and found out that was the best thing I ever did in my life." and he will say "I will pass over you."

"Government is not reason; it is not eloquent; it is force. Like fire, it is a dangerous servant and a fearful master."
George Washington

Now this is the same Washington that is the founder of our country so if he was alive right now and said this he would be deemed a terrorist and probably killed because of the patriot act, and so if he was here today, you would vote to kill him and then brag to your friends how wise you are. That is just a slight indication of what you are going to face, when you pass on I assure you of that. I might not be sure about anything, but I am nearly positive Washington is looking forward to meeting ones who vote.

Here is one definition of reason: sound judgment; good sense.

Washington said the government has no sound judgment and no good sense. So Washington said the government has unsound reasoning skills and bad sense or bad common sense or is illogical in its conclusions. So that is saying the government cannot be trusted to make decisions. You do not have to remind me we need a government to function, because I am already aware to sold your soul to the government, and your children's soul, and all voters that come after you. I am aware you are a slave's and you are unable to make sound judgments on your own so you decided to vote and let the government make "unsound judgments for you." You are unable to make good sense so you voted to allow the government to make bad sense for you. What you have done is a symptom your mind is operating with the conscious emotional aspect, dominate. Translated; "You do harmful things and make harmful decisions because you get scared easy." Fear is an emotion one should be mindful to condition their self away from.

Here is a fun definition of reason: normal or sound powers of mind; sanity.

So now if Washington was here he would be saying the government is insanity.

"Government is not reason"

 And then you would pass the patriot act and make sure the government killed him for saying that because certainly he would be a terrorist if he said that. So now you have killed Washington twice and that is just by passing or voting to allow others to pass the patriot act for you.

So now here is another definition of reason: the mental powers concerned with forming conclusions, judgments, or inferences.

So Washington said the government does not have the mental power to form conclusions , judgments or inferences, meaning, the government only has one goal, which is to convince the voters to give them everything they have including money, their offspring, their home, their land, their soul.

The government will take everything you have, and then pass a law that makes you a terrorist if you say anything about it, and then make the others voters kill you. The government wants everything. You no longer matter, your children do not matter, and the generations that come after you do not matter. You are just simply a slave and are simply too blind to see it. I am not a slave because I do not do anything at all. I am free. I type words and publish infinite books and hope the tyrant knocks on my door because you deemed me a terrorist for using free speech. Then the revolution will start and I will be certain to knock on your door first. I will not be passing you over my fellow citizens who voted me down the river.

In all seriousness, I perceive I am attracted to Washington because this subconscious aspect likes revolutionaries. I like Einstein, I like Helen Keller. I like some of the bigger names that stick out in my mind based on history that I am aware of. So essentially all the information I have stored in the subconscious mind from my entire life now makes perfect sense. But also I hear some music from pop stars and their words make perfect sense. So I am simply biased. I perceive everyone is revolutionary.

 I perceive the government is a revolutionary, and the voters are, and I am, and Madonna is. But that cannot be possible. So I am biased. I see wisdom in everything I read, so I am biased. I am blind to the FACT everyone is not a revolutionary, or full of wisdom. It simply appears that way to me because my perception is altered. I can convince myself a Swiss cheese commercial is full of wise sayings. The good news is, I can write about anything, and that plays into my hands because my goal is to write infinite books or at least give it one hell of an attempt.

 I am not concerned about quality I am concerned about quantity. I do not mentally have the ability to determine quality any longer. Everything looks wise and perfect to me. That is bad in some ways and it is great if your goal is to write infinite books because I have lots to write about. That's this subconscious aspect. It has a hard time finding something it doesn't like. The way I used to be was nearly the reverse. There was very little I did like and especially myself and my body, and my talents, and my situation, and now I have no concept or self consciousness about my body, about my talents, or about my situation. So in some ways it is accurate to suggest I went from caring too much about things, to not caring much at all.

 My gamma waves were slightly altered and that changed my perception or outlook. The upside is I do not have any stress at all. I simply do not care what anyone thinks about me. I use to care a lot what people thought about me. I care about myself now. I didn't use to care about myself because I was too worried about caring what others said about me. So perhaps this accident made me do a mental 360. I do not care enough about others to physically harm them. I simply do not care enough about you to ever even raise a finger to you physically. Others in general are simply illusions to me and I no longer fight physically with illusions. Now the line in the sand is verbally. I will verbally convince anyone of anything, and the only way they will be able to escape total defeat in an argument is to get emotional and leave. They will say "I will not argue with this madness", but I would never do that, because I am aware they will lose any kind of logical or rational argument with me. It is not I am a great orator it is simply I am subconscious dominate and apparently it can make a case for anything.

It is not a matter of I have strong convictions about things. It is a matter of this subconscious aspect thrives on arguments. It thrives on verbal jousting. Sometimes the argument gets heated, but that's ok, that's good, that means people are thinking and pondering and sometimes that creates emotions. The trick is to never let it get you to a point of physical harm of others. Physical harm to others caused by argument means the beings mental faculties have failed them so they resort to the losers tactic of physical violence by making up some illogical reason to stop and argument like "I don't have to take this." Or the very popular "I do not have time for this." That is simply a way of a being giving up.

All of this is simply the fact that subconscious learns from arguments. I strictly work in real time because my pronounced sense of time is gone. So I seek arguments in order to keep the conversation going to keep the monologue going to reach further understandings. So one can see I do not have a personal attack nature on others, it is simply I can only learn from monologue. If someone insults America I will assume the role of the patriot. If someone insults the government I will assume the role of the Public Servant. If someone insults a religion I will assume the role of a member of that religion. If someone insults Physics I will assume the role of a scientist. I debate issues and reach further understandings. So many assume I am many things, or an expert on many things but I understand I just take the position opposite of what ever is said. I am a devil's advocate or a doubting Thomas. So now after the last hundred words on monologue and figuring that out, I am aware why I decided to write infinite books. I am aware why I made a decision to write infinite books two months after the accident. I am an infinitely long winded monologist. No one with conscious dominate mind can give me the satisfaction to argue as much as I want to, so I write my arguments in books because I have infinite things to argue about.

I am a protagonist's antagonist. I write 1000 words why the world is a nightmare and follow that with 1000 words why the world is perfect. Then I pick another topic and repeat into infinity. And I never reach a final conclusion. This is of course cerebral jousting with myself. I argue points about anything with myself and then I ponder which side I am on. I unable to pick one, because both a very good arguments. So then I go to the next topic. I sometimes like to explain popular wise quotes. That is my method to rest my poor fingers and attempt to keep my books small. So this subconscious is a powerhouse that has no quit. So I am not anything but a monologist. Nothing else is relevant at all. Only seeking further understanding and that is done mentally so I am harmless to ones with physical concepts of war and hate and anger. They won't stand a chance against me in a verbal joust and I won't stand a chance against them in a physical joust. I prefer that. I prefer to be a thinker because thinking and questioning is in itself a purpose.

I perceived I had no purpose before the accident and now I may not say many wise things or accomplish much physically but mentally I am in another world and I am having a ball. I am one with this new mental state I accidentally fell into. I perceive I understand how others can "unlock" or become dominate subconscious. There are some perks such as a "telepathy" aspect and some other interesting aspects such a some sort of "esp" but some things are lost, such as sense of time and sense of taste and sensation of pain is changed and some memory adjustments and cravings and desires are greatly diminished.

So I am not anything in particular, but I can play the role of anything in particular. I also am aware of this "speed reading" aspect. I see it is really the ability to skim a paragraph and get the spirit of the paragraph and not pay much attention to each word, so I can get through a book swiftly. But the down side of that is, when I take a thought and try to put it on paper I sometimes skip words or write a word twice and it is difficult for me to detect it because I speed read when I edit. So I may have to read something I edit 10 times to find a spelling or word out of place in a sentence. So one might suggest I do not judge a sentence by its words but by its spirit. A misspelled word does not bother me or a comma out of place does not bother me because I cannot honestly tell anymore where commas are supposed to go, same with paragraphs. Everything looks like the same thing to me. So if I break a paragraph I assure you it was just a lucky guess. One should not become emotional or judgmental or upset over a misplaced comma or a misspelled word or they simply have emotional issues. People are not stupid if they misspell a word or misplace a comma. It also does not mean they are not educated. That is crazy talk by ones with too many emotions. You are a valuable being whether you spell a word properly or not. That is reality. That is a harsh reality for some to accept.

I honesty try to do the best I can based on my situation and I am aware that perhaps is not good enough for some.

When I say "I", I mean "you" and when I say "you", I mean "I".

I am extremely ashamed of everything I write in all of my books that is why I publish them.

May 2 2009 2:47 PM EST

I prefer quantity over quality because I can't figure out what quality is.

When quality is important quantity dies.

Quality comes and goes but quantity has no limits.

My inability to write proper books is only exceeded by my willingness to keep trying.

A leader's corruption is only exceeded by the ones who follow them.

A voter votes for someone to vote for them.

All are students and some are more clueless than others.

All stand in front of a tidal wave; some find, it cannot not knock them over.

Attempting to avoid stress causes stress, and thus encourages more attempts to avoid stress, that in turn causes more stress.

Lust is knowing what you want; wonder is trying to understand why you want it so bad.

Buddha vowed to find the truth or sit under that tree until he starved to death, and karma enabled that girl to find him on the bank of that river, and a river never ends, it is an infinite flow.

Some sought a cave to find the truth, and a cave is an infinite empty space that goes on forever.

True terror is waking up one morning and finding out you're not running the country.

Sometimes the easiest way to fight a mental battle is to fight it swiftly and fiercely.

Psychology is a mental battle that never ends; physical battles end when both sides understand they lost.

It takes many mental strokes to cross the river of Styx because the sticks keep popping the raft.

I can't complain about what any other person says because they are most likely right.

When a person loves the world that is a symptom it has mentally defeated them.

Life takes no prisoners so mentally follow its lead.

When one accepts death mindfully they are still the same mental being they are now they just lose some physical cravings and desires, such as the strong cravings to hate and the strong desires to eat.

The difference between life and afterlife; one takes much longer vacations and the air fare is less.

Find some friends who can tolerate cuss words and see who can cuss the most, yet say the least. This tactic is emotional conditioning. No matter what anyone says in the universe, nothing is going to happen by saying words, unless your mind is in a mental tyranny or you live in a physical tyranny.

Everyone is looking for a fight; some perceive they are not looking; some never stop looking.

Mental suffering entails working ones way out of slight suffering so they can achieve higher forms of it.

Mindset set means everything once the proper definitions to words are mindfully realized.

So one may perceive I am humbled but I understand my eyes are black with hate.

This is in relation to being self centered. If one is self centered they may actually fix their self and in turn be able to indirectly assist others. This is exactly what "worry about the log in your eye" is all about. I was so self conscious I experienced so many things in the 40 years of my life, I decided to do the most self centered thing one can do. Kill their self.

But I messed up and I did not physically die. But it planted the seeds in my mind that freed my mind. So I laid the proper ground work to free my mind accidentally as a result of being extremely self centered. Of course this is in hindsight. I could just as well have died. I certainly was trying to I assure you of that. So I messed up in that sense. I "let go of life" mentally and as a result I opened up my mental power. This is rare to ever happen. It simply was unplanned. I simply fell into this state of mind as a result of being the most selfish, which is to say, " I have the power over my life or death." That is the extreme of self centered. That is also the extreme of "worrying about the log in your own eye." I was not running around trying to help others, all I understood is I wanted the hell out of this life. But I messed up and took enough pills to get sick enough to believe mindfully I was going to die if I did not seek medical help swiftly, and I mindfully decided, so what, I will die then. So whether I took enough pills to actually physically die, I recall about 25, it is not important. What is important is, mentally I believed it was enough to die. So one could suggest, if they put another being in a situation that being understands mentally they are going to die, this accident could happen to them.

Near death experiences are a good example. But this technique is not legal. The scenario would be. You kidnap someone and they are not aware of what is about to happen. Then you strap them to a table and tell them for about an hour how you are going to inject them with poison and kill them. Now that being understands you are going to kill them. Then you take another shot and shoot it into an animal and that shot is real poison, and that animal dies. So then the test subject understands the poison is real. So then they are more convinced you are going to kill them. But the test subject cannot be aware this is a mental conditioning tactic. The test subject has to believe this is a kidnapping and they are beyond the reaches of getting help and they will die when that "poison" is shot into them. So then after all this done, it is important to shoot them up with something that will make them slightly sick, then suggest to the test patient "This is simply a slight dose of the poison just to torture you", then the test subject mentally understands the next dose is going to make them so sick they will die. Then finally the test subject is made aware the final shot is coming. And this I perhaps a point in which the subject will beg and plead. That is a good indication that the subject believes death is coming.

Then the shot is given and it is a sedative that makes the patient go to sleep, perhaps for some hours. And before the patient awakes, they are put back into a safe environment where they came from. This is not legal to do. It is legally kidnapping and legally torture from both psychological and physical aspects. This is why my many years of suicide attempts were also mental and physical torture. I believed at the time I was trying to kill myself, but now I understand I was torturing myself. I could have just as easily went to the skyway bridge in Sarasota and jumped off, or went and got ammo for the shotgun in the house. I certainly considered it many times. So this whole principle to go to extreme subconscious dominate mind is a rare thing to happen because so many things can go right.

I had to be very poor at killing myself for many, many years. I had to be a loser in the quest to kill myself. Many suicidal people are winners at it, and some eventually get so medicated by drug's they cannot go to the end to be winners at it. There are simply too many things that have to go wrong for the extreme subconscious dominate mental conditioning to happen. This is in direct relation to "the least among you" or "the stone the stone cutter threw away".

I am the loser of all losers to fail at 30 suicide attempts and not physically pull it off.

So the whole concept is, if I could do anything right in this suicidal 15 years and in reality more like 25 year process, I would not have had this accident. Now in hindsight ones might say well if you made this discovery and it may help others reach this subconscious state then you are a good loser, or it is very lucky you were such a loser. That is exactly why it is so mysterious and so strange. It is a blessing I was such a loser that people did not accept me, and then I felt I was a loser, and then I failed at many things that reinforced the suggestion of others that I was a loser, and that encouraged me to really want to kill myself, and then when I messed up in my many attempts that made me feel more like a loser and made me want to really kill myself then, and somehow after 25 years or so of doing this, maybe 15 years openly attempting suicide, I finally came so close my mind believed I did die, and stopped registering time, and it was not enough to actually physically die, but enough that I mentally believed or my mind believed I did die. This is in relation to people who have a terminal illness and near the end make their peace. They mentally understand they are going to die no matter what, and they are at peace with that. They are no longer fighting to stay alive. They let go of life because they understand they simply cannot fight the reality of this fatal condition or disease they have.

So, the ones with fatal illnesses mentally open up the subconscious mind just before they die because they finally let go of life mentally. But the thing is they die shortly after, so they never figure out what they did. It took me 2 months after the accident to even be able to write words. I was what one could easily suggest was extreme mental shock. I could not mentally function. I was mentally in a daze. I was mentally adjusting from sequential limit based emotional conscious mind, to infinite, random access subconscious mind. The mental shock was so great I am still in mental shock. I am just letting go of some it with each passing day. I can tell my first book was a nightmare. It has one sentence and huge spaces between it. That is a symptom of how much mental confusion I was in. I was mentally a new being. I mentally had to learn everything over again. It is like I was born mentally again, and everything in my past 40 years was wiped out. All of the lessons I learned in my life up to that point were erased or no longer applied or no longer were relevant. But the further I get away from D-day so to speak, the more of it comes back and is applied to how I am now. I can tell I am more at ease forming sentences now than I was. But I am still having trouble with comma placements and determining where paragraph end or start because this absence of contrast. Mentally I can look at a section of words and I simply can't tell where the idea stops and goes to another idea, because my words are in random access, or subconscious form. Diminished emotions, means I lost contrast, and thus my judgment is altered. I type in real time. I still see everything is one thing, and a paragraph denotes contrast or separation. If one mentally see's everything as one thing, then a paragraph is not possible. I could go through and just randomly split the sections of words from others and fake that I wrote a paragraph but it wouldn't work. People with conscious left brain aspect dominate perhaps can hardly even read my writing.

 The words are there, the sentence structure is there, but the ideas caused by the arrangement of the words is perhaps beyond the sequential dominate minds ability to grasp. I am all over the place as far as my ideas. So I appear confused to ones who are sequential thought based. But I assure you I am very far from confused at this stage after the accident. I am aware I am mentally fighting with myself less. I am more confident in myself mentally. I at first doubted everything I said and now I am slowly warming up I am not so angry or fighting as much. What I understand is the subconscious dominate aspect is killing off the last vestiges of these things called emotions. The emotions are self doubt and doubt of others and self hate and hate of others. I am losing that. I am pleased to suggest my early books were simply me hating myself or attempts to, because after all I spend a good part of my life hating myself. I never in my life tried to kill anyone else but I tried many times to kill myself.

The truth is, I would have a hard time writing a book about how great love is and how great peace is because in order to do that I would have to be the world's greatest liar. I know nothing of this love concept and I know nothing this peace concept. When I heard the word love and peace and conformity when I was suicidal all I was reminded of is how bad I stuck out as an individual. And because of that, I hated and wanted to kill myself even more. The ones who are depressed and suicidal are the only ones in reality who are slightly in touch with the situation they are in. I write my books for the depressed ones to let them know, you just ignore all the insane ones who say you are "sick" because in reality the ones who say you are sick are the sickest of them all. I submit some beings are certain they want to kill their self and some beings rather isolate theirs self from society. That is none of my business and that is none of your business. That is their business. Every time I got baker acted for attempting suicide it gave me a three day period to consider how I would accomplish the suicide the next time I tried. Every time I went into a psychologists office I always came out with the understanding, I am glad I am not so insane I prescribe beings drugs that confuse their thinking so they will never work things out mentally and just remain in a mental fog of stagnation. I am pleased that I never became as sick as those psychologists are.

I look at war and violence and anarchy as an opportunity for beings to kill their self into some clarity. Physical War is a nice way of saying "Look how retarded we still are." So war and violence and anarchy are opportunities to come to further understandings. Sometimes being kills their self in many varieties. Some beings get drunk and drive fast and die. There subconscious knows what is happening, that being has a death wish. Some beings are trapped in some materialistic mental state. They spend their whole life making money and when they have more than they could ever use, they come up with other ways to make more money. So they work their self to death in order to make tons of money that they are fully subconsciously aware, they cannot take with them after they die. Yet these beings still hurt others and lie to others and swindle others and cheat others to get that money they already know, they cannot take with them. So they are clinically delusional and confused and mentally unstable. How much money does a being need to be an important being? The answer is zero. If you doubt that you are mentally unstable. You are essentially mentally imbalanced. You forgot who you are somewhere along the way.

Beings tend to want to make life easier but they only end up understanding life is not easy. Life is not fun. Life is not luxurious. Life is harsh and life is tough and life kills you. One can go around suggesting life is wonderful but the reality is, life is killing you every second of everyday. Some kill their self with too much food. So they are suicidal. Some kill their self with too many drugs so they are suicidal. Some kill their self over ideals or concepts of what is true or right and what is not, and they are suicidal. If you are a being who has a sense of time and a sense of having fun and a sense of hunger and a sense of daily aches and pains and a sense of I need to eat because I am getting weak and you get tired after just a few hours of mental effort, you are simply conscious dominate and thus you are physically suicidal.

13

I am mentally suicidal in respects I am extremely self centered, but I would never dream of harming myself or others physically for any reason but strictly self defense. What I mean is; When an army invades my country as in my state, I will attack them. If a being comes in my house I will attempt to defend myself. But before I start killing other beings in those situations I am going to sit down and think about how I can resolve this situation with words or with ideas suggested to that perceived enemy. I do not mean I will consider doing so for a moment. I mean that is my form of attack. Words spoken and arranged in such a fashion I will be able to talk that being down from their desire to physically invade my area. That is proper war. And the reality is only the master generals can ever even attempt it. All the other generals are not generals but jokes. Anyone can control others with physical means, but that is the folly of idiots. People go around and shoot off their mouth and say things like "We had to fight world war two because we couldn't reason with the Axis." What that really means is "We had to fight world war two with weapons because we have no brain function to persuade others with words."

There is a friend in a chat room I meet not more than a month ago and I have no idea what his real name is, but I am aware he is due to go back to Afghanistan soon. He suggests to me" I will go back to Afghanistan because I do not want to dishonor my country or my parents by telling the army I no longer wish to fight in a war I now understand is just an empire building scheme for war hawks and the military establishment" You do not know what you do to these young beings. You kill these innocent offspring with your guilt trips and suggestions of fear to satisfy your own insecurities caused by your own lack of mental clarity. Every single day I lie, I mislead, I say whatever I can say to that single being in my infinite attempts to get him out of going back to Afghanistan because I am fully aware he is only going to die mentally or physically to make a government unable to reason, and his parents not think he is loser.

This innocent being is self conscious. He is afraid to not be accepted by the ones who suggest he should die for their gain. I want to see the generals and I want to see the Senate and I want to see the House get their ass up in the hills fighting the Taliban.

No more talking advantage of the offspring. Those days are over because I have arrived. I have arrived which means you are on your way out. And the vote has already been taken, and it was a landslide. Your side did not do as well as expected. Perhaps you need to pump that into your calculator to figure out what that means. I am not late; I don't hesitate; I seal fate.

Freedom of speech is a wonderful thing because if you get in the way of my freedom of speech, I have 300 million bullets that will assist your skull in understanding what lead feels like.

I will sum up my sentiment of the last few sentences with wise comments.

A fanatical cult leader can never compete with the amount of innocent lives a government kills.

A war run by a government is a slaughterhouse run by a butcher.

A government understands the veal of the population makes the best eating.

The military complex encourages wars because it does not want to go back to making tractors.

The military encourages wars because it cannot live without them.

The space program is the only solution to war; put the war mongers on the leaky shuttles.

If you like to physically kill other people there is a huge battlefield called space but you have to be able to hold your breath to enter it, so bring your snorkel.

The militaries only goal is to figure out how to kill people faster, if you support that in anyway, you are a murderer, do not talk to me about why you are not, because I will just laugh at your delusional mind.

Okay I need to calm my mental fury with some jokes. This is a tip for everyone. When your mate or lover or wife or husband is sound asleep, cuss them out but quietly or let them know how you feel and let it all out, do not hesitate. This way their subconscious hears you, you get to lose your fear of saying how you feel to your mate, and only you know you did it. Then the next time a fight starts you will be docile and humble to your mate, because you know when they fall asleep you are going to verbally butcher them. So this is harmless to them and it makes you feel mentally better. It is a secret way to always win an argument. A being does not have to be consciously aware of what you are saying. They do not have to consciously be awake. You can just whisper how they upset you while they sleep. And they will subconsciously understand what you mean. So what this means is any being who just read this comment will have to think very carefully before they go to sleep again because their mate may been cussing them out while they sleep. There is simply nothing the one who is sleeping can do about it. The one doing the cussing can say anything. So the being doing the cussing is liberated and they understand now, the subconscious never misses a beat. If any sound happens the subconscious hears it, and even if that being is deaf, I am aware somehow the subconscious hears it. I am uncertain how I know that at this stage of the accident, but the truth is some of these beings who are deaf and blind and even paraplegics, they still have a mind and thus subconscious aspect, so they are as powerful potentially as any being ever will be. This whole physical focus is in error. It is not how strong you physically are, it is how well your mental engine is oiled. And that is not in relation to how many books you have read, that is in relation to how many mental battles you survived.

 Some beings fight a couple mental battles and then decide to avoid ever doing that again. That is because they are weak willed. They simply unestimate their mind. We got to the moon is 1968 and we have not done anything since. Why? Because we got all hesitant about our abilities. We got all paranoid about things. We became afraid. We became mentally paralyzed. We became exactly what one being suggested we should not be. "We have nothing to fear but fear itself." We haven't taken over the solar system because we are to afraid to try to swiftly, because we think there is something to fear, but in reality, there is never anything to fear , ever. There is no such thing as fear, there are only mentally paralyzed beings.

 The Hatton vs Pacman fight is starting and I am predicting Pacman will win by KO in the 8th. It is not important if I am right, it is only important I can see if I am warming up or still need much warming up to do.11:32 PM Pac won with as second round KO. 11:45 PM But I discovered a great truth from that boxing match outside of the fact sports for money is no different than dog fighting. Making a human being physically harm their self for the sake of money is insanity. But then I have to fight that illusion and understand that suffering leads to understanding. Wars lead to understanding. Pain leads to understanding, on a personal level and on a collective human species level. So then I understand. Countries that have militaries have not even progressed out of ancient times yet. In ancient times they made huge armies to control other people and countries. So that means we are still at the same maturity level as a species we were 5000 years ago. We are no different at all in any respect. We are barbarians totally and completely, except now we can butcher people for no reason much swifter, so in that respect we have actually gone backwards. The ones who butchered people with their weapons 5000 years ago were far more mature then we are right now. One is not more mature because they can kill other beings faster they are in reality much more insane. A person who murders one person is in trouble but is a good person compared to a butcher of many. A mass murderer continues to mentally persuade their self what they do is right or righteous. The reason is mental delusions. The end result is that a mass murderer convinces their self to kill again. That is the psychology of countries that have a standing army. They will eventually convince their self there is a righteous cause to break out the guns and kill people. From outside of the box, they are simply a mass murderer that is delusional and likes to kill people. That's all that is happening.

So I am always mentally reduced to the one truth that the land of the free, which is in fact the human species, does some pretty interesting things psychologically speaking and somehow this leads to further understandings and that is the momentum that drives our species.

 It very hard for me mentally to judge anything or anyone, I am unable to say the worst criminal is bad. Or the best saint is good. I am only able to mentally understand beings do things that lead to further understandings. This is why I feel this space exploration needs to be nurtured by mankind so that mankind will stop fighting itself. Some sort of slush fund for the exploration of space on a world scale so a set space exploration base can be built. The sole purpose is to see how many spaceships it can send into space in a year. And then try to top that every year. There is no reason to put all of our eggs in one basket. We should strive to have infinite baskets and infinite eggs because we never seem to find what we set out to look for in space exploration but we tend to accidentally discover many things we didn't set out to look for. This whole aspect of "We can't send astronauts in space in unsafe spaceships." is nothing but delusional thinking.

There are millions of beings who want to go to space and that being the case they have already made up their minds they are willing to die to just get a chance to go to space. They subconsciously, by saying "I want to be a spaceship person." have already gone through the whole mental process of decisions required, and when they hit the question "Are you willing to die physically to go to space?" they answered mentally, "Yes, no question about it.". So all one can do is build spaceships with reasonable safety and balance that with reasonable time scales. People suggest we may get to mars in 20 years. What on gods earth are you talking about 20 years. We should have as a world, 1000 space ships in space with people in them and exploring the whole solar system within 3 years. Last time a huge asteroid came close to earth it was extinction sized and they didn't see it until after it passed. That means it will be too late to do anything. That requires the world to get on board. No country can do it alone period. There are beings in every country who are masters at something. So why rob ourselves of the fruits of mankind by suggesting, "You are not from my country so I cannot

15

listen to you." That is delusional isolationism. I am not intelligent enough to know who is going to make a world changing contribution. It might be a street person in a 3rd world country that will invent a spaceship that can go the speed of light with one simple discovery while they are living in a cardboard box on the side of the road. I am not so intelligent I can discount that, because it is in the realm of possibility. Realm of possibility is a powerful concept. Washington said to the first couple of people who started listening to his revolutionary ideas "It is in the realm of possibility we can make a free country based on freedom of speech and freedom of press for every being." Everything else is history now.

We are only human beings so we cannot underestimate any one of us. We simply cannot afford that luxury. Let's look at this from out of the box. If an alien race attack humans who would you want as a tactician and strategist? A general in the US army or Bin Laden? That's right. If it was a matter of the human race I would pick the one who I can clearly see is a master tactician. When it comes down to it, you go with your strong suit. Right now we are fighting him and we hate him because he is so dam tricky. So we love to hate him. We are in love with how dam good Bin Laden is at evading our traps. If we caught him what would we do? We would have to pull out of Afghanistan and all the military industry would be crying. The military would be crying because the war would be over. If we catch Bin laden there will be Americans who will cry in anguish because his presence sustains them. So you see the psychology of this war on terror is very deep seeded. Some American makes jokes about it. It is almost now a punch line. It is as if Americans are already aware our country is unable to ever catch this guy in sandals who lives in caves and it just truly pisses them off into infinity. We as a country can destroy the whole world with nukes but if you asked us to catch a guy in sandals forget it. But the truth is, that is because human beings can adapt. Bin laden is a human being with a subconscious aspect which is probably pretty close to dominate because he has to adapt every single minute. He has to use his mind every move he makes because he is aware his life is on the line. He is aware satellites can track him. So by this time in this war on terror, he is so "wise" that there essentially is no chance in hell anyone will catch him. He has survived long enough to have mastered survival in the fire. So even if we catch him there will not be celebration in the streets. There will be beings who realize they gave up so much just to get one being and they will feel saddened. That is why the greatest truth is, avoid getting in physical fights with humans because they adapt. That is the problem. In all the wars in history no one has been able to wipe out the human race. So it is pointless to have wars with humans. We should be at a level of understanding we cannot wipe ourselves out, only other species. I do not think you are able to grasp what I just said, but I said it anyway.

Where does zero start and where does zero end?

Here is an alternative to the death penalty. The being is placed out in the middle of nowhere. With maybe a small amount of water and small amount of food. Their fate is left up to their ability to adapt and adjust to their situation. So once one is judged to be put to death, they are given a second chance. They can learn to use their mind to survive or they will die. This way the US will not be known as murders of their own citizens. If that being actually survives they will appreciate the power of their mind and they will never harm others again. All the death penalty really is from a psychological point of view is a revenge killing. Nothing happens. The "criminal" kill some people and then we kill them. Nothing good comes out of that because the ones who kill that death penalty person, also feel guilt subconsciously. The guards who lead that person to be killed in the death penalty also feel guilt. Everyone associated with killing that "prisoner" comes away with guilt subconsciously. Ask any soldier if they have any regrets about killing others in combat, and the problem with doing that is the ones who feel the most regret usually kill their self after they come back, the ones who feel no regret are the ones with no brain function at all.

I killed myself because I understood this world didn't want me, so don't you dare start saying you want me now. Helping one who is mentally struggling, takes a bit more words than just saying, "Pray about it" or "Take this pill three times a day." One has to actually be in a mental state of understanding they can detect what that being needs to hear. That means they have to have "telepathy" and then they have to have "understanding" and then they have to have the ability to arrange words in a proper way to assist that being to feel good about their self but not just sugar coated crap like "Love is all you need." One must have a mental ability to adapt to the colors they detect in the being who is seeking mental assistance. Throwing vague cliché's and pills at that being are the methods of beings that have no business attempting to assist anyone but their self.

Beings trained in methods of madness are only capable of encouraging madness in the ones they speak to. The blind leading the blind means a mentally blind being can only lead other beings off a cliff. A psychologist has decided to help or assist other beings. That means you put yourself second to the beings who seek your assistance. That means your pay and your life is secondary to their needs. That means you forfeit your desires for their desire to become more enlightened to the way things are, so they are less confused. This means your goal is to talk. Your goal is not to listen to them your goal is to talk to them. I can get a rock and place it in a chair and charge people 50 dollars an hour to talk to it. If you think medicine is a better healer than your ability to form words to assist others, you need to get the hell out of the business of psychology because you are killing people.

If you cannot mentally heal one patient a day in 8 hours you are not a psychologist, you are a delusional being who someone said is a psychologist. I am able in a chat room to talk a being from being depressed to a being who has decided to think for their self and question and assume all others are insane, if those beings insult them in any way. I can do that in about 1 hour on my bad days. If you can't at least do that in 8 hours you need contact me and I will train your properly in psychology so you won't go around killing people who seek assistance. And I will never ask any payment from you because I don't do things for money I do things for no reason at all.

The last I checked they don't accept Visa or Master card where I am at.

Perhaps my emotions have not been completely silenced after all. Hopefully by the time I write infinite books they will be slightly silenced.

I cannot come back to the world you are in, but I can attempt to suggest you can come to the one I am in. I will clarify. I am unable to go back to sequential conscious state of mind I came from, but I am allowed to say infinite words and you may decide on your own to come to subconscious random access state of mind I am in.

One should be cautious of anyone who say's "I keep secrets from you for your own protection and safety." Because all that really means is they like the fact you are gullible and the secrets are about you.

One loud word can wake the whole chicken coup.

A psychologist bases their practice on the delusion they want to help people based on the promise they will make lots of money.

Compassion is staying in the world that led you to kill yourself in the first place.

Post I made on boxing forum post fight:

There is a problem in fighting pacman.
He is a being who grew up in poverty and perhaps faced the reality of actual death if he did not focus mentally to work his way out of his situation as a youth. He was in a situation as a being that no one was going to save him. No one was coming to his rescue. So he was literally in a do or die situation. And that means he is mentally invincible. The problem with that is he is also lightning fast and as Hatton found out he can end your career with a punch that you will never see. So I understand pacman will not be losing any fights, but he will be retiring within 3 to 6 years. So age will dethrone him, but I do not detect any boxer will be able to. He is simply a legend, so one is wise to enjoy it while he is still fighting because in 100 years they will remember who pacman was. Floyd took out Hatton but it was an amateurish attempt compared to what pacman did to Hatton and Hatton by himself is no slouch. I do not even see anyone who would fight pacman except for a payday and understanding they would be getting the losers paycheck. Speed kills and speed and power annihilation.
We saw annihilation tonight. Pac's mental speed and mental power leads to his physical speed and physical power. He is always smiling. He smiled at Hatton at the weigh in when they were toe to toe, because pacman saw Hatton was just about his height. He frickin smiled. He is a legend.
What else can I say.

END

Mental speed and mental power trumps physical speed and physical power. Abject poverty can lead to legendary minds. A human being that is forced to adapt to do or die situations is a human being that understands defeat is sweet and never considers retreat. Perhaps one is wise to consider that before picking fights with beings in third world countries again.

Love leads to love of war, and love of hate, and worst of all, love leads to depression when love is scorned.

Avoiding marriage is the easiest way to secure a happy one.

You only break the law if someone tattles.

Everyone goes about things differently and my books prove that.

It is easier to ruin a good thing than to encourage a bad thing.

I am not sure what that last wise saying even means but maybe you will figure it out.

I crossed the river of Styx six sixty six.

The ride was rough but not enough six sixty six.

The hate is great but wont dissipate six sixty six.

You hated me into the sea six sixty six.

I won't hesitate to seal your fate six sixty six.

You can't talk to me, I drowned in the sea six sixty six.

I do more drugs in 2 sentences than most people do in eternity.

The only thing one has to fear is that they will eventually understand fear does not exist.

I am very high trying to figure out if you guys are real or just some cruel joke afterlife is playing on me.

Solipsism is the philosophical idea that "My mind is the only thing that I know exists."

My problem is I do not think my mind exists either. I am not sure what mind even is. Maybe it's spirit and not mind . Then that changes things. So then I am stuck with, what is spirit. I am unable to tell what spirit is because just like mind, one is unable to prove it exists. So then I can only say, the only thing that exists is the only things one cannot prove exist. Like a True Vacuum.

There is only one way to find out if you have too many emotions. Find a location reputed to be haunted like an old house or an old cemetery. Go there at night, when it is pitch dark. Go alone. Go into the house or into the center of the cemetery where you are far away from an exit. Stand there and do not whistle and do not talk to yourself and do not bring a cell phone and have to possible way to get away in time if something goes bad. Then you stand there or sit there if you are that brave. And wait about 90 minutes. Listen very closely and intently to every sound you hear. Do not stand near lights or even in a way you can see lights. It has to be pitch black. If you are unable to do this you have so many emotions they literally are driving you mad. The slightest sound will set you into pure shock and you will run as fast as you can to get away from the slightest noise. So then you will know you mind is way out of conditioning. It is not working properly. Even if a ghost appears in front of you in that house or cemetery you should not run unless you are way too emotional.

But the truth is, you will never get to see that ghost because you will run in terror from the slightest sound. You will run in terror because it is dark. Darkness causes a beings mind that is not working properly to panic. One cannot see in the dark if one's mind is not working properly so one panics. The darkness isn't anything, so you should not panic unless your mind is abnormal. You are simply blinded in darkness if your mind is not functioning properly.

One who is afraid of the dark is one who makes rash decisions based on delusional thoughts. Their mind is playing tricks on them in the dark and they are physically reacting to it. That is what delusional person does. They believe what they think is happening and act out in physical ways. Typing words is not acting out in physical ways. It is simply monologue. A person who writes words down is putting their thoughts on paper. So a person can write a book about a world war but they do not have to fight an actual world war to consider what it would be like.

One can write about what it's like to be in combat and kill other people in combat, but one does not have to actually be in combat to write about it. So they are simply imagining what it would be like. Hemingway did not go out in a little boat and catch a huge marlin and fight it for many days. He imagined what it would be like as he wrote the words down. I do not have to experience a physical war to understand what it is like. You do not either. You understand what it is like or can be like, yet you still are okay with encouraging other citizens you suggest you care about, to go fight in them in other lands. That is a symptom of a confused mind.

Sunday 03 2009 2:25 PM EST

They cannot handle talking and only respond to wise sayings so I will give them what they can handle.

Love is all you will need when I am finished with you.

"A man who won't die for something is not fit to live."

Martin Luther King, Jr.

A man who won't mindfully accept his own die is mindfully dead.

One who is afraid to die is terrified to live.

Living poorly is worse than dying happily.

A man who won't put his life on the line for his friends won't put his life on the line for himself.

Facing death when you are alive get's you use to the fact.

If you can't face death you will never be able to face life.

If you are afraid of something you cannot avoid you will be tormented by what you cannot hold on to.

Fraud in the business world is achieved when one being sells another being an item they know that being can get for less from their supplier.

A wholesaler defrauds the retailer and the retailer passes on his revenge to the customer.

A wholesaler defrauds the retailer and the retailer seeks justice from the consumer.

Death of a salesman denotes a being who decided to stop scamming people for a living.

People do not kill other people for money; money has value and people are just in the way.

Death and taxes denotes you will die so they will have spending money for toys.

If you are afraid of this life you will be a waste in the next one.

If you are scared to serve your purpose in this life you will have no purpose in the next one.

It is easy to live when you only have moments to live; most never figure out they only do have moments to live.

You have zero time to master life and all eternity to figure out why you failed at it.

You have zero time to master life and all eternity to figure out why you didn't.

You have zero time to master life and all eternity to figure out why you do.

Don't worry about figuring out life there will be infinite time for that later.

Don't worry about what you do right or wrong just make sure you do something.

They don't give out diplomas for effort but that is the only one that counts.

Washington countered the argument "No one is above the law" with, No law is above ones freedom to ignore law.

Inalienable right to be free means no law can compete with that reality.

You cannot trump ones alienable freedom as a being with a well legislated sentence.

I went to the hospital today because for the last two weeks I have felt a slight discomfort in my abdomen. They ran all the tests and said I checked out but then said from the urine sample they tested I may have a slight, slight urinary infection. Then I realized this definition of Heimdall being able to hear the grass grow. Essentially I am so in tune or sensitive to the slightest change in taste and hearing and now feeling my body itself. So I detected a slight infection and to me it felt very strong but in reality, it was not even enough for a person with emotions to even detect at all. So I am in a situation I have to discount any discomfort until it is unbearable because I am too sensitive to the slightest changes in my body. Everybody has infections all the time in their body but the white blood cells usually kill them off before the being with emotions even detects any physical pain. So something is strange. I am in a sense numb or nothingness sensation so the slightest stimuli is detectable as being very loud, or "hearing the grass grow".

So in a way this accident has made me very heightened to sensation but in order to be that way it has to turn everything all the way down. The nurse was inserting an IV needle and she couldn't find the vein and was digging around attempting to and I felt the needle but no real sense of pain. Then she tried the other arm and got and said "I am sorry I couldn't get it the first time." And I said "No problem." Because it honestly did not hurt me at all. The slight pain was quickly gone. So then I am really talking crazy talk because I am saying things hurt but they don't hurt. They asked me what level of pain does this sensation in your abdomen have, on a scale of 1 to 10. And I just said 4 because I mentally cannot tell. I detect something that is not like I usually am which is "numb" physically. But on their scale of pain it might be .00001 and to me that is discomfort but to them, they would not even notice it.

My only hope is to remind myself it has only been seven months since the accident and I am still getting used to this state of mind.

When I was in the waiting room I was aware I was in a catatonic state because I was looking at these other people and I could "read" how they were doing. I could see who was sick and who was there with them, and not sick.

I was so mesmerized by what I was "feeling" with vision from looking at them, it essentially put my mind a catatonic state because it is unable to think or function properly because the "feeling" from vision is so strong because all the people that were there, it literally tired me out. I was in a sort of zombie like state but perhaps no one else noticed it.

I do not perceive I type fast in chat room but I am lightning fast compared to others. I get kicked from chat rooms because I can flood a chat room with my typing and people with a sense of time just assume no being can type or think that fast. To me it is normal or I perceive I am just typing and coming to conclusions at a normal pace but in reality my thinking or thoughts to type is so fast, they are unable to figure how I pull it off. I do not perceive writing a book a month is fast, I actually perceive one month is a very long period of time. One day is a very long period of time but also goes by like a flash. So this subconscious state I am in is literally an entire new world to get use to mentally.

I listened to some Madonna tunes today and before my accident I perceived she was looking for attention in the things she did and says, but I understand one great truth about Madonna, she is a being who uses her craft to suggest some very deep messages. She is very deep in her lyrics. She perhaps may not be consciously aware of it, but her subconscious is in control, I am certain of that. I submit I may be delusional but that is how I perceive her. She is fascinating.

I pondered some things while listening to her music and I realized every being by nature is looking for trouble.

A man marries a woman, he is looking for trouble and usually gets way more than he can handle. A women who gets married finds infinite trouble especially when she marries a man. When a person decides to do anything even if that anything is nothing, they are looking for trouble. When a mother has a child, she is looking for trouble.

I hate the clarity this accident has caused me, I cannot take it. I am not strong enough to handle the clarity because I understand every human being is perfect and I am unable to handle that truth.

It simply is not important if you know or understand Nirvana or this state of nothingness really means one has conditioned their mental being to a point they are subconscious dominate and have clarity that is beyond the understanding of ones with a sense of time. It simply is not important if you are aware that because I am aware of that.

It only took me 4.2 books to figure out how to use a timestamp. So that will save me much time and now I can write faster. I am a transforming adapting author.

Trusting another human being is the most sadistic thing a human being can do; trusting yourself is the most masochistic thing, trust me.

In a court of law insanity is decided on a case by case basis.

Sometimes beings who do very illegal things pretend they are insane to get off the hook legally, so they are not that insane, and sometimes people say "I didn't know that was wrong." but in reality they did know. So they are not so insane after all.

Tell someone they shouldn't do something and they will prove you right.

All proper relationships are enriched with a healthy dose of disrespect.

My infinite wrath potential reminds me of how bad I am in bed and I am swift to remind her why.

Suffering is a well disguised blessing.

I add some of my chat room conversations, because talking to people gives me great contrast.

Please be mindful I am not religious. I do not correct my spelling in chat rooms so you can understand how poorly I spell in real time. I understand with no sense of time, I type very fast, and very rushed, but I cannot tell.

{10:03} <Heimdall> I have pondered this story where buddha was found by teh river nearly dead by a little girl who said, he reminded her of a spirit she "once met"

[10:03] <anatta> with the fasting he was trying to find out if you can stop all suffering if you ignore the world, ignore yourself, your body, if you denie all this and just take what is neccessary to stay alive

[10:03] <Heimdall> thats is perhaps to obvious to me

[10:04] <anatta> but that was not the way

[10:04] <Heimdall> yes anatta perhaps one who is depressed isolates their self from teh world and one method to end sufefring is to let go of ones own life

[10:04] <anatta> and after he gave this up he found the way

[10:05] <anatta> if you are depressed you wont be able to get a calm mind

[10:05] <Heimdall> but sometimes a little girl finds you before yu let go all teh way

[10:05] <anatta> and so you cant even attain the jhanas

[10:06] <Heimdall> perhaps buddha was searcvhing for an end to suffering but was not aware he would find it until he did

[10:06] <Heimdall> he probably did not say "honey i am leaving home for 10 years to find truth, see you at dinner time"

[10:07] <anatta> well, you are not interested in what he did find out are you ^^

[10:08] <Heimdall> No i am simply interested in pondering his life and perhaps i will get to the teachings at a later stage, so to speak

[10:08] <Heimdall> I guess i am asking myself "what on earth was he thinking"

[10:08] <anatta> do you only care for his life before enlightment or also for the life after?

[10:09] <Heimdall> yes i perhaps only care about what led up to the nirvana

[10:10] <anatta> i see

[10:10] <Heimdall> he may have been a bit biased after teh fact due to the fence he sat on

[10:11] <Heimdall> perhaps he suggested teh fence or "do not take teh word of a blind man" because he hoenstly couldnt tell what was right or wrong or porper or improper afetr teh fact

[10:12] <Heimdall> he saw suffering to go in search of an end to it, but then found suffering may simply be a way to reach furtehr undertandings

[10:12] <anatta> well he said what made him leave home

[10:12] <anatta> so no need to make any theories just read it ^^

[10:13] <anatta> there was this question, is it possible to stop birth, sickness, old age, death

[10:13] <Heimdall> maybe if buddha did not see suffering when he looked outside, he would never have reached nirvana, so the suffering he saw was to encouarge him to find a greater truth

[10:14] <Heimdall> so the suffering was in fact a blessing

[10:14] <Heimdall> so maybe that is thr truth

[10:14] <Heimdall> suffering is a well diguised blessing

[10:16] <anatta> yes

[10:16] <anatta> only when he went out of his palace he saw it

[10:16] <Heimdall> yes

[10:17] <Heimdall> maybe went outside of his palace denotes, he let go of himself, he let go of his life, by not eating for 38 days, and so he reached a mental state of being outside of the box of life looking back at it, and saw thinsg differently

[10:18] <Heimdall> it perhaps is hard to see suffering as a blessing when one is in teh buddle of life but outside of the buddle it is obvious

[10:18] <Heimdall> bubble

[10:19] <Heimdall> but what i ponder is, what if that little girl did not find him near death by that river

[10:19] <Heimdall> there would be no buddhism

[10:19] <Heimdall> so that is perhaps a great lystery or what karma is

[10:19] <Heimdall> mystery

[10:20] <anatta> hmm u know... ^^

[10:20] <anatta> u just need to read in the pali canon to get information

[10:20] <anatta> the ancient scriptures

[10:20] <anatta> then u can get some more insight in the whole thing

[10:20] <anatta> there was not only one Buddha

[10:21] <anatta> time is endless

[10:21] <anatta> now we have to opportunity to get out of the rebirthing cycle

[10:21] <anatta> and in future it there will be this opportunity again

[10:21] <anatta> after Buddhism disappeared

[10:21] <Heimdall> i ponder if Buddha was the only Buddha because one has to let go of life truly and then hope that a little girl find them before they physically die, and that is very rare

[10:22] <Heimdall> it is as if one has to kill their self, but then at the last second not physically die

[10:22] <Heimdall> but do it in earnest

[10:23] <Heimdall> so it might be impossible to accomplish on purpose

[10:23] <Heimdall> it has to be an accident

[10:23] <Heimdall> i ponder if Buddha knew all he had to do was starve for 28 days we would just ahve done it

[10:23] <Heimdall> but he didn't know

[10:23] <Heimdall> so it was an accidental discovery

[10:24] <Heimdall> he tried many ways

[10:24] <Heimdall> and finally one worked so it was an accident

[10:24] <Heimdall> 10 years of experiments

[10:24] <anatta> 6 years i guess

[10:25] <Heimdall> i hear he went from one thing to another searching or experimenting like he tried one way and then tried another way and then said i will sit under this tree or else

[10:25] <Heimdall> kind of like a do or die mentality

[10:26] <Heimdall> and then he got lucky because that girl found him just in the exact right moment

[10:26] <Heimdall> 5 days later and no Buddha

[10:26] <Heimdall> so its a mystery who was that girl

[10:26] <Heimdall> was that girl a metaphor

[10:27] <anatta> ^^

[10:27] <Heimdall> like some angel that saved him or maybe a spirit that girl said he met earlier that reminded her of Buddha

[10:27] <Heimdall> she

[10:27] <Heimdall> she says Buddha reminded her a spirit she met earlier

[10:28] <Heimdall> so who was that spirit and did it manipulate her to go down to teh river that day

[10:28] <Heimdall> so maybe Buddha got tapped

[10:28] <Heimdall> and it was not as much of who he was but he got tapped

[10:28] <Heimdall> he got tapped to be the Buddha of the age

[10:28] <Heimdall> he didn't have a choice

[10:29] <Heimdall> something tapped him

Humans perhaps have always had language but the invention of written language enabled humans to have planned language. So the invention of alphabets and thus written language enabled planned language and planned language encourages emotions because if one misspells a word they are judged. "You can't even spell properly."

That is a direct symptom of emotions. "You spelled that word wrong and so you are stupid." That is impossible. Everyone can say the word and even if they do not say it properly everyone knows what they meant. But then you have language invented and then you HAVE to spell the words right and if not, you are wrong. Right and wrong are symptoms of going from evolving language with no written language to a point of planned language as a result of writing. If there is no writing then it is impossible to spell a word wrong and so it is impossible for one to ever judge you because you misspelled a word. That is a direct symptom of what brought about this mental concept called emotions or judgments or verbally hurting someone's feelings.

When you tell a child they got it wrong on the test, you are hurting that child's feelings. You are not helping that child you are hurting that child. That child has no concept of what is right or wrong until you cram it down their throat while you hurt their feelings. A child does not know what killing people is until you teach them how many people we can kill in a war. Then you have the balls to say, "What is wrong with my child?"

They do not know what murder and hate and judgment and bitterness and anger and hate and killing is, until you show them how to do it. And then you say, "We do not know what went wrong." You teach the children what you are and they become just like you. So you need to not be so stupid to wonder why they are messed up. They are messed up because you taught them how to be messed up because you are messed up. The children learn from the masters of insanity and then you encourage them to be just like you, and do it just like you do it, and teach their children to hate and murder just like you taught them to hate and murder. That is exactly what you do. Only beings with mental fortitude can handle a great truth like that and the rest of a weak minded beings will simply attempt to write infinite books to explain how that cannot be truth.

Perhaps "suffer the children to come unto me." Really means "Why do you make the children suffer like you do? Why do you ruin them like you have been ruined? Why do you take the innocent ones and make them like you are which is hateful and bitter and angry? Because "You know not what you do."

Your intentions are honorable and the children's suffering as a result is infinite. Only beings with extreme mental fortitude can ever face that reality. Everyone else is just weak minded, delusional, confused, attempts at being a being. But the trick is, to look at a great truth that may cause suffering inside as an opportunity to adjust ones strategy. An adjustment is easily conceived and can impact the universe.

An email to someone about something.

I am humbled by your background story about why you write, and about your grand mother.

I perceive much wisdom in it. I feel the struggles your grandmother faced in the war lead to her becoming a wise being and in turn instilling that wisdom in you.

I am aware you write books to encourage love and I find now fault with that. I understand I am attracted to you as an author because my books explain how all emotions simply lead to cravings and desires and control and that in the end only leads to suffering of the being. This attachment caused by love is dangerous from my perspective. I suggest to my readers the whole reason I was so suicidal for 15 years is because i perceived everyone disliked me, from teachers who said i failed their test to people i knew who said I could never get it right. This all led up to me talking a hand full of pills after many attempts to kill myself , and then when i saw i would certainly die, i did not seek help. I let go of my life, and then I woke up the next day and eventually found i lost my attachments, my sense of time, my sense of taste my, sense of right and wrong and thus judgments and i also lost the most important thing of all, my emotions.

So i am unable to Bond with others now, but i would not trade that for the universe. I am unable to care if others insult me. I am unable to care if others pass on. I am unable to care if people suggest my books are not worthy because I write one needs to avoid love because love only leads to attachments and hate and control and thus suffering. So I am truly free of the bonds of this world. I am on the outside looking in and nothing in this world can harm me. So i say what i feel and nothing in the world can phase me any longer because this world and its wisdom is why i took the pills to begin with and the last thing I will ever show mercy for is the ones who suggest I am not an important being because i can't spell words properly.

So I am attracted to you as an author because you are my arch enemy. So i understand without you writing your books preaching about how great love is, I would have no motivation to write infinite books, so you are also a blessing to me.

Love is suffering in disguise.

END

When I stop doubting myself you are doomed.

I am an undiscovered author and I go to great lengths to keep it that way.

One thing I am unable to know is, as some have suggested, I got tapped, and so it may mean it could all be over very soon, but I am unable to tell because I am in the dark about why I was tapped. I do not know what "all over soon" means. Ones understanding of Karma or Fate is relative to ones inability to understand what causes it. Beyond understanding denotes events that defy logic. I write about my accident because I keep doubting it was one. Children are not supposed to grow up to be what you want them to be because they always grow up to be what they are destined to be. Only the most humble parents can face the reality they are not allowed to pick their child's destiny because it had already been determined when that cell divided into two. Okay I am getting weird I will go back to wise quotes for a while.

"All our knowledge merely helps us to die a more painful death than animals that know nothing."
Maurice Maeterlinck

Our attachment to wanting to know makes it so hard to let go of knowledge.

Letting go of physical life leads some to kill their self in their attempts to hold onto it.

We miss our enemies when we defeat them and thus are stuck with our friends, and despise them instead.

The hardest part of letting go of love is; understanding it controls you.

 Love of life encourages hating to let go of it.

We are all afraid to die because we are afraid our understanding of what comes after is wrong; only the dead are not afraid any longer.

I understand enough to know i do not want to understand any more.

I set a very low bar for myself so i never fail.

I am beneath the mountain while everyone else is attempting to climb it.

<Heimdall> I once said in a Christian chat room, disbelief does not change the fact he is lord of all, and i got banned

because that was saying, their attachment to belief is irrelevant.

<Heimdall> their belief is what makes them relevant

<Quentin> lol

I am one who understands battles should be fought with words and I am in a battle with ones who believe weapons are the best way to fight battles and so the battle is waged, and I never lose a battle. That is my creed and I die by it. Now you know the definition of an epic battle.

Okay back to the "wise " quotes.

"Death is a very dull, dreary affair, and my advice to you is to have nothing whatsoever to do with it."
W. Somerset Maugham

Death is the only teacher you will learn something from.

Death of emotions is only scary because you are afraid of the light.

It is much less expensive to destroy the universe in your mind and takes infinitely less time.

Once you understand no one is talking to you, one can observe some beings with some interesting quests. The path is relative to who is on it. One is the first step to infinity.

If you have emotions you are an emotional wreck, if you have no emotions you miss being an emotional wreck. You taught me well how to teach you. Let it go in one ear and plug up the other. I need help because others are so hard to help. Motivation is driven by panic.

One cannot win so they can only try. The fear is, you might write a book someone will like.

It is impossible to be hated by all. The world only discourages my sanity. A word never meets its definition. A schedule is one thing i can't keep. Holding onto what is important means you have to let go of what really is important. The last thing anyone wants is to die when they do.

Responsible people attempt to suggest everyone else is not. Always write horrible books so you are in the mindset to try again. There are beings in this world who manipulate you in much clever ways than writing infinite books, I assure you of that.

"Death is no more than passing from one room into another. But there's a difference for me, you know. Because in that other room I shall be able to see."

Helen Keller

This is such an inside joke. Helen Keller could see much better with no vision than others will ever see with vision. It is easy to see reality as long as you have no vision or hearing.

Death: when women no longer have to wear makeup and men no longer have to mow the lawn. It kills me to read such elegant quotes by such an elegant being. I can't say that quote any better than she said it; I can only infinitely try to. Helen underestimated me because I am blind, deaf, and a loser. Death is no more than life. If you have a sense of time and cravings and desires you will assume life is much different than death; if not you will understand there is neither. You will never leave the mental room you are in right now. Actual sight blinds you to what is important, and hearing complicates things further. I am quite certain women rule the world and allow men to think they don't. Mental clarities advantage is universally confusing.

It's illegal to read this sentence, turn yourself in or you are evil.

I don't catch fish to eat; i just catch them to see if the fire still burns them.

I am only concerned about the fires heat and i use fish to test it. There is nothing worse than being the best. You are only good at nothing when you get tired of losing at everything.

If you are afraid to say something in public, you should say it to see if your fear is delusional or if the ones who hear it are. Fear is the worst delusion; hesitation is the most complete.

I am not certain where we are at, but I am certain where we are not at. My worst accident led to a string of meaningful ones. My last accident was the first one on purpose. God always takes the wise ones and lets the idiots live. People either live to die or die to live. Soft spoken lies are loud truths. The kingdom is within; the illusions are without; truth. Fortitude separates the weak minded from the absent minded. I am certain it will sink in who i am, eventually.

If I don't even get my own comments till later, then who the hell is coming up with them?

The harmony is; my moments of clarity are equal to my moments of rage.

"Death most resembles a prophet who is without honor in his own land or a poet who is a stranger among his people."
Kahlil Gibran

Life and Death have no morals and especially no class.

Life and Death is a cold drink that never quenches the thirst.

"Die, v.: To stop sinning suddenly."
Elbert Hubbard

Die, v.: closing your eyes and being able to see.

Death, n.: breaking a date easily.

Died, v.: excuse accepted everywhere.

Death, n.: fastest growing theology in history.

Death, n.: doctrine we all follow.

Apparently we have comedians amongst us.

"For death is no more than a turning of us over from time to eternity."
William Penn

For Death is no more than one turn for a worse turn.

Death only bothers people who anticipate it.

Heavy emotions cause sense of time; silenced emotions cause no sense of time, or a sense of mental eternity.

Tuesday, May 05, 2009 12:08:05 PM

Facing the truth is all about accepting a reality you hope is just a lie.

A stranger to life encourages one to cry so hard they usually end up laughing.

Love is for ones who cannot tell the island they are on is far away from everyone else's island.

"From my rotting body, flowers shall grow and I am in them and that is eternity."
Edvard Munch

The flowers that grow on top of your grave let everyone know you now are a slave to them.

Everyone gets to choose how fast they die but the duration after death has already been decided. If your body rots it is an indication you didn't use enough scotch guard.

A life insurance policy does not delay the body rot in you or the recipient of it.

Physically rotting in a box six feet under is far less painful than mentally rotting in a box on the surface. Video killed the radio star and cravings killed the lights of all the stars. If everyone had a sneak peak of what happens after death they would be a bit more humble and much more panicky. The only difference between life and death is the check out times. Chaos & Misery, Hate & Darkness; describes life or death, but not both.

"Home Secretary ..... said she decided to make public the names of 16 people banned since October so others could better understand what sort of behavior Britain was not prepared to tolerate."

http://www.independent.co.uk

If one desires to be an isolationist in matters of views and words that is fine. The very reason Washington killed these guys to begin with was because they didn't like to hear others opinions that did not agree with their own. One must be mindful the British are not free, they are in a tyranny. We as Americans are in the land of the free so we must have compassion on other countries because they simply are not to a level of understanding, freedom is the only way to ensure tyranny will not take control over the people of a country and the right to bear arms is the insurance policy in that equation.

I asked for some advice on how I might best go about doing something to make my books a bit more aesthetic and I explained my situation to them they simply said , "We do not find anything interesting about your situation and we after all are most interested in profitable ventures." And when I read that I realized who I am, and what I am going do, and I what I am going to exterminate with my words. And I recalled that is the exact same sentence I read in general in my mind over and over in my many years of attempting to kill myself. "Todd you are not as important as money." So I pray to god that any one of you will attempt to get in my way because I will eat you alive and you will beg for mercy and I will offer you none. How is that for a lesson to live by. Your money will offer you no defense from me. What you think is important is what I will use to strangle you with. I bet you still think I am concerned about petty things you are concerned about.

Before I hang myself further I will jump back on the translation of wise quotes.

"Clocks slay time... time is dead as long as it is being clicked off by little wheels; only when the clock stops does time come to life."
William Faulkner

When one has a sense of time they never have enough time when one does not they have infinite time. Ones with a sense of time are always in a rush; ones with no sense of time cannot tell they are in a rush. Reality does not pander to a ticking clock. If you sense time; you do not have time to help others because you do not have time to help yourself. If one has too many emotions they mentally sense time and everything else goes to hell because of that.

The only thing that is certain is the past, and the few who understood it are now in it.

Clocks tell time and people who believe the clocks physically slay people. As long as you have a mental clock you will not see reality, you will just see illusions caused by that time delusion.

One can hold onto a sense of time by clinging to emotions that cause a sensation of enjoyment or satisfaction, or one can grow up and climb the mountain with no top, but most beings do not have the fortitude to make the harshest choice. It is impossible to alter the future or the present but some humans are able to clarify the past. My paranoia is only exceeded by my ability to convince myself I am delusional. How little money one has is not the problem, it is what one is willing to do to get the amount of money they wish they had that is. Double standards lead to narrow minded-ness, which sometimes encourages personal adjustments.

5/6/2009 1:59:07 PM

I was going to discuss something that I recently became aware of, as far as some mental aspects that have recently come about but I will ponder that for a bit and just translate some quotes for a bit.

"All of us failed to match our dreams of perfection. So I rate us on the basis of our splendid failure to do the impossible. " William Faulkner

If you think you cannot do much better than your dreams you are dreaming. Splendid failure is a symptom of persever-ance. Failing 1000 times in a row suggests you have mastered something. Failing at everything you do takes much prac-tice. Dreams are simply what you would settle for if you do not try. I will try again in case I said something right. Several arrogant statements are a sign a large humble statement is on its way. When people remind me I misspoke I swiftly convince them they misspoke. Your dreams are never as scary as your thoughts.

I am extremely "gentle" right now because I pondered something. I will explain to you why we should be in full "slavery" in America. I attempt to be in verbal "compassion" but I understand I am delusional. It is too late for verbal "compassion"

TERRORISTIC THREAT

(a) A person commits an offense if he threatens to commit any offense involving violence to any person or property with intent to:

cause a reaction of any type to his threat[s] by an official or volunteer agency organized to deal with emergencies;

place any person in fear of imminent serious bodily injury;

prevent or interrupt the occupation or use of a building; room; place of assembly; place to which the public has access; place of employment or occupation; aircraft, automobile, or other form of conveyance; or other public place;

cause impairment or interruption of public communications, public transportation, public water, gas, or power supply or other public service;

place the public or a substantial group of the public in fear of serious bodily injury; or

influence the conduct or activities of a branch or agency of the federal government, the state, or a political subdivision of the state.

I will now explain why whoever passed this law is a tyrant and will swiftly be watering the tree of liberty and I will also explain why, whoever allows this law to stand is also a tyrant and a domestic threat to my freedom of speech and freedom to communicate and they will also be watering the tree of liberty swiftly.

There is no law above defending the constitution. The constitution is not a LAW. The constitution is not questionable by anyone ever. Anyone who attempts to pass a law that interferes with the constitutional rights afforded to everyone in the land of the free is automatically deemed a domestic threat to the constitution, PERIOD. They are automatically deemed a tyrant and thus need to be shown how to water the tree of liberty which is the constitution. The tree is the constitution and any law passed to infringe on freedom of speech is a tyrannical law passed by tyrants. No beings life is more important than upholding the constitution, period.

"Occasionally the tree of Liberty must be watered with the blood of Patriots and Tyrants."
— Thomas Jefferson

You need to spend the rest of your "infinite" life trying to understand what this comment says and trying to understand the being who said it.

Occasionally people will pass laws that will say you cannot say certain words and that is a sign from god you must "do-nate" your "water" to water the tree while attempting to donate the tyrant's blood that passed that law. So you see I simply do not give a "Thank" who you think you are because you passed a law that negated a constitutional right given to me.

 It means it is my duty to make sure no laws are ever passed to harm the constitution or I must die to uphold the consti-tution. So you just spilled your own water and you also signed mine. I would insult the founding fathers if I did not make sure the constitution is intact for the next generation. So you "loved" me and you "loved" yourself when you passed that. I am bound as an American to die to protect the constitution from all threats foreign and domestic. A law that is passed in America that says I cannot say a certain word is a domestic threat to the constitution and I must die to make sure whoever passed that law waters the tree of liberty or I am in reality a tyrant and a threat to the constitution. So I do not know when it is going to happen but I am an American and I am willing to "love" to uphold the constitution, and I have deemed whoever passed that law is a domestic threat to the constitution. I am a patriot of the constitution and I have just realized the constitution has been compromised with that law that says people cannot speak what is on their mind, so I have just realized we are in a tyranny and I am bound by Jefferson's understanding that as a true American I must be willing to "donate" my "water" in my attempts to "donate" the tyrants "water" to keep the constitution sound.

I do not like that. I am not a founding father. I can only detect what they said and understand it's a crappy situation. I do not want to have to "garden" just to make sure the next generation has freedom of speech. That is not fair. So let's just throw away the constitution and just declare this a fascist state and a dictatorship and then I won't have to shed my blood for the tree of liberty which is the constitution. So here are my options.

Allow the terrorist threat law to stand that says I cannot say certain words and thus negate my freedom of speech de-clared by the constitution ; and switch over to a tyrannical state system and burn the constitution and never speak of it again or Prepare to do a lot of watering.

That is the only two options I have now. That is it. What I want is certainly not what is before me. There has to be a typo in the constitution so I will review it carefully because these founding fathers cannot possibly mean I actually have to prepare for death to keep the constitution alive. We need to stop teaching our kids what these founding father said, be-cause they were a bunch of crazies. And we need to burn that constitution swiftly because it is a suicide pact from hell. All they are really saying is," If you are not willing to die literally for freedom, you should not be in the land of the free because you are worthless and have no fortitude and do not deserve freedom to begin with."

And what really sucks is they meant, you might have to die in conflicts against your own fellow Americans if they pass a law that negates your freedoms, such a freedom to say anything you want, ever. So then you see that and understand you are not an American you are a just a delusional loser who goes around saying you are an American. The Americans are the ones who died to create the constitution. You are just a freeloading whore on their coat tails and you will never be anything else because you only care about yourself and your life and you care nothing about keeping freedom alive. I have no fear because you cannot beat a dead horse.

Before I get to the constitution I will go through that law and maybe I am mistaken about it. Maybe it does not discourage ones freedom to say words.

"A person commits an offense if he threatens to commit any offense involving violence to any person or property with intent to:"

If a person says they will water the tree of liberty to uphold the constitution they are a terrorist. If a person says I am willing to attack the tyrant and kill him to uphold the constitution which the founding fathers said I better be willing to do from time to time, I am a terrorist. So if a tyrant passes a law and says you must all jump off a cliff and you say you are going to kill that tyrant, you are a terrorist. If you say you are going to water the tree of liberty with that tyrant you are a terrorist. Perhaps I am mistaken so I will look at another aspect of this law. I am attempting to talk myself out of what I understand my obligations are as an American.

"cause a reaction of any type to his threat[s] by an official or volunteer agency organized to deal with emergencies;"

So if you say anything to anyone deemed an official and it causes them to get emotional you are a terrorist. If one suggests to an official I will never vote for you again you retard, you are a terrorist. If one says to that official, "You will make great fertilizer for the tree of liberty", you are a terrorist. If one even makes the most vague statement at all to an official, you are a terrorist. That is in direct violation to the constitutional freedom of speech. Therefore this 1st aspect of the law is a tyrannical law and I am bound by my duty as an American to sacrifice myself to water the tree of liberty.

Perhaps the second clause will negate the first one.

"place any person in fear of imminent serious bodily injury;"

FEAR OF IMMINENT serious bodily injury. That is exactly what the government said we should be, which was why they tricked us to invade Iraq and Afghanistan, So the government should be locked in prison for scaring us and tricking us into doing what they wanted to do. They clearly said "If we do not go to Iraq and Afghanistan they will come over here and kill us and they will do it swiftly." So they threatened us with "FEAR of imminent bodily injury". I only detect many things are going to be watering the tree of liberty very swiftly. Perhaps you need to look up the word swiftly, swiftly. Now that last phase of the tyrannical law did not satisfy my need to be satisfied so I will look into the third aspect.

"threatens to commit any offense involving violence"

I understand "threatens" is a nice way to say "you do not have freedom of speech". That means you do not have freedom to assemble peacefully. You cannot say anything you want and so you cannot assemble peacefully. Assemble peacefully means you get to say whatever you want, but you cannot do anything physically. So we are in fact in a tyranny and if you doubt that you can go "Thank" yourself because I do not give a "Thank" what you say because you killed the constitution and I am bound to water the tree of liberty.

"Congress shall make no law respecting an establishment of religion, or prohibiting the free exercise thereof; or abridging the freedom of speech, or of the press; or the right of the people peaceably to assemble, and to petition the Government for a redress of grievances."

Congress passed that law that said you cannot threaten others verbally so congress passed a law that infringed or prohibited freedom of speech, so congress is the tyrant and they destroyed the constitution and the worst part of it, they took out the first amendment,

"Congress shall make no law.. abridging the freedom of speech".

"to shorten a written work by taking out parts." That is what abridging means!

So Congress and voters who elected congress changed "freedom of speech" to "freedom to say some things, but not all things or you are a terrorist." So since they abridged the constitution they are a tyrant and need to be assisted in how to water a tree swiftly. There is no hesitation or room to second guess. They hung their self. We are just here to pull the lever. Simply by breathing they spit on Washington's face, so do not assume I like you. The only difference between me and you mindfully is, I am looking for the fastest way to check out and you are looking for the easiest way to stay a slave.

I herby want to delete everything I typed today and I am ashamed of everything I typed today and I am embarrassed by everything I typed today, and so I will publish it to condition myself away from my emotional delusions of fear. No being cares what an insane person says. It is time for some gardening in the land of the free and in a couple hundred years they will write about the patriots who won, so nothing else matters at this time outside of that, so try to water properly and maybe they will write something right about you. They certainly will not negate the first amendment to go after an insane person. It is simply a delusion in my mind and the worst thing that can happen is they will hang me on a cross, and that sounds like fun. I prefer long infinite suffering when you kill me. Look at that as my last request so you do not have to ask me what it is, when the time comes.

Apparently subconscious likes to hang me often so I will now revert back to wise quotes to take a little off the edges of a spear so that makes a sharp spear to pierce me with. I mention in my earlier books I have more faith in freedom of speech than any being in the universe, and now I know why I said that.

Your life is not important at all in contrast to making sure the constitution is always intact. You can pass a law that says" I cannot speak my mind about some things.", but the minute you do, I deem it a domestic threat to the constitution and it is my duty as a defender of the constitution to water the tree of liberty. No questions no hesitation. I am an American and that is the burden Washington places on us when we are born here. We have to be willing to die to protect the constitution against any domestic threats such as laws that say one being cannot say something because another delusional tyrannical being passed a law and say they can't say something.

So do not ever say you are American. You are simply a delusional being that is in denial.

Only a tyrant would pass or allow a law that abridges the principle; absolute freedom of speech.

A being who says "If you threaten someone with words I will throw you in jail" in fact threatens you with words. They are saying "If you say words I do not like I will throw you in jail and in jail someone may kill you." So in fact they threaten you with imminent bodily harm if you say certain words. So that means the ones who pass that law should be thrown in jail for doing exactly what the law they passed says one is not allowed to do. So I am not sure who passed that law but whoever it was should be thrown in jail for making terrorist threats by passing that law, PERIOD. So the law is not as important as the constitution ever. The constitution is not negotiable. It is off limits. You did not create it. You do not have a right to cancel it out no matter how many people vote to do so. It would be called the Law of the United States of American instead of the Constitution of the United States. So now it is important see what the hell a constitution is.

"the system of fundamental principles according to which a nation, state, corporation, or the like, is governed."

A fundamental principle means, if you erode or abridge that fundamental principle you lose the principle. If you erode absolute freedom of speech you lose freedom, period. So if there is any law that says you cannot say a certain word or sentence and they enforce it, they reveal their self as a tyrant and you have a duty to water the tree of liberty with them and you may also have to water that tree with your blood in order to do that, period. Dam I lost my train of thought. Oh yes, you are bad, I am good.

So here is the only logical solution so you do not keep passing laws that abridge the constitution and keep spitting in the face of Washington.

Block your emotions and desires and cravings by saying perhaps a lot. This will loosen up your locked mind. This will also encourage you to question things and ponder things you read and hear so you do not end up being a mental sheep that no longer has brain function. This will eventually lead you to going into a dominate subconscious state of mind and you will be insane like me and then you will just say a bunch of stuff in infinite books but never actually do anything physically so you will just wait for the tyrant to show up at your house and kill you so that will start a revolution and everyone will assist the tyrant with the definition of "watering the tree". That is the logical solution.

The monks offer to house me, looks better and better by the sentence.

This is the exact moment I decided to put perhaps in front of every sentence in this book except this one.19:20:13

Lawmakers pass resolution claiming Oklahoma's sovereignty..

"We're going to get it done one way or the other," said the resolutions' author, Rep. Charles Key, R-Oklahoma City. "I think our governor is out of step."**www.Newsok.com**

"We are going to "get it done" "one way or another"" That is a terroristic threat. Saying "I am going to get you one way or another.", is a threat. And in this case the person is saying "The government is out of step and we are going to get it done one way or another." What does "done" mean? So now he is PERHAPS certainly being watched by the NSA as a potential enemy combatant. You can PERHAPS bet your life on it.

I am mindful I keep forgetting I am not talking about the present in my books I am strictly telling the future.

16 year old homeschooled child arrested, held under 'patriot act'.

"We have no rights under the Patriot Act to even defend them, because the Patriot Act basically supersedes the Constitution," she said. "It wasn't intended to drag your barely 16-year-old, 120-pound son out in the middle of the night on a charge that we can't even defend."

"They're saying that 'We feel this individual is a terrorist or an enemy combatant against the United States, and we're going to suspend all of those due process rights because this person is an enemy of the United States," said Dan Boyce, a defense attorney and former U.S. attorney not connected to the Lundeby case." http://www.wral.com/

I submit I am delusional. I submit I am insane. I submit everything is just fantastic.

Here is what I perceive about America. We are going to "vote" ourselves into such a tyrannical nation that we all will "vote" ourselves back into total freedom with our arms and I perceive this cycle goes on forever. After we start locking up small children for threatening to steal their preschool mate's toys, we will start voting down all these laws and swing back into the opposite direction. Already there are states considering legalizing drugs that have been illegal but where legal before they were illegal. Already there are states that are starting to allow same sex marriages. The psychology of this is simple. Freedom of speech. Freedom of speech means you are supposed to have arguments. You are supposed to get angry with your words so you do not end up getting angry with your fists. So this terroristic Law is a way to force people to use the word perhaps and maybe. If someone says "I will harm you." That's a terroristic threat. If someone says, "Perhaps I will harm you." That is perhaps not a terroristic threat unless this is a tyrannical state or police state which I am certain it is.

If someone says "I will destroy the universe" that is a Terroristic threat and since that person is in the subset of the universe, they are suggesting they are suicidal by saying they will also destroy their self, so they should be baker acted, and then they are also a threat to every being in the universe because they are suggesting they will destroy the universe and every being is in the universe. But if they say "Perhaps or maybe I will destroy the universe." That means nothing and is not a baker act offense or a terroristic threat. So again the mindset aspect comes into play. So a being mentally switches out the word in their mind "love" with the word "Kill" and then they can go around and say "I love the government and I love all voters." Now to other people they sound very sane and fine and not a threat. But to that being who is saying that, they are saying in their mind "I kill the government and I kill all voters." and they are within the law. So it is all mindset. One is unable to stop a person from switching out the definitions of words. It is impossible to stop that. So they pass a law to make it illegal to say certain words arranged in a certain fashion. So the solution is to use words that are legal to substitute for the words you want to say and then throw the word perhaps in front of it. It is called a veiled threat. It is relative to the observer. It is all mindset. One does not have to believe the definitions they are told to believe. But psychologically what is delusional is if a country declares war, all of their laws no longer apply. So people say "No one is above the law." But that is a delusional saying because in fact, anyone in the military is above the law. They have free reign to kill innocent people and blame is on the rain or the war. They can kill infinite people and then say "Yeah but". So they are in fact above the law that the voters created. So all the military has to do is create an enemy and then they can say "We killed all these innocent people but they were neat the enemy, so it was not murder." And then the voters will say, "Yes you did not spit in our face by breaking our laws, so ""Thank You" kind beings."

Of course no one gets anything I say so it is rather funny I continue to monologue to myself into infinity.

"Despise the enemy strategically, but take him seriously tactically."
Mao Tse-Tung

This is a brilliant saying. It is saying, Argue like mad with everyone but at the end of the day, think about what they said and attempt to learn from their argument. This is really what America is all about. Say anything you want and act like you mean it, in hopes someone will argue with you and set you straight. Only a fool pays the first price that is recommended. This means every state should be declaring sovereignty and threatening to succeed every single day. It is okay to say "I hate the government." That is fine, that starts a discussion that will lead one to appreciate the government. The government is your fellow citizens. You should argue with them as friends argue over a girl. No need to get physical, you are just arguing for the sake of understanding. Only weak minded beings need physical weapons. So you should hate me and tell me you hate me and explain why you hate me so that I can form a good argument to counter your delusional argument and at the end of the day you may actually learn as much from me as I learned from your delusional argument.

There was a Russian comment I may have mentioned in an earlier book and they said something to effect, America will split up like we did. That is perhaps possible. That is okay. That will enable others to appreciate what they had in a solid unified nation. But that is no reason to go to war with physical weapons and kill each other. Nothing is worth that much. No state that succeeds is worth one beings life. You are delusional if you do not understand that. That is the whole point. Oklahoma can succeed from the union but they can't move their state. It is still in the middle of the United States. They can do anything they want and pass any law they want, but they are stuck in the middle of the United States. So in reality they only leave the United States on paper not in actuality. That is what freedom is all about, to see how many different ways you can arrange things to give the illusion we are not one nation under "god". We can pass laws and attempt to break free, but we are still one nation under god. We are landlocked to each other forever. So there is no point in fighting actual physical wars to keep us as one nation under "god". We are one nation no matter what happens. You can look at it like this. America or freedom is in our blood for the duration. That is why it is so important perhaps to argue about everything and make threats about leaving and running away and declaring sovereignty. It's verbal posturing. No matter what anyone says ever, IT IS IMPOSSIBLE TO BREAK THE LAW UNTIL YOU PHYSICALLY DO SOMETHING. If that is not the case then we should all be locked up. We are all potentially criminals so we should be locked up. They should preempt us and lock us up.

If someone suggests "I will get drunk and drive home tonight." They should be locked up for drunk driving. They make a terroristic threat by saying "I will get drunk" because getting drunk means they will be out of control. Then they say "and drive home" now they are threatening their self and other people.

So I am scared and fearful of imminent danger for my safety, so if you are at a bar you should be locked up because you will drive home intoxicated and perhaps kill me when you wreck your car into me. So anyone who even drives a car; I am in FEAR OF IMMINENT serious bodily injury. I am in Florida and I can tell you the old people scare me to death and I am in a constant state of FEAR OF IMMINENT serious bodily injury. So they should all be locked up. The teenagers they are also very unpredictable rushing around buying rap CDs so they also create a sense of FEAR OF IMMINENT serious bodily injury in my being. So they should also be locked up. If someone says we need to go attack another person in another country I understand that might piss those people off in that country and they may come an attack me , so that person who suggested we should go attack someone in another country also created a sense of FEAR OF IMMINENT serious bodily injury in me. So they should also be locked up. And then when someone decides to lock me up they are putting me in with other beings who I cannot trust and so they are also cause a sense of FEAR OF IMMINENT serious bodily injury in me. So they should be locked up for locking me up with beings I do not trust.

Einstein suggested it is all relative to the observer. That is right. Who determines what FEAR OF IMMINENT serious bodily injury is. Who determines it? Some being who gets paid money to lock people up so they can get kick backs from their friend who builds prisons?

As long as the NSA doesn't tell my infinite wrath potential about the Asian porn sites I have "experimented" with, in the last 10 or so years, testing out my photograph viewing software, I pretty much do not give a dam what they do.

Now I am going to experiment with alcohol again to try and kill this "subconscious dominate aspect".

I talked myself out of it so I will attempt another day.00:11:42

5/7/2009 8:35:14 AM

My ability to take a hint is only exceeded by my inability to tell it was a hint.

 Every night I get to a stage of wanting to give up on books and then in the morning I am reminded no being is ever going to read them and I feel much better.

Love reminds one of all the things they desire to control but are unable to. Love has control strings attached; Compassion just is. Translating thoughts into physical actions is a dangerous affair that should be questioned diligently. The trick about humanity is: Everyone learned everything from the ones who came before them, so the very first humans knew nothing.

I will now form a new religion.

The doctrine of the new religion is to use psychological conditioning methods to get to a dominate subconscious state of mind.

One is not allowed to insult ones who chose not to take the route to get to a subconscious dominate state of mind.

One is not allowed to talk poorly of ones who decide to stay in the emotional conscious dominate sense of time state of mind, it is no one's business to make decisions for others.

Ones priority must focus on making their self more subconscious dominate using the subconscious dominate methods.

One has no teacher but their self; they are allowed to consider the suggestions of others.

No one member of the religion is able to assume the role of the authority figure.

Questioning everything anyone says is the conversation topic of the meetings.

Some emotional conditioning methods include:

Using the word perhaps and maybe as much as possible, to ease ones mental state into a state of questioning.

Avoid cravings and desires for a short period to condition one away from emotions to start the subconscious dominate unlocking process.

Avoid strict "I know this for a fact" arguments but attempt to consider all arguments with an infinite grain of salt and most importantly one's own arguments should be considered with the infinitely larger grain of salt.

The new religion will be called: Psychological Conditioning to become Subconscious Dominate.

There is no founder of the religion because everyone knew this all along.

If I needed the government's permission to make this new religion legitimate, I would tell them I would have to do that, and they would be awe struck by my compassion. "Thank You."

Safety in numbers is a threat to ones who are able to think for their self. The only danger to a herd is one who is outside of and not a part of the herd. One who uses words to solve a conflict will avoid becoming the enemy he is fighting against.

I will sum up my situation as I perceive it. I spent a good part of 20 years in major depression and mental sorrow and a recent string of events allowed me to mentally work my way out of that emotional nightmare and I am factually verbally willing to perhaps annihilate the entire universe perhaps if it attempts to do things that would steer me back to that emotional nightmare I came from by attempting to suggest writing infinite books is worse than where I was before the string of events happened. So the universe would be perhaps infinitely wise to avoid attempting to "help me" in any way, shape, or form.

Now I will discuss something of importance.

The weight of the stone around your neck is equal to the burden you have placed on others.

The easiest way to avoid hurting others feelings with words is to never say anything at all.

The best way to respond to someone who insults you with words is to convince them with words they are right. The best way to learn compassion is to remind yourself everything you know is wrong. I learned the fewer people in a chat room with me, the less my chances of getting banned increases.

New song with an old message. http://www.youtube.com/watch?v=h4BKrlq5BC0 – LifeLike

If you give me 800 billion dollars I will burn it all, and because I tell you that up front, you will not feel robbed and foolish, you will just feel foolish.

I am fully aware what really happened to me was I became conscious dominate which means before the accident I was unconscious dominate. Other words when I had emotions and a sense of time I was in an unconscious mental state. As in the suggestion by Freud "The goal of the therapist is to make the unconscious conscious." I will avoid mentioning that reality in this book because some beings would simply be unable to face a great truth such as that. A more positive way to look at it is: With no sense of time and thus being subconscious dominate I am not as delusional and prone to halluci- nations as much as I was before the accident. With that said, I submit I am not even starting to be warmed up yet. When I have started to get warmed up I will remind you. Perhaps one might suggest, If I had to try, you would be in trouble. The problem is I do not see anything anyone can possibly do to harm me further then they have already harmed me if I make statements like "If you have a sense of time and feel aches and pains and get tired easily, and have strong hunger desires, you are literally unconscious and in a complete mental state of hallucinations and delusions and you are a threat to yourself and everyone around you, so you should seek mental help swiftly because you are extremely dangerous."

I simply do not perceive there is anything one who is unconscious can possibly do to me that would make me even blink, for making a comment like I just did. I know enough about psychology to know that many delusional and psychotic patients avoid taking their medication because they start to think they are normal. This is very dangerous because when one is in a full delusional state of mind and seeing hallucinations all around them they might start acting on the delu- sions they perceive and thus should attempt to swiftly get back on their medication.

The sad thing is many of the completely psychotic patients go undiagnosed for their entire life because they actually believe sense of time, strong cravings for food, and daily aches and pains are simply normal, when in reality they are extremely abnormal and a certain indication one is in full psychosis.

Perhaps I could have used a more strategic wording method to explain a great truth such as that. Perhaps I could have used far more compassion and mercy to explain such a great truth such as that. The greatest truth is: I do not have any compassion or mercy and I do not plan on working on my strategy to develop compassion and mercy. "Thank You."

Anyone who assumes a government is being honest with them needs to have many aspects of their being examined, and they should perhaps focus on their upper regions first.

"Intelligence officials released documents this evening saying that House Speaker….. (D-Calif.) was briefed in September 2002 about the use of harsh interrogation tactics against al-Qaeda prisoners, seemingly contradicting her repeated statements over the past 18 months that she was never told that these techniques were actually being used." Washington-Post.com

If a parent will lie to their child about Santa Clause why would they assume they are not being lied to by their "parent" in Washington.

The first lie ever told was when a human said "Lying gets you nowhere." Because the truth is lying gets you where you need to be, of course that's a lie, because lies also get you where you are. The major disconnect in society is the ones who say they are not liars, are lying, and the ones who say they are liars, are telling the truth.

The ones who say they are not liars are infinite liars and the ones who say they should not be trusted can be slightly trusted.

One might suggest I am lying when I say, "No one has a right to read any words I write in my books because of what I had to mentally do to myself for 15 years to reach the clarity I am at now to write these books", so we will both find out if I am a liar, in give or take 120 years, that is certain.

Perhaps if one has a sense of time they perceive they have plenty of time to find out, but I have no sense of time and I have already started preparing the welcome wagon for you for invading my privacy and insulting me by reading my personal diaries. One might suggest there will be a seat at my table for any being who infringes on my personal diaries.

There are no laws where I am mindfully at because when one arrives, they arrive in the prison.

The viper is the one who knows because the viper has bitten off the tree of KNOW-ledge and fallen off the LEDGE.

5/8/2009 1:37:08 AM

I am not pleased so I am getting an early start on writing today.

I have noticed one thing in chat rooms for certain.

<Heimdall> perhaps we have come to an understanding.

<Heimdall> talk about out of context.

<grace> are you on drugs?

Now let's contrast that single comment by grace with this comment.

Act 2:13   Others mocking(GRACE) said, These men are full of new wine.

Act 2:14 But Peter, standing up with the eleven(Ones who also went subconscious dominate), lifted up his voice, and said unto them, Ye men of Judaea, and all *ye* that dwell at Jerusalem(The World), be this known unto you, and hearken to my words:

Act 2:15 For these are not drunken (They speak in random access words cause by subconscious random access thoughts), as ye suppose, seeing it is *but* the third hour of the day.

Act 2:16 But this is that which was spoken by the prophet Joel;(Joel also was subconscious dominate and from the old testament or Torah)

So this is exactly what is happening. A being with extreme subconscious dominate mind usually caused by a rare accident arrives. Some they hang around or are close friends also become subconscious dominate. One thing to note is John the Baptist was in some relation to Jesus. They killed John the Baptist why? Because he talked like he was drunk because he spoke in Random Access sentences which is the reverse of what one who has conscious emotional dominate mind speaks in, which is sequential access sentences.

 So of course I sound like I am on drugs to ones who are unconscious or conscious dominate or ones with emotions and a sense of time. And of course Joel knew some of the other beings in the old testament, and they were known as prophets or wise men, but in reality one who is subconscious dominate is literally light years beyond ones with a sense of time mental potential simply because subconscious is the powerhouse of the mind.

 No one can argue with that but the trade off is, the world is full of people with a sense of time and have strong hunger, so these ones with subconscious dominate minds sound like they are on drugs, as grace suggests.

It is a simple principle. Kill what is different than you. That's what they do to me in every chat channel. I am alien to them and they are alien to me, so they attack me and I attack them because we assume each other must be on drugs. Dam I lost my train of thought.

Now the next verse is rather misleading to some.

Act 2:17 And it shall come to pass in the last days, saith God, I will pour out of my Spirit(Subconscious dominate aspect) upon all flesh: and your sons and your daughters shall prophesy(Know the future or be able to tell what will happen), and your young men shall see visions(Telepathy), and your old men shall dream dreams:

Now this is all misleading. Subconscious is the powerhouse of the mind. I certainly have developed some sort of feeling others through vision. I certainly can sometimes tell what others are thinking or are going to say before they say it, but that is because the subconscious calculates and has so much information at it finger tips so to speak, it can tell what other are thinking or are going to say. One can simply sedate a person into a comma and then hold a conversation with them and be able to say, "I am clearly more coherent than that person in a coma."

So it is misleading to say one is so much smarter than the one in the coma. It simply is a matter of, one is using the powerhouse aspect of the mind and one is using a weak aspect of the mind. It's no contest. But the good news is everyone has a subconscious and it can become dominate with some simple emotional conditioning techniques. Now remind yourself the words "subconscious" and psychology did not exist at the time the Bible was written. So they perhaps substituted some words to explain this powerhouse we call subconscious. So then one might suggest these beings did the best they could based on the fact they did not have the luxury of those words at that time. So this subconscious is perhaps what was unlocked and made these beings appear "drunk" and "insane" and "out of place" with the "regular folks" so they butchered them.

That is pretty much the expected characteristics of human beings with left brain of emotional aspect dominate. They tend to butcher what is different than them. They mock ones who are different than their set herd.

 Do I need to give examples? Racist people dislike other people who are different than them. School kids mock the ones who do not dress like they do and do not like what they do. Then you get stuff like Columbine, and when that is over the people say the kids who did Columbine were evil. But the great truth of it is, the kids mocked those beings to the point those beings determined they are going slaughter the ones who mocked them, and because those beings did not have dominate subconscious aspect, that led them to get pay backs using physical means instead of words.

I get mocked in chat rooms more times in 1 hour than most people get mocked in their lifetime, but I am clever enough to understand it is simply I am dealing with beings who perceive I am on drugs because I type in Random access thoughts and sentences and they can only grasp sequential access thoughts and sentences. So they say I am retarded, but I laugh because I fully know: If I am retarded they are simply brain dead.

So one should be mindful I am not a racist I was fully conscious dominate with a sense of time up until the accident of about seven months ago. It is impossible for me to truly be racists when I know everyone has a subconscious, they simply do not know how to make it dominate. I found out by accident but I certainly would not go around saying I am something special because to me that is not possible. I found out accidentally. There is nothing special about that. Now there is one aspect that is perhaps going to throw a wrench in all of this. I am certainly on the fence about everything I say at all times, and that is my right.

Gen 1:26 And God said, Let us make man in our image, after our likeness:

So perhaps, and I am using an infinite "perhaps" on this one, the likeness of god is subconscious and he gave man a conscious emotional aspect to his mind, and a subconscious powerful aspect. Now this could mean, god is mother nature, god is just "the way it is" or god is a supreme being, and that is why we are different than all the other animals because we can tell each other how to unlocked the "god aspect" of the mind.

So I am going to stay on my fence and you can go jump off cliffs if you want, but I am not warmed up yet so I am going to let it be. I am going to ponder which it is until the end of time. I am not falling for the "I know" trap anymore. I do not know a dam thing ever. I am much safer that way. I am not concerned about what you think you know; I am only concerned about avoiding knowing anything ever. So perhaps this whole concept of "saved" or in the "light" is simply saying if you have a sense of time you are under the influence of the "dark side" of the mind, or emotional conscious aspect. So that would perhaps mean if you subscribe to the "god" concept in the major western religions and you have a sense of time and have strong cravings for food, and hunger for food, and have daily aches and pains, and you are not in a constant wide awake state when you are not sleeping, you are what a religious person may perhaps call "not in gods graces", period.

You draw your conclusions, I will write mine. I fully submit I do not know, so you are on your own. I know therefore I am. I am careful to avoid that trap.

You do not want me to get into the blame game about columbine, but you better be dam sure you are not unconscious and delusional when you start throwing your stones at people in relation to that event. You contact me if you have problems about anything I say ever, because I do not care who you think you are. Every time you take a breath you remind yourself I have infinite compassion.

I will regress back to the wise quotes because clarity tends to be a bit "hang myself friendly".

"A bird doesn't sing because it has an answer, it sings because it has a song."
Lou Holtz

A bird is experimenting with singing a song but it never accomplishes it.

Birds learned how to sing so they could insult you as you walk by.

A little bird suggested it only insults you with its songs, and never me, after I mentioned I crave roast duck, for no reason at all.

"A hen is only an egg's way of making another egg."
Samuel Butler

Humans are nature's way to exterminate all other species.

A human is bullet's way of making another gun.

This book is my way of writing another one.

The quality of this book is only exceeded by the quality of all other books.

Hair is a great way to hide the embarrassment just underneath it.

The skull protects a person's brain from further injury.

In some people the skull only covers up the obvious injury.

In some people their skull is their most valuable asset.

Without a skull some people would only have legs to stand on.

A skull attempts to keep the mind from wandering.

One is simply not allowed to love another being, they are only allowed to observe that being and attempt to understand: What the hell was that being thinking?; so they can then look at their self and ponder that same question.

07:10:11

I am weird today so I want to attempt to explain what I see in the last words of some major figures in history.

The Buddha's final words were, "All composite things pass away. Strive for your own liberation with diligence."

It is suggested Jesus said on the cross: *"Father* forgive them, for they know not what they do."

Mohammed: Among his last words were: "We the community of Prophets are not inherited. Whatever we leave is for charity."

What I understand from a psychological point of view is these sayings are indicative of what subconscious aspect is all about. It is very cerebral and so it is anti-physical or earthly or material possession based. "All composite things pass away" that is the same as "Give unto Caesar what his is and give unto me what is mine." That is also in relation to "Whatever we leave is for charity." Because that comment is the same as "Give freely." This is a direct result of the cerebral aspect that dominate subconscious thrives on. It is not money is bad or material things are bad, it is one's mind is so mental based with subconscious dominate it is no longer material based focused. This is complex though.

I cannot speak for what they perceived, but I submit I am not charitable. I reached my depression state and suicidal state because I didn't have money and I didn't have a good job and I didn't have luxuries, and so that is why I was depressed so now I am mentally weary of valuables such as material things. I simply do not want to go back to that "See how much money you can make so when you lose it all you will be depressed."

My mindset is, forget money, I would rather have no money and have no profits from my books then get caught up in that insane rat race, that I can never win. So as a tradition in all of my books starting with the second volume, I remind the reader I have the copyright to this material and I will never enforce it, so give these words freely.

As for the "for they know not what they do comment." This is a direct comment about ones with conscious dominate, sense of time, beings. They are simply unconscious as Freud suggested. They killed Jesus because he was different, he spoke about things they could not grasp so they determined he was crazy and so they butchered him. This is simply because he was speaking using dominate subconscious mind and it was beyond the conscious dominate beings ability to handle. His words were beyond their understanding so they butchered him. That means I go to Christian channels and they say "Are you on drugs." I go to any religious channel and speak and they all say "You are on drugs, a robot or insane, so please get out of here or we will ban you from the channel."

So they literally know not what they do. They perceive I am the one who is messed up because they are unable to know, they are unconscious. I am simply unable to communicate with them. They are essentially brain dead. They think I must certainly have a problem, it cannot be them. So they ban me and say "You are a bot and a idiot and on drugs." What this means is, if I was around 2000 years ago and said what I say, I would be butchered by ones with a sense of time and thus emotional dominate minds, because I would say things that is simply beyond their ability to grasp because they are unconscious in contrast to one with a subconscious dominate mind. So it is a complete and utter disconnect.

So I am pleased with the religious leaders or "founders" of these religions. So I get very upset. So before you go running your mouth about who killed Jesus you just determine if you have a sense of time and have cravings to eat and you can look in the mirror and know exactly who butchered Jesus, and most importantly, you would butcher him again because you would say "What drugs are you on?, you are crazy, you are not like me, so I am going to butcher you." Do not assume you would not because you are delusional and unconscious.

People who have a sense of time butchered Jesus, do not kid yourself genius.

Why does a hunter shoot a deer? The deer is different. That is how the unconscious think. If it is different, kill it and then you will have control over it. Emotions make one controlling and silenced emotions eliminate that desire. Emotions cause isolation that led to control and the reverse is silenced emotions lead to freedom. I understand I am not allowed to enforce a copyright on my books because that is a form of control. I understand I am not allowed to tell anyone what to do other than think for their self. I understand I am not allowed to preach. I am only allowed to write books in the form of a diary, that suggests I am taking to myself . That is my emotional conditioning required to get away with what I do.

Serial killers usually start off by killing animals because they think it is fun. Do you think hunting an animal and killing it for the trophy is fun? Serial killers keep trophies of the ones they kill, a lock of hair or maybe a necklace. People who fish sometimes keep the fish to eat. That is one thing. Sometimes people hunt for the food. That is one thing. Sometimes people just kill things because they can and because it is fun. That is abnormal. One is psychologically unstable to kill things for fun or for sport or for meaningless gains. Things need to be killed so we can survive. That is unavoidable. That is bad enough. But then people who are unconscious think they need three meals a day because their mind has stopped functioning. One does not need three meals a day because we have multi vitamins. So if you need to eat breakfast because you wake up and have hunger, you are mentally unconscious, delusional and hallucinating. You should not have much hunger. You may be thinking your hunger desires to eat often is real but it is simply a strong illusion and a strong hallucination caused by an excess of the drug, emotions. It is nothing more than that.

Some people live their whole lives based around when they get to eat next because they are always hungry. They get physically weak if they don't have food to eat every 4 or 5 hours. People say "I need to get something to eat." That is called hunger. That is a symptom one is unconscious and is mentally abnormal. I do not hold that against anyone. They have freedom to be mentally abnormal because that is none of my business, but it is factually true none the less. One's disbelief does not change a fact. I decided to write infinite books so I might as well write about something. The great truth of my writings is what I do not say. You just get the slim pickings. You won't be getting any of the good stuff. Just keep telling yourself you are just like me so you do not panic.

15:24:54

I have been avoiding writing today because I keep remembering who you are.

"A people that values its privileges above its principles soon loses both."
Dwight D. Eisenhower

A being that clings to physical luxury avoids mental struggle and ends up a waste of humanity.

One with material advantage is no match for one with the mental clarity who is able talk them out of their possessions.

Mental clarity can only be earned, not purchased or partitioned by set plans and mass production schemes.

"those who sacrifice their liberty(absolute freedom of speech) for security , deserve neither"

"Do not waste your time on Social Questions. What is the matter with the poor is Poverty; what is the matter with the rich is Uselessness."
George Bernard Shaw

The poor are the raped and the rich is the rapist.

A carpetbagger is one who has decided to take advantage of others instead to share there blessings.

The rich will convince their self, their wealth is their own doing when it is really their undoing.

Every decision one in poverty makes is a life and death decision; every decision the wealthy make has no consequence.

The rich would never give up their money because they are aware they are useless without it.

One who is poor in material wealth is rich in mental struggle, and one who is rich in material wealth has given up on mental wealth.

The ones in poverty seek the mental challenge the rich do not have the fortitude to handle.

In an economic downturn the poor get wiser and the rich cry like babies.

Ones in poverty have no weaknesses; the rich have millions of weaknesses.

 The rich do not know who the poor are, but the poor know what the rich are.

Money mentally liberates the poor and mentally drowns the rich.

When money loses its value the poor get mentally tough and the rich mentally crumble.

The rich need millions of safety nets to cover their poor decisions; the poor do not need a safety net because they only make rich decisions.

This Shaw guy is dangerous with his words so you should avoid him at all costs. He clearly flaunts the norms of society and should be locked up because he is just a downright threat to society by making comments like he does. He is evil and bad and should be watched carefully.

The poor know the wealthy are useless that is why the wealthy have so much security around their homes. The rich believe the fence keeps the poor out, but the poor have tricked the rich into an isolation trap because the poor are trying to contain the fatal disease the rich have.

A wealthy man buys many nice items to let everyone know he is not mentally wealthy.

I have no morals because I see what they have done to you.

The wealthy turn the physical blessing of abundance into a mental curse of isolation.

The problem you are facing is, I simply do not know what this accident means. I only know everything makes perfect sense to me now and not much made sense to me before the accident. It happened on Oct 31st 2008. Do not expect me to tell you what it means because I am honestly in the bubble and all I know is, I decided to write infinite books about two months after the accident. I do not remember what is in my books. I am in the bubble. I just type letters swiftly. That is as far as I go in understanding what this accident means. I am on this date, no longer even on a mental plane to be able to speculate what this accident means. I am strictly reduced to the role of a sounding board. I go with the flow and am unable to explain what the flow is. I am not here to save you. Perhaps you misunderstood my intentions. You should perhaps punch that into your calculator swiftly. I told you I am insane but I am not on drugs but you wish I was. I had an accident so please have mercy on me because you will not be getting any mercy from me. "Thank You." You will pray in vain I was capable of mercy before I am finish with you. You will pray for death but your prayers will be ignored. Perhaps we have come to an understanding. "Thank You."

I will get back to these stupid quotes.

"Most of the change we think we see in life is due to truths being in and out of favor."
Robert Frost

All truth is relative to the delusional capacity of the observer.

The suicide victim has determined the greatest truth is to distance their self from society.

The rich have determined the greatest truth is to ensure everyone else remains poor.

My greatest truth is: I write infinite books to remind you I am not the loser as you suggested I was and I pray to god your guilt will drive you mad. What that means is: When you do understand I am not a loser after all and you want to be my friend, I am going to tell you to go to hell. So save your critics for ones who give a dam about what you think. You already told me what you think about me so you no longer get to speak to me ever. Ponder the concept "the shoe is on the other foot." and multiply that by infinity infinite times. A monk suggested I was tapped and I only have one chance to take advantage of the tap and I swiftly reminded him he is not allowed to advise me ever, and he took my advice.

A government's greatest truth is that the slaves are easily manipulated.

A government's greatest truth is that the slaves will do anything if you scare them enough.

A voter's greatest truth is that they perceive they know the truth.

A psychologist's greatest truth is that if they make enough money from pushing pills they won't go insane.

A cop's greatest truth is that one day they will have to lock their self up for enforcing laws.

A workers greatest truth is that they are working up the nerve to kill the boss that enslaves them.

A writer's greatest truth is that one day they will be able to write.

A scientist's greatest truth is that one day they will discover what they cannot believe.

A child's greatest truth is that one day they are doomed to become like the adults.

A parent's greatest truth is that they cannot be like a child so they take out that rage on the children.

I don't hesitate, I seal fate. You just wait, that's your bait.

I am not concerned with surviving this world (emotional aspect) I am too busy ensuring you do not survive the next one (Subconscious aspect).

My inability to write is only exceeded by your inability to understand what I write about.

For those just join us this is the plot of my infinite books. Video game, such and such, end of time, such and such.

I just watch some sort of comedy show with Bill Mahr and it had Seth Mcfarlan on as a guest and it was such a hilarious show because they just essentially cracked jokes about everything. I did not detect one serious comment it was all just a laugh fest but I think they at times were trying to make valid point but it always ended up with a punch line. If I spelled their names wrong that means I wasn't talking about them.

43

So from now on I am going to write comedy books and I am going to try never to be serious because I always end up getting mad so I will be a total comedian about everything, starting now.

Religion is one idiot telling another idiot they are not as big of an idiot as they could be.

Government is a group of idiots trying to steal from idiots who were too lazy accept a government job.

Jesus hide all his writing because he was smart enough to know idiots would never figure out what he was talking about, and he was right.

I am not an idiot but I am prefect at detecting 6 billion of them.

An atheist is an idiot because they cannot figure out who surrounded them will all these idiots.

An infant is an idiot because in a few more years they will be an infinite idiot.

The dead are idiots because it took them so long to make up their mind to get the hell away from all these idiots.

Before a religious person preaches religion they should show us their penis while they talk so we can see what inspires them.

Religious women have to show us they do not have a penis while they preach, for our safety.

Whoever decides to accept a leadership role must make comments in the nude; that will guarantee only women assume the position.

Okay I am bored with stupidity. Suffering is much more fun, especially when I am inflicting it on you.

Apparently I get consumed with rage in the evening and if you do not know why you have not been listening. A religious person asked if I wanted to join their movement; I declined but suggested an extortionist who would be good at it.

Do not ever listen to anything I say, I am a loser and a failure and do not ever think otherwise.

Now is a good time to try and kill this subconscious aspect with liquor I cannot take any more of it.1:05:52 AM

I drank 2.4 shots of this nightmare tasting vodka at 1:12 AM

My first observation is do not drink, it tastes like shit.

No burning sensation but when I thought about how bad I remember it tasting I gagged out the last .6 of the three shots. So my next words of wisdom is, Some people take drugs to gain clarity and I take drugs to try to lose just a tiny bit of clarity so I can function.

Whoever teaches, one should become subconscious dominate, should be hung on a cross or fed poison lamb chops, I will take either option or both options at this point.

Ignorance is bliss once one realizes they can never go back to it.

I will try some quick quotes and take another shot after.1:17:12 AM

"A man has free choice to the extent that he is rational."
Saint Thomas Aquinas

The unconscious are not capable of being rational; IE conscious dominate ones with a sense of time.

"All that is true, by whomsoever it has been said has its origin in the Spirit."

44

Saint Thomas Aquinas

When one becomes subconscious dominate they understand the only truth is what they perceive is true.

One shot taken at 1:21:37 AM. A tad bitter but no after taste.

"All the efforts of the human mind cannot exhaust the essence of a single fly."
Saint Thomas Aquinas

Thinking about writing infinite books does not scare a fly, but writing infinite books gives one many ways to kill that fly.

"Beware of the person of one book."
Saint Thomas Aquinas

Beware of idiots who think their religion is the only way, and idiots who believe their beliefs are the only true beliefs; everything is relative to the observer.

"By nature all men are equal in liberty, but not in other endowments."
Saint Thomas Aquinas

All beings have a subconscious but few ever become subconscious dominate.

"Clearly the person who accepts the Church as an infallible guide will believe whatever the Church teaches."
Saint Thomas Aquinas

If you have no doubts about your religion then you should have no questions when they say you should die for it.

One who knows has lost the ability to question.

"Faith has to do with things that are not seen and hope with things that are not at hand."
Saint Thomas Aquinas

Faith is intuition and hopes are delusions one wishes were intuitions.

When I was in high school I played on a football team and we played the Saint Thomas Aquinas football team and they kicked our ass so this guy can kiss my ass. They are an all boys school so they had way too much hormones and thus cheated. So technically we won that game.

Took another shot 1:31 AM

"Good can exist without evil, whereas evil cannot exist without good."
Saint Thomas Aquinas

It is possible to be subconscious dominate and not be under the influence of confused emotional aspect, but that is a theory as far as I am concerned.

One who is subconscious dominate is good although they perceive they are hateful, ones with conscious dominate aspect are evil yet perceive they are good.

Clarity can turn one into a mental mad man and emotional confusion turns another man into the physically evil insane.

Ones with clarity fight with their self with words and the sane kill each other with weapons.

"Human salvation demands the divine disclosure of truths surpassing reason."
Saint Thomas Aquinas

One must reach their own salvation by conditioning their self into subconscious dominate; that is every beings only truth. When they accomplish that you won't be having any trouble from them anymore. Surpassing reason means they will "appear drunk" with their words. They appear drunk to the sane. You know the sane that destroy children with their drugs because the child is not sane like they are. You know the child abusers. Subconscious dominate state of mind is not about reason; it is more interested in questioning what reason is.

"If the highest aim of a captain were to preserve his ship, he would keep it in port forever."
Saint Thomas Aquinas

Those who want mental peace prepare for mental war.

A rock can throw itself at someone; try moving that rock with your mind and you will understand conflict.

A rock can achieve conscious emotional dominance, only masters can achieve extreme subconscious dominate mind and live to tell about it. Once in a while a total loser who cannot even kill himself after 30 attempts accidentally reaches extreme subconscious dominate mind and he is such a loser he cannot even kill it with vodka. Killing subconscious with vodka; now you know I am a complete loser.

1:46:08 AM okay another shot has been taken. Tastes like water. This Aquinas fellow sure does not sound very religious to me. Sounds like a comedian. Avoid him at all costs. NSA, spy on his ass. I will shift gears.

"A constitution is the arrangement of magistracies in a state."
Aristotle

Once a government is in place they will ensure the constitution is no longer important.

Once you elect a leader you are not longer the leader of your own destiny.

"A friend to all is a friend to none."
Aristotle

Stay the hell away from me, I already have one friend more than I can handle.

A person who is not a friend to their self is unable to be a friend to anyone.

I am harsh on my one true friend and that is none of your business.

"A great city is not to be confounded with a populous one."
Aristotle

A room full of 10%ers is no contest to one being using 100% of their mind.

A herd of sheep is no contest against one crazy fox.

A fool on the hill defeats a million wise men in the valley.

"A true friend is one soul in two bodies."
Aristotle

A real being has subconscious dominate and the torn aspect; the torn aspect is in awe.

When you understand your physical body and your mind are two different things you will be a true friend to yourself. This comment he has made is so out of context. I will correct Aristole's horrendous quote with a horrendous clarification. Psychologically speaking. A person has emotional, emotionless and torn aspect to the mind. Or Conscious emotional aspect and subconscious aspect and then the torn aspect; torn between the two.

"All men by nature desire knowledge."
Aristotle

All being desires understanding but many rest on their laurels and thus are trapped in isolation of knowing. The beings who knows you are the enemy, knows you should die.

Knowledge is fine as long as you look at it as a stepping stone, so you avoid hanging yourself with it.

Beings ate of the tree of KNOW-ledge and fell off the LEDGE. So they became the fallen angel, that fell off the ledge. So the perhaps and questioning attitude is the only way to climb back up from the dark mental pit they have fallen into.

Took another shot. Tastes like a rain drop.1:59:28 AM

"All virtue is summed up in dealing justly."
Aristotle

If you base your life on scamming people to make a living your will never live; IE capitalism.

Show me someone who charges interest and I'll show you an extortionist.

Virtue is about assisting others at a loss.

All of you who say "I need to make a living off selling service for a markup" , I pray hail stones rain on you for eternity. How is that for wisdom?

The ones you rip off in order to make a buck, are there to see if you can assist them for free, you heartless fools.

"Bad men are full of repentance."
Aristotle

Your apologies to the ones you rape will not save you from my wrath.

Do not bother to repent because you hang yourself with every word that comes out of your mouth.

You are already dammed you are just in denial.

Shame, embarrassment and repentance are emotions and one with subconscious dominate is in a state of compassion. Extreme subconscious dominate means that beings feels nothing but rage induced by the clarity but others perceive they are curious.

Enough of this idiot Aristotle I will convert the quotes of someone who is wise.5/9/2009 2:07:45 AM

"A free life cannot acquire many possessions, because this is not easy to do without servility to mobs or monarchs."
Epicurus

One who thrives on material wealth neglects the mind which stores the only true wealth.

Once you are subconscious dominate you will understand physical wealth is a joke for fools who have no mind.

You can gain physical wealth; all you have to do is assume the life of a rapist and murderer of ones who are there to test if you can lend a helping hand, without hanging yourself in the process.

You take all my money and my wealth so in the next life you will find out, who get's their turn.

You mentally murdered me so I would be able to mentally murder you for eternity.

You should avoid this Epicurus he is some sort of terrorist and revolutionary so kill him swiftly.

You take everything I have in this world, because you already have.

I need to take a shot to dumb myself infinitely down so you have a chance to understand me.

I am one being you wish you never taught the language.

I will remind you when I start to try so you can dawn your death shroud.

Shot taken. 5/9/2009 2:14:58 AM

I get more pleasure playing my video game than thinking about you.

"I have never wished to cater to the crowd; for what I know they do not approve, and what they approve I do not know."
Epicurus

The herd is always the ones to avoid being like.

The herd is always getting ready to drink the cool aid.

You go ahead and jump of the cliff with the herd and I will stand back and document it in my diary.

What the herd knows is exactly what I question.

Apparently this Epicurus being was quite a comedian.

If you do not think for yourself you will not last long in my world.

"I would rather be first in a little Iberian village than second in Rome."
Epicurus

I would rather be an outcast from the herd than a member of it.

You stay in the herd because I am a lone wolf and I eat the herd, by the herd, that's what I heard.

Give me liberty to be a being or give me death.

"Give me the freedom to accomplish what I perceive is important or kill me, because if you don't I will massacre you with my words."

I quoted that last one because none of you sheep will.

"If God listened to the prayers of men, all men would quickly have perished: for they are forever praying for evil against one another."
Epicurus

Beings with conscious dominate emotional aspect are sadists and masochists at the same time so lock them up, swiftly.

If there was a god you would not be here because if he favored anyone he favors me.

God ignores idiots and allows the wise to change the world.

Okay I finished the bottle of vodka at 5/9/2009 2:28:39 AM

I am no longer subconscious dominate the vodka killed it so now I will attempt to translate wise quotes but will fail at every attempt.

"It is folly for a man to pray to the gods for that which he has the power to obtain by himself."
Epicurus

You have subconscious and you are an idiot because you do not choose to make it dominate so stop bothering god, it already knows you are an idiot.(Extremely out of context)

When you are subconscious dominate the only god you will be mentally preying on, is yourself.

I do not pander to those who know because their wisdom is already apparent.

I will go play the video game now because you bore me. The video game is a challenge.

If you are not subconscious dominate do not attempt to do anything because you will only harm it. Assuming I am your friend would be a fatal mistake. You are a joke to me so do not assume I am your friend.

I submit everything I wrote this far in the book is just lies and stupidity I will start the book for real tomorrow.4:43:50 AM

5/9/2009 12:46:51 PM

The great truth I understand about all drugs now is: When one is in a subconscious dominate state of mind, emotions are altered and this state nearly turns off most contrast feelings. Most of the senses related to contrast are silenced, such a sense of taste, sense of pleasure, sense of depression, so drugs are not effective. Drugs only work properly on ones with a sense of time and thus emotions, because emotions give the contrast of pleasure and suffering, mentally speaking.

The sensation of "high" is not possible on drugs when subconscious is dominate. All drugs work on one principle no matter what the "drug" is. You take a drug, be it a recreational drug or a psychological altering drug and you get "high", then when the drug wears off you come down.

With subconscious dominate aspect there is no high so there is no low. One does not go up so one cannot come down. One is mentally trapped in the middle; the middle way or limbo. So I feel physically a bit different but I do not feel relaxed as drink is supposed to make one. I get a little haughty and maybe a cuss a bit more but I do not get this sensation of satisfaction from drinking. The drug is only effective on ones with emotions, and thus have contrast high or not high.

Depression itself is a "depressed" state of mind. One is depressed 24/7. Manic behavior is a state of mind and one is manic 24/7. In a subconscious state of mental limbo that is impossible. I can swing from manic to depressed in a period of about 3 to 4 minutes and never stay at any stage for very long. I can go from mentally happy to mentally angry but never rest on those extremes. I tend to fall back to the middle. So I am neither or nothingness mentally. So recreational and psychological drugs work wonders if you are an emotional wreck and they do not do anything if one is subconscious dominate and thus has emotional aspect altered. Now this is not taking about medical drugs such as drugs made to fight infection and things along those lines, this is strictly talking about mind altering drugs such as psychological drugs and recreational drugs.

So the only people who have problems with recreational drugs are ones with emotional capacity. So, ones who say, recreational drugs are bad because they make you high are in fact mistaken. The proper way to say it is, recreational drugs get one high, relative to ones emotional capacity. So I understand the reason I do not have cravings for drugs to excite pleasure is because my mind is aware they no longer work. So addiction to drugs their self whether it is physical or emotional addiction is only possible if one has emotional conscious dominate sense of time mentality, or, if one has hunger pains from not eating 3 meals a day, because emotional capacity is what gives one contrast to the sensation high or not high.

So one who goes to subconscious dominate state of mind is not able to be addicted to things anymore, they simply would lose the attachment aspect that many physical things encourage. One simply cannot be addicted to a drug that does not emotionally "turn one on". One simply cannot be addicted to food if that food creates no "satisfaction" mentally to that being. So a being in a mental state of limbo or "so so" means after the drug is taken there is no satisfaction and after the drug wears off there is no "coming down" so the drug is not even noticed, and the fact that memory is altered in a way that does not allow one to recall the sensation, means there is no mental attachment to the drug.

When I was on antidepressants I recall how I would feel "high" or better when I took them and then feel "bad" or depressed again when they wore off. So then I wanted to take more and more to feel "high" again. That is simply what mental addiction to drugs is. Emotional capacity means one gets high and then comes down and then needs more drugs to reach that high. It does not matter if the drug is aspirin, psychological drugs or recreational drugs. A mental high is a mental high and is always followed by a mental low and that is caused by emotional capacity being present caused by conscious emotional dominate state of mind.

So young beings that are conditioned into emotions from the subconscious state of mind they start with at birth, by being judged at school and being told what to do, are new to this emotional state of mind and thus take a liking to drugs because they get high. A new born child is in a subconscious state of mind because they could not function for months in the womb if they had a sense of time, and nervousness and claustrophobia. The fear of being enclosed in small places is a direct result of emotions and being in a conscious emotional dominate mental state.

So a fetus would go berserk in the womb if it was in an conscious emotional dominate state of mind. It would become berserk because it would be aware of time. With no sense of time, months on end in a small confined space such as the womb means a fetus would not really notice time passing so it would just be a short stay. So perhaps parents who have children should be very delicate with how they treat a child so they do turn it into an emotional abomination like they are.

Telling a child they better do what you say means you turn them into an emotional judgmental hateful abomination like you are, but a child is born in a perfect mental state of mind until you get done with them. And then parents have the balls to say, "I do not know what happened to my child so I will put them on psychological drugs to fix them." You literally make me sick. You all come at me at once because I eat for no reason. I will go consult with the video game about why I am never wrong.

50

I do not fear death, and I do not fear god, but if you perceive I should, please contact me because I am amused by beings who like to explain why delusions scare them.

A terrorist is a being who persuades people to do their will on threat of some sort of punishment. A religious terrorist is one who persuades other beings to give them money so god does not harm them. A governmental terrorist creates imaginary enemies to persuade the tax payers to give them money so they can protect the tax payer from these imaginary enemies. A psychological terrorist is a being who persuades other beings to ingest pills so that being will not go insane. A military terrorist is a being who starts wars and then persuades governments it is a just war so that military terrorist can justify its own existence.

A scientist or researcher on the other hand never assumes there is anything to fear because they are mindfully attempting to find stuff to fear. They are looking for fear but only seem to find understanding. A space explorer is only afraid they will stop making space ships.

Marie Skłodowska Curie was so interested in discovery she actually ended up dying from the radiation she was studying. She literally died to reach understandings. Space explorers are willing to die to reach understandings. That is healthy. That is what progress is. Progress is not made by manipulating beings and extorting money from them and scaring the hell out of them. So being's that likes to scare the hell out of people to make a buck to justify their self have serious problem now. The butcher of extortionist's has arrived. You may perceive I am being haughty because you cannot mentally grasp I am actually being infinitely humble. So if you are one who thrives on scaring the hell out of beings so you can line your pockets with money and manipulate them to serve your delusional goals, you are extinct, it simply has not caught up to you yet.

If I needed an army to accomplish that I would have one.5/10/2009 1:18:56 AM

I will attempt to translate quotes because I am feeling extremely out of context.

"A belligerent state permits itself every such misdeed, every such act of violence, as would disgrace the individual."
Sigmund Freud

The intense emotions that cause cravings and desires in beings that have conscious emotional dominate mind can lead that being to disgrace their self while they perceive they are doing good deeds.

A delusional, emotional, conscious dominate state permits a being to not be able to know what they do or know what they say.

A being that has strong hunger cravings eventually eats their self to death believing hunger is normal.

Physical War is the eventual conclusion of harmless desires.

"A certain degree of neurosis is of inestimable value as a drive, especially to a psychologist."
Sigmund Freud

A psychologist is crazy to believe they can assist others with words and in psychosis to attempt it with pills.

Every being is insane, but some beings do not act out their hostile delusions by causing physical harm to other beings.

A psychologist prescribes pills because they have already determined their words are not a powerful enough drug, so they should prescribe their self pills until they are less delusional.

I laugh because you do not understand that is what Sigmund is saying with this quote.

This is a meaningless song I wrote today so I will not bother posting the link to it in my book.

http://www.youtube.com/watch?v=3o1-W2MMC8w - Failure

"A man should not strive to eliminate his complexes but to get into accord with them: they are legitimately what directs his conduct in the world."
Sigmund Freud

Your insanity is your strength because it enables you to reach further understandings about what the hell your purpose was for saying what you said.

Mental self control has caused the death of many beings and other beings lack of physical self control is the reason why.

Everything a person does is an opportunity for them to question their actions.

When you figure out what is wrong with us, call so I can validate my findings; When you figure out what is wrong with you, I will be in full agreement.

"America is a mistake, a giant mistake."
Sigmund Freud

I see Sigmund is quite the comedian.

Tell a being they are free and they will test the definition of it.

America is an asylum full of psychologists.

"America is the most grandiose experiment the world has seen, but, I am afraid, it is not going to be a success. "
Sigmund Freud

This is a serious comment by a wise thinker. He is wise in his comment. The sad reality about democracy is: One day 51% will vote that 49% are the enemy and there will be a blood bath.

America is based on one principle. Freedom of speech and the right to bear arms in case a law is passed to negate freedom of speech. Freedom is a suicide pact; it takes blood to keep it alive with no distinction between your blood and your brother's blood. There certainly were governments in history that tried to make democracy work and allow every- one to act freely, and they are not here any longer for that reason. If we yell "We are free" loud enough the world might start to believe it. In America you are free to rip your brother off and claim it is capitalism. America will collapse when the greedy discover her weakness. I am truly saddened by this quote by Sigmund because it is a great truth. Lady Liberty is being slaughtered by bankers and corporations and the military complex and simply by beings that will do anything to our lady just to make a few more bucks. These beings greed knows no bounds. They kill lady liberty for a nickel. What is tragic about America is: One is free to kill lady liberty for a nickel and capitalism encourages it.

 Sigmund understood this because he could take it to its logical conclusion. What is America today? Who is really in control? First we have the spy agencies, and they spy on everyone and who knows what they do with their secret funds they do not even have to account for to anyone but their self, on the premise it is for our safety. So the spy agencies are literally able to kill people and they have to answer to no one and if they do have to answer they just say "They were an enemy." And no being will ask questions.

 The great truth about that is the tax payers allow it so they are accomplices in cold blooded murder. So if there is a being in these spy agencies that sees some kind of cold blooded murder, they are bound to never say a word to anyone about it or they will be thrown in jail as a traitor. That is just one aspect. Then we have the military complex that has only one goal. Keep wars going so they can make better weapons to kill and control others, and so they can line their pockets with blood money. Then we have the banks. The banks make their living off of taking other people's money by offering gim- micks to trap one into servitude. The mortgage companies are in the same business as banks. In a capitalistic monetary system people are conditioned to cheat to make as much money as they can so they can feel worth. If it is illegal in a monetary system it means everyone is doing it.

So you have tax payers cheating on their taxes to save money. They get caught and thrown into jail as traitors. You have beings in poverty that have to do "illegal" things because they want money and do not want to think of their self as one with no worth. So they get caught attempting to make money in the best way they know how and they are thrown into jail.

Then you have the rich who are the most adept crooks in the system and they pay to have infinite ways to rob other people. They are the cream of the crop of scam artists in a monetary capitalistic system. They are not wealthy because they play fair. They are wealthy because they can find the biggest loopholes. Their goal is not to enrich America; their goal is to exploit freedom. They are not bad, because they are free to do this in America. The rich are free to rape lady liberty into hell; that is what freedom is, simply put; to each his own.

"Usury (pronounced /ˈjuːʒəri/, comes from the Medieval Latin *usuria*, "interest" or "excessive interest", from the Latin *usura* "interest") originally meant the charging of interest on loans. This would have included charging a fee for the use of money" WIKIPEDIA.COM

So at one times banks made loans and paid interest on deposits. Then a person got the idea if they make a new business called mortgage companies they could loan money to people for a much higher rate and avoid the usury clause, which is charging an unfair interest rate. One percent on a loan is an unfair interest rate unless you can say "I have to make living you know."

Then they can raise that interest rate to whatever they want. So one has to give up on helping others so they can focus on raping others, and then explain to their self they are just making a living like everyone else. They are not evil or bad, they are free to rape others and free to rob lady liberty and free to kill lady liberty.

That is exactly what Sigmund was saying. He was afraid the experiment would not work. Which is a humble way to say; There is no way in hell that experiment called America will work.

Freedom is simply doomed to civil war. Freedom is doomed because people do not play fair when they play to make money. They will rape whoever they have to , to do it, and it is usually the ones who need the money the most who are raped the most.

There are not any millionaires taking out mortgages on houses or paying huge interest rates on credit cards. That is why they are millionaires to begin with. They are absolutely not bad or evil, they are encouraged to do that and take advantage of the less fortunate in a monetary system in a capitalistic society. That the name of the game in a monetary system: Take advantage of your brother who needs some help. There are no good Samaritans in a monetary system. You see a minister or priest giving out money to the poor. They got that money by telling other people they would go to hell and be dammed by god if they did not give them money. Then they will say "I have to make a living somehow." So they are not evil or bad because they are free to exploit money out of people using fear tactics in the land of the free.

It is important to avoid suggesting anyone is good or evil because it would only be an absolute judgment on yourself. Since the accident I cannot allow myself to make money off of my words. I have to take my books in PDF formats and upload them to download sites in hopes people will just take them because I cannot mentally allow myself to charge anyone for my words. I do not want you to think I am crying why I am typing this sentence either. You just leave me alone. I hate my fate. You may perceive I am big and arrogant but I only perceive I am cursed with this clarity. When I die I have faith the clarity will stop. So I do not want your money because that may keep me alive longer than I have to be. So I essentially go from a mental state of gnashing of teeth to heaven about 100000 times a day and it seems like eternity because I have no sense of time. So I am not really sure what happened to me or what caused this accident or even what this accident is. But my theory is I get very emotional at night around 2 AM because that is about the time I started to convulse when I made my last suicide attempt and decided to not call for help.5/10/2009 3:00:48 AM

So just look at me as crazy and just ignore me because you cannot help me anyway. So do not contact me and do not suggest you can help me because all you will do is torment me further with your suggestions and promises of assistance.

So I play the video game so I can go into some sort of meditative state or catatonic state and have a little of mental peace although it is always short lived because I only come up with more things to write in my infinite books. Now I will discuss something of consequence.

"Being entirely honest with oneself is a good exercise."
Sigmund Freud

If one cannot defeat their own demons they are unable to fix others demons.

It is simple to cast stones at others and harsh to cast stones at one's self.

Being (one with no sense of time who is in the now) can attempt to be oneself (as in at peace) but the mental clarity will always result in mental suffering, so it is a good exercise, but one that will never be accomplished.

To translate that: One with no sense of time can attempt to be at peace and that will ensure further torment.

Being, subconscious dominate, is a friend who breaks your heart when you come back for more.

I submit it has only been seven months since the accident and I submit I am currently in some sort of denial stage. I am writing books explaining how one can become subconscious dominate and then I am telling the reader why they should avoid becoming subconscious dominate. This is what the epic mindful struggle is. This is what mindful self doubt is. It is in reality healthy. It helps one to question their self and face their own actions. It is emotionally painful to face one's own demons, but I understand it always leads to further understandings. So that is why it is healthy. It keeps one mentally grounded.

Having a mind a difficult enough; mastering it is out of the question.

5/10/2009 1:03:55 PM

I am mindfully full of self doubt today. I just noted I have lost 10 pounds since I weighted myself about 2 weeks ago. I am still quite heavy though at 180 LBS. Self doubt and self esteem rely on each other.

"Civilization began the first time an angry person cast a word instead of a rock."

Sigmund Freud

Words start wars and rocks end them; mental struggles often end because of rocks (emotions).

Ones that have no faults usually have the biggest guns; the ones with infinite faults can only afford words.

If you believe weapons will end suffering why don't you do a self demonstration.

I will start throwing punches if I ever finish explaining why I should.

Civilization never started a war, only the ones who claim they are part of it do.

In case you are wondering, Sigmund read the saying "let those without sin cast the first stone.", and translated that into his quote. That initial quote is simply saying: A wise man has the mental capabilities to fight with his words and a fool can only resort to physical means to say what is on his mind.

Words were invented so ones with brain function can compete with ones who have no brain function.

A being is supposed to talk back to authority figures or they will eventually consider physical means.

If a being insults you with words, verbally convince them they are talking to their self and then wait for them to implode.

A war of words is preferred over a war of blood.

If a general cannot convince their enemy to surrender using words they are their own worst enemy.

I honestly felt normal today and assumed I lost my clarity. That is what I have noticed, as the day wears on I get mentally sloppy or tired, but do not physically feel tired. I can tell I need to rest because the emotions start to creep back in. I perceive there is nothing I can read that I cannot translate since the accident and all I am really doing is trying to find something I have trouble understanding. If I can just find one sentence I cannot grasp then maybe I am not as crazy as I think I am.

"Civilized society is perpetually menaced with disintegration through this primary hostility of men towards one another."
Sigmund Freud

Sigmund was not a psychologist as much as a great thinker trying to talk sense into ones he understood were delusional. He was a revolutionary like many before him. No question about that. This quote is not about psychology. It is about explaining why humans are so stupid to still be at the mental state of physically fighting each other. He was more a philosopher and religious type figure or a figure that was at a level of mental clarity, he was tormented by what he saw happening around him for stupid reasons. If humans goal is to just kill their self off as a species let's do it; If not stop doing it. One cannot kill off humans because they adapt and come back wiser and harder to kill off. If you kill a human being you are a mental midget. If you think you are not an idiot for killing a human being then that proves you are an infinite idiot, whether it is directly or indirectly. No being has the balls to kill all other human beings so stop your delusional insanity.

You do not have the balls to wipe out all of civilization so give up; you are mentally weak and foolish. You do not have the fortitude to accomplish what you want to. You talk war and death and then when you are at that stage you back off and try to not kill others. That means you're a schizophrenic weak willed delusional insane person. If you want to fight a physical war and kill people then kill everyone, if you don't have the balls to do that find a new profession. You are not a killer you are just flirting with that idea but you are not cut out for it. So you are delusional because you think you are a killer but you do not have the fortitude to be a killer. You are in a state of half steps. You kill people you say are the enemy, but then you cannot kill other people who are associated with them. If you are unable to persuade someone with words who poses physical harm to you to cease and desist their physical actions, and discuss their problems peacefully, that is subconscious's way of telling you, it is your time to die because your mental abilities are not up to snuff.

A mental corpse can get a weapon and physically harm others. Beings that use weapon to get their point across are an abomination to mental mankind. I do not care who you think you are, you contact me and I will convince you, it is best if you pass on swiftly. Show me someone who is religious and uses weapons instead of words and I will show you the first one you should lock up.

Religious people who use weapons instead of words to get their point across should be cast out of society. They should be isolated from all others and not given food or water and left out in the desert so they can test their weapons on each other. Any sane being should simply ignore these delusional beings that choose weapons over words because these beings are simply mentally incapable of thoughts or reason. They are in fact insane and delusional and that is a very dangerous mix. They are not righteous they are mental abominations. If you are a religious being and you support others in your religion to help them kill other beings with weapons in any way, shape, or form, you should get a weapon and end your own life because you failed at life.

The moment a being understands they are not allowed to kill other beings, but are only allowed to talk to other beings, they become a human being. Only the devil kills other human beings when he has the option to discuss things with them instead. If you cannot talk sense into an enemy you need to find someone with brain function who can. Weapons multiply the problem but have never solved one. I will remind you if I ever try. I will remind you if I ever detect I am starting to get slightly warmed up.

Right now I have no brain function but I hope to have at least one brain cell functioning. My IQ right now is zero, but if it ever gets to 1, that will be the first thing you know, and that last thing you understood.

"Everywhere I go I find that a poet has been there before me."

Sigmund Freud

Yes Sigmund. I understand I am only stealing everyone else's material as well. They may copyright my books but I am certain I just stealing the material of the poets that came before me. What this really means is one who has dominate subconscious mind see's everything as one thing. This is exactly in accord with early American Indians who saw everything as one spirit. Everyone is one thing. That means there is only infinity. If everything is the same thing then one is rather foolish to try to control anything. Nothing I say is original or a new concept because it has all been said before. All of these "poets" down through history have all been saying the same thing and it never seems to lock because they are talking to the brain dead. They are all saying, you have subconscious aspect of the mind and with simple emotional conditioning techniques you can start to be awake and aware and intelligent and stop being an abomination to the word human being. There is no other point to life but to attempt to get to a stage in your mind where you are not a delusional insane abomination. I am not allowed to preach that to you. I am not allowed to say that is what you should do. I am talking to myself in my diary. I no longer talk to you after what you did to me.

Luxury encourages a delusional mind; mental struggle makes one noteworthy. Humans are not here to have fun; humans are here to fight a mental epic battle with their self. You will not survive that battle but it still must be fought. You cannot avoid that mental fight. Ones who progress in that epic mental fight are remembered and ones who are annihilated by that epic mental fight are the ones who believe life is about luxury and comfort.

The mentally blind see life as a miracle and blessing and the mentally strong see life as a battle they can never win, at every turn. You are not allowed to talk about Sigmund because you think he was a bad being for taking his own life after his struggle with cancer because you are not at a mental understanding he took his own life to get away from you and the cancer was his best opportunity.

Sigmund spoke with Einstein because the mentally living tend to speak with each other and crack jokes about the mentally dead they are surrounded by. If you wake up in the morning and feel you have to gets something to eat and also feel you have to go to the bathroom that is a symptom you are mentally dead. You simply should not feel that much unless your mind has stopped functioning to the point it is delusional. You are unable to even believe that. Things like hunger and "I need to pee real bad" that is because your mind is so confused it no longer is registering reality. Hunger should not be felt. Not eating food should not affect your state of being as far as feeling weak and feeling tired. One with actual mind function that registers actual reality should be able to go long periods and not feel hunger. One should not have hunger pains even if they do not eat, and also they should not get weak if they do not eat for long periods. If one has true mental function they should be wide awake whether they eat food or not. They should be at a heightened sense of awareness whether they eat food or not. What this means is people who are subconscious dominate or ones with no sense of time in reality eat food for no reason at all. I will translate that. People with subconscious dominate minds eat food because they decide to remain in hell, which the ones who are conscious dominate call life. I will now go play my video game because I am aware I am just wasting my time with these stupid books.

I am mindful I am not allowed to assist you or help you or even suggest what you should do that is why if you read my diaries you are invading my privacy.

When the mind is not working properly it will create panic when there is no need to panic. When a being with too many emotions is in a situation of facing others for the first time, they may start to pee or feel the need they have to pee. That is called nervousness. That means their mind is tricking them into think there is a reason to be stressed or nervous because their mind is not functioning properly. Essentially they are like a toad that when picked up it pisses all over the place. A being perceives hunger because the mind is not working properly and the next thing you know, that being is 300 pounds and near death physically, and will say, "I just like to eat."

Others will say I just cannot stop eating because they assume hunger is normal when in reality it is a symptom their brain is not functioning properly and they are in fact abnormal and perceive they are not. They are delusional and perceive they are not delusional. It is one thing to be insane and understand one is insane. The ones who are most dangerous are the ones who perceive they are sane when they are certifiably totally insane and delusional. I am not jumping for joy because of my new found understanding. I fell into this new found understanding by accident, which denotes I did not want to know this. I did not wake up today and have the urge to pee and it is 3 pm and I have not eaten all day yet I am not physically weak, and I notice no difference in my mental clarity. So maybe everything I have typed today and in all of my books is in error, but if my theory is in fact a valid theory based on my understanding of things after the accident it means the vast majority of civilization is delusional and hallucinating because their mind is not functioning properly, and they perceive they are not hallucinating and delusional.

So essentially I had an accident and woke up to the fact I was hallucinating and delusional and I am stuck in a world of insane and delusional beings that have not woken up to their own sickness, yet. So now you understand the definition of a living nightmare. Do not tell me about problems you have because you do not know what a problem is.

A problem is not lacking in money, a problem is waking up in a god dam insane asylum and being aware the insane perceive they are normal and perceive I am insane. It is 6 billion against one and they do not stand a chance in hell against me. That's a problem. I openly cuss in my books because I hope it pisses you off and then you start thinking I am evil and angry, and then you read a little bit further and realize, you should not even be thinking at all, if you think I am evil and angry. You are unable to detect what evil is, because you are evil.

The insane perceive everyone is against them. I do not perceive anyone is a threat to me. I am at a state of mental clarity. I wish someone was a threat to me, but I understand there never will be anyone that is a threat to me, ever. That is what sanity is. That is what being conscious is. If an insane person kills me with a physical weapon, that is not a threat to me. That is simply what happens in insane asylums. The insane at times attack perceived hallucinations they believe are a threat to them. I expect to be physically murdered for my words, because I am after all trapped in an insane asylum. I wish I had the keys to escape the insane asylum but life does not care what I wish for, because life does not care. Life is not fair. Life has no morals and no virtues. Life exterminates and creates, but it never hesitates and it is never late. Life does not end suffering because only delusional beings perceive there is suffering. A delusional being suffers when they perceive they are hungry, and if they do not get food soon they will die, so they must kill and rob to get that food so they do not suffer further because the society brainwashed everyone in the concept "Without money you are worthless."

I believed that brainwashing is why I took a handful of pills on my last attempt and my mind believed I did die. So society did exactly what it was supposed to do to me, to wake me up to its delusions. So I find no fault with it. I am humbled by its perseverance, because now I am going to do something that will change society forever and ever.

There is no such thing as hunger it is just one's mind is no longer functioning properly so they perceive there is hunger. You should attempt to understand who I am declaring war on, so you can reach a level of awareness about who I am.

Only powerful beings declare war on the universe, the others just declare war on their sandboxes. You fight your sandbox war and I will declare war on anyone with a sand box. You fight for your little crop of land and I will fight a war against the universe that created that land. When I stop doubting myself the game will be over. Perhaps you should punch that into every calculator you can find because my intuition just suggested I type that last sentence and I have no idea what it really means.

My only guess is after the initial mental shock in the first two months after the accident I got this feeling I was in such mental progression I would overload physically or mentally. But now I understand what that perhaps really was. It is my first inclination of doom or an end is coming. I at this moment do not want to speculate further than that. I hope that feeling is an extreme delusion and hallucination and I hope I am in reality completely insane and out of my mind. I have faith that I am infinitely paranoid about all the intuitions I get. You should pray with all of your might that I am just infinitely paranoid. I fear nothing and I am certain you fear everything.

You should be seeking out the wisest beings on the planet so they can convince you nothing I write in any of my books is right. The reality is, I hope nothing I say in my books is right because I am not writing them, I am just running my fingers over the keyboard. I do not remember what I write in any of my books because I am writing what comes to mind. I am just writing what I am told to write but I am not wise enough to figure out who is coming up with all of these words, but I am certain it has infinite things to say. So you should pray with all of your might it is just the power of dominate subconscious mind because if it is not, you will not be in need of all of your money very much longer.

I can jump back on the fence must swifter than you can, and now you know why.

"He that has eyes to see and ears to hear may convince himself that no mortal can keep a secret. **If his lips are silent, he chatters with his fingertips; betrayal oozes out of him at every pore.**"
Sigmund Freud

You are unable to understand what this quote means even though I just explained what it means in the above comments. I will move on to the next one because some of these are far too deep for your snorkel to reach.

"If youth knew; if age could."
Sigmund Freud

One in subconscious dominate mind has no sense of time so they have found the fountain of youth, they do not KNOW they are aging, they are eternally youthful, mindfully. Ones with conscious dominate mind sense time so they have things like midlife crisis, impatience, and say things like "I do not have time to speak to you." They are essentially in a rush their whole lives, so they can hurry up and die. So this quote is saying. If youth knew age; age could know youth. This is the common disconnect. Ones who are subconscious dominate speak in random access and ones with conscious dominate minds speak in sequential access, so they can never reach each other. So to ones with sequential thoughts the ones with random access thoughts appear wise or special. It is not logical that I could live 40 years and be a nobody on a scale of nobody, and because of a video game accident I now understand everything because my final suicide attempt was about 3 months prior to my decision to master that video game or else. That perhaps is simply not possible unless I unlocked the intelligent aspect of the mind and became subconscious dominate as a result of playing a video game to an extreme. Why don't you write infinite books about what you think really happened so then we can all buy your books to determine how infinitely delusional you are.

"It is impossible to overlook the extent to which civilization is built upon a renunciation of instinct."
Sigmund Freud

This is an inside joke for the ones in the loop. Humanity is conscious emotional dominate so all the disasters it creates are simply the results of it delusional cravings and desires. Desire for land, desire for control, cravings to control, cravings to have fun, desire to kill each other. All of these cravings and desires that humanity is based on are simply delusional symptoms caused by an emotional conscious dominate mind.

If there is anything in my books you have never heard before that is a symptom you are detecting true original thoughts and concepts.

I just gave my third book to my girlfriend's daughter and she said she had a dream that she saw a commercial about amazon.com and in the commercial she saw my books sitting on a table. I understand that means the only real books Amazon has ever sold are the ones on that table. Of course that is just my interpretation of her dream. I prefer to give all of my words away for free because I have absolutely no attachment to them because I cannot exactly remember what I write in the books. I have a spirit of what my main goal is in writing but I cannot remember the details. I perceive I am just saying the same thing over and over into infinity with the sentences arranged a bit differently each time.

I am mindful that eventually I perhaps will go back to a emotional conscious dominate state of mind and then I will have my books to read to attempt to figure out how to get back to where I am right now. I publish my books because I am mindful I perhaps will go back to where I came from and I will have no guides to get me back here if I do not publish my books. My nightmare is that one morning I will wake up and have a craving to eat food because I am feeling weak. Emotions use physical weapons to fight battles because its forked tongue is unable to fight his battles effectively. If your mind is weak your words will reflect that.

A well formed sentence created by a well tuned mind has no adversaries. The ones who attempt to teach me learn much slower than the ones who accept I am the teacher.

"Men are more moral than they think and far more immoral than they can imagine."
Sigmund Freud

Sigmund is quite the comedian. This is just a retranslation of "They know not what they do." And that is translated as: Ones with conscious emotional dominate minds have a sense of time and are having cravings and desires that are based on delusions caused by their minds because their minds are not actually functioning properly.

Imagine a person who takes PCP and dives out of window because they think they can fly. That is exactly what is happening when a person has a desire to eat food because they perceive they are getting physically weak without 3 meals a day. When a person is in a "nervous" situation and perceive they must swiftly go pee, they are falling for the hallucinations in their poorly functioning mind.

I perceived I was worthless because I did not have enough money so I determined the best solution was to kill myself, or jump out of a window. People who lose their jobs and go home and kill their self and their family perceive it is wise to jump out of a window. People who determine another person should be killed with weapons because that initial person assaulted them, when in reality that person who attacked them lives across the world and is really no threat at all, has decided to jump out of the window.

One can write infinite books about how a being is a threat to me in the land of the free when that perceived enemy they write about is a world away. That perceived enemy will never be able to actually invade the land of the free, and remain alive for more than a few seconds, and all that being will accomplish is to convince me beyond a showdown of a doubt, they ingested far too much PCP.

I will translate that. If a being throws a rock at your window it will not make your house collapse unless you try to fix that window with dynamite. A true general attacks the enemy in a certain fashion because they have already determined how the enemy will react and have a trap set up to accommodate that understood counteraction. A well placed trap appears like a righteous crusade to a master of self immolation. Translated further. Beings attacked America on 9/11 with the sole intention of making America come to their land so they could destroy America.

So America did not have wise beings in control that could detect that trap and now America is being dissected because of that. America is passing laws to kill freedom of speech and turning its own citizens into terrorists. America is dying because it voted into an office of power beings who are not wise in the ways of traps and trickery. If any being wishes to invade America I welcome them with open ARMS. Until then they are nothing. No matter what they say or what they do, until they have the fortitude to arrive on the shores of the land of the free with their armada's they are nothing and are no threat to the land of the free.

"Neurosis is the inability to tolerate ambiguity."
Sigmund Freud

Sigmund the comedian.

If someone who is different bothers you mentally, you are in psychosis.

If you hate someone that is a symptom subconsciously you wish you were like them.

This is why love and hate is the same thing. They are simply mental attachments. They only lead to one thing, mental suffering. If you hate someone you will love killing them. If you love someone you will hate to see them die. People who love their mates kill their mates when their mates scorn their love. It happens every day. This is the scenario. Women divorces man and man shows up at her house and shoots her dead and kills himself. Then society announces it loud and clear, Love is all you need. Love is wonderful. If you do not love you are bad. Society itself needs to be baker acted because they are saying things that is making others around them go insane and do insane things.

You are a human being and you are born and your only purpose is to mentally condition yourself using mental self control so you do not love and do not hate because both are the exact same thing: Mental attachment that leads to suffering. I am not telling you what to do. I am reminding myself of what I will never do again. One should strive to become subconscious dominate not because it is easy street but because it is the harsh street. Mental living is harsh; if you think mental living is easy, it is because you are not mentally alive.

Dominate subconscious living does not make it easy on you and that is exactly what makes it easy on you. Once you reach a state of dominate subconscious mind you will understand physical problems are nothing at all. You will understand the definition of a true epic conflict. I cannot think of any physical event or battle in the history of mankind that even compares to the mental battle I have been in for the last seven months. It does not matter what you think. That is reality. Disbelief does not change reality. One who cannot think clearly cannot act properly. Sigmund's humor is right up my alley, I am certain he wishes he could have reached the heights I have reached without any effort at all. My purpose is to explain what Sigmund was unaware he was explaining. It does not matter what being I quote. All I am doing is correcting their misunderstandings. Do not kid yourself.

"One is very crazy when in love."
Sigmund Freud

Now Sigmund is stealing my material.

One is crazy if they have cravings and desires like strong hunger, need for acceptance, need for attachments.

If you are mentally uneasy with the reality; you are all alone in an infinite void; you are mentally unstable.

When a being accepts the fact they are not allowed to love anything or anyone, they will understand the harsh reality of the situation they are in.

When you love something you give it permission to torment you into infinity.

I torment Sigmund because he loves me and he loves it.

"Religion is an illusion and it derives its strength from the fact that it falls in with our instinctual desires."
Sigmund Freud

I am declaring copyright infringement after this comment.

Religion, Government, Institutions are simply ideals to scare the followers into doing the will of ones who are too scared to allow the followers to think for their self.

Psychological manipulation through scare tactics is called terrorism and is only hurts the ones who have been manipulated. This is why politicians do not fight the wars they vote to engage in. This is why pharmaceutical companies do not take the medicines they create. This is why parents that home school their children do not suggest the child is a failure if they do not understand the information, because the parent teachers understand it is their failure if the child does not understand the information.

A home school parent does not judge their child; they learn to become a better teacher.

A soldier in the military would never kill a person unless the military dangled a carrot of wealth in front of them.

A human being would never kill another human being unless that initial human being had a delusional treasure of gain in their mind. Human beings only kill other human beings for delusional gains. Life is going to kill all of us, so it is delusional vanity that encourages physical killing of other beings.

"Sadism is all right in its place, but it should be directed to proper ends."
Sigmund Freud

Now Sigmund is really treading on thin ice and perhaps is delusional in his assumption it is not all my ice.

You are a sadist so masochistically direct it at yourself and visa versa.

Sigmund is stealing my material from my second third and fourth books. He is doing illegal things. I do not give a dam when he died he is still pissing me off.

I will go into broken record mode about sadism.

In bondage a submissive tells the dominate partner how far they are willing to go, so the submissive is in fact the dominate one because they are calling the shots. The dominate one is the submissive one because they will not go further than the submissive one will allow them to. So there is no such thing as a dominate one or a submissive one. So the word dominate is not real. The word submissive is not real. So people are going around believing words that have no meaning. So they are delusional. Beings are going around saying you are evil so I will kill you so I will be good. A war is one delusional being killing another delusional being while both beings are claiming they are good for doing so. That is the text book example of an insane being acting on delusions in their mind in a physical way. So my only suggestion is, if you have strong hunger cravings that is proof you are a delusional being and you would be wise to stay the hell away from me because I shoot zombies on sight because zombies crave brains because zombies no longer have brains.

I do not respect any being in this universe because their ego is already infinite; I do tolerate one being and that is why I am infinitely compassionate.

"Sometimes a cigar is just a cigar."

Sigmund Freud

This is an inside joke to all the idiots who go around saying one is evil if they use recreational drugs. Drugs are just drugs. If your mind is not functioning to begin with drugs will not hurt you; If your mind is functioning, drugs are just something to experiment with because you are bored by all the insane beings you are surrounded by who keep saying drugs are evil.

If you have no mental function drugs are evil and if you have mental function drugs are just drugs.

The more you say pot and cocaine and other drugs are evil and bad the more money you put into the drug dealers pockets and the more the children hear about things they need to experiment with next because they certainly do not want to grow up to become like you are. If you introduce a law that says you are not allowed to speak ever again, I will vote for it and convince everyone else to vote for it also.

I will run for dictator of the universe when my current infinite term expires.

I will now discuss something relevant.

"The goal of all life is death."
Sigmund Freud

Now Sigmund is stealing other beings words and those beings stole my words so he is a triple threat.

"Those who try to save their self will lose their self."

Those who crave for safety caused by emotional fear you will end up in emotional conscious dominate wooden boxes of isolation.

If you give up mental conflict for a little emotional fear induced security you deserve neither.

I will translate all of these thoughts because you are simply unable to.

A being under the influence on conscious emotional dominate mind is afraid. Everything they do is based on fear. They fear death, they fear embarrassment, they fear pain, they fear uncertain ground. They fear change, they fear, fear. They fear anything they can think of. They fear life and fear death. That is what emotions cause them to behave like. Everything they do is based on delusions caused by emotions.

They fear change so they fear they will lose control and then they fear that loss of control may make it unsafe for them. They shoot their self in the foot to avoid shooting their self in their good foot. The emotions cause them to be mentally blind to the reality they are mentally blind. So it takes one with an extreme mental capacity to form the proper sentences to attempt to wake them to their blindness. The only way such a being can reach that level of mental clarity required to form the sentences that can reach the mentally blind is if that being lets go of their own life mindfully.

That is the only way one can reach a level of subconscious dominate mind that everything they say will come out in random access thoughts. So that being is not only in a state of nirvana or no sense of time, they are at the extreme of that state of mind. That being cannot say anything that is sequential based thoughts once they get warmed up from the accident. It is always going to be accidental because one has to be suicidal and then fail at it. So this being has to want to die but they do not physically die but their mind believed they physically died after a very close attempt.

Many may reach no sense of time or subconscious dominate aspect from listening to the words of that initial being but they will never attain the extreme subconscious dominate mind that being who had the accident reached, because they reached the subconscious dominate state the easy way. One cannot say the being who reaches that extreme subconscious dominate state is some great being because they reached it simply because they were such a loser they could not even kill their self properly, but their mind believed they made one hell of an attempt and thought they did. So what I am suggesting is, only a suicidal person has a chance of having the accident, but if they are not a total loser even unto their self, they will accomplish suicide and the accident will pass over them.

So one literally has to be the least of the least or as some suggested "the least among you" or " the stone the stone cutter threw away". So I understand everything any being can ever suggest because I am such an extreme loser I could not even kill myself after 30 attempts over 15 plus years. So my conscious emotional aspect certainly wanted to die, and my subconscious aspect always made sure I never did enough to actually physically die. So I was torn between wanting to emotionally die and subconsciously not wanting to die, and my mind finally believed I did die and stopped registering the cravings and desires caused by the "norms" of this world. And so I understand everything clearly because the dead understand everything clearly, because they are outside of the box of "life" and are looking back at it, and hindsight is 20/20.

 Of course everyone has been trying to tell us this for all of recorded history and we as a species just never got point. When a human being knows they are cursed they understand they are blessed. You may have thought you knew what religion was about and now you understand you never knew a thing about anything. You have just been babbling insanity for your entire life.

Think about all the beings that have been killed because they knew what religion was about and then you will understand what kind of insanity this species is capable of. We will kill our self off as a species unless we understand the religious leaders of history were in fact the first psychologists. Dam my train of thought derailed.

"Love and work... work and love, that's all there is."
Sigmund Freud

 Mr. Comedian has showed back up. Don't mind Freud he was light years beyond your mental ability to grasp and he is light years beneath my mental ability to misunderstand.

Only one with brain function can grasp this comment. Consider this comment.

"One is very crazy when in love."
Sigmund Freud

Freud is saying all there is are crazy people working their self to death at jobs to satisfy their love and cravings and desires for money and fun and insane reasons or physical reasons and not mental reasons.

In this life you are either gratifying your physical desires and killing your mental clarity or killing your physical desires and developing your mental clarity. You do not get both. You take one or the other. You grab one and let go of the other. I certainly will never attempt to tell you what you should do. If I say you should do something I am in error. You should kill everything in the universe if that is what you think you should do. There is a reason for everything you do and I am not intelligent enough to second guess those reasons; I am only intelligent enough to question my reasons for tolerating you.

In this world there are great experimenter's and everyone else are just lab rats. Apparently my brain is now in my finger tips at this stage since the accident because I cannot even tell if what I type even makes sense. If anything I type makes sense make sure you call me.

I notice I have trouble with past, present, and future tense words. If it should be "everyone else is just lab rats" or "everyone else are just labs rats ". They both sound the same to me. So one has to be right and so whoever made up the syntax for the language was completely out of their mind with emotions because they think one way is the right way and the other way is the wrong way. I am attempting to use a language syntax invented and developed by an insane person and I am having trouble mastering it because I am so far away from the realms of insanity at this point in the accident. That is the truth and I do not expect you to be able to grasp the truth, ever. I will go hunt in my video game now because you are an honest bore. When I detect a being is trying to advise me I do the exact opposite of what they suggest in the off chance they made an honest attempt.

"What a distressing contrast there is between the radiant intelligence of the child and the feeble mentality of the average adult."
Sigmund Freud

"Suffer the children to come unto me" because the children are subconscious dominate which means they are not delusional, judgmental, anal retentive, emotional fools. Children cannot build crosses or hammer nails, but adults can with the greatest of ease. That essentially is what Freud is saying. So in reality when your children becomes spoiled little brat and says you are an idiot to your face, understand they are telling the truth. They subconsciously hate you for making them become like you are. Do not take it personal they are simply telling great truths. I get delusional and start to believe I am insulting people with my words, but then I remind myself I am only talking to myself, and I am nothing and thus have nothing to fear.

Once I thought I heard you talking to me and now I understand you are not allowed to.

I focus on translating the quotes of dead people because the living people have yet to say anything that catches my attention.

The Taliban represent a great philosophical question. No being is intelligent enough to understand what the Taliban's exact purpose is, in the scheme of history. On one hand mother nature could have decided there are simply too many being on the planet and has determined the Taliban will be the first to be wiped out. This would explain why the Taliban are so eager to die. So this means nature is allowing these beings to die for delusions in their mind because nature needs to find excuses to persuade humans to kill their self because nature is aware there are simply too many humans attempting to be alive at the same time. Clearly if there is a heaven no being who physically butchers people, will be going to it no matter how many other beings say they will be. Disbelief does not change the fact it is lord of all.

Now on the other hand if the Taliban is some sort of revolutionary force that is attempting to make civilization grow away from this materialistic mindful thinking aspect then they have a valid purpose. But that valid purpose is cancelled out by the fact they are forcing people to do things they do not want to do. So the Taliban are attempting to "free" others and in the process they are isolating and enslaving their self. The Taliban are asking their own brothers to die for the sole purpose of helping others. So they are shooting their self in one foot to save the good foot. This is a symptom of "hurry up we do not have much time.", which is impatience. They are not patient so they are making mistakes.

One huge mistake is killing people physically who do not believe what you believe. That ideal is caused by delusions of an insane mind. So clearly if there is a god it simply knows nothing of them. If there is only mother nature then we have to salute her ability and her efforts to persuade humans to kill their self because there is simply too many humans on the planet.

Mother nature is making the Taliban kill their self and then making the ones who try to stop the Taliban kill their self as well. Once a being kills another being they are never the same again. There subconscious mental rage and mental regret usually ends up destroying them. So in fact they kill their self as a being by killing another being. One can go on and on about how great it is to kill another being but that is because on a subconscious level they understand all the money in the universe will never allow them to undo what they have done.

Once a being kills another being they cannot rectify that so they consciously make up lies to justify that. Soldiers who say "I would do it all over again." are subconsciously saying "I relive it all over again every single day in my mind." That is called infinite suffering. So these "combat" beings usually end up running into a bullet on the battle field subconsciously. They are perceived to be "brave" but that is because subconsciously they want to die because they cannot live with what they have done.

A clarification: One who is emotional dominate gets a subconscious signal they are doomed. That subconscious signal is translated by the emotional dominate aspect and then that being physically kills their self. Subconscious dominate beings are very violent but mentally, it never reaches the physical emotional part, because they are no longer physically bound.

One can get over cussing at someone. One can get over an argument with someone. One can get over hitting someone. One mentally can never recover from killing another being because subconsciously they understand they just destroyed a universe forever and ever and ever. They end up wondering for the rest of their life what the world would be like if they did not kill that being. It does not matter if it was from shooting a rocket from 5 miles away or dropping a bomb from 30,000 feet or hand to hand combat with knives, or shooting someone in the street while robbing them. The being that does that killing is subconsciously mentally doomed to mental hell.

So in reality they must be approached like a rabid animal. But the flaw with that tactic is more people have to kill them, and then those people are mentally doomed. Soldiers do not come back from combat and have emotional problems because of the loud noises they experienced. All of their emotional problems stem first off because they have emotions because they are conscious dominate and then it is because they witnessed other beings being killed or killing other beings.

Many soldiers associate their self with their outfit or squad. They say "Our outfit killed 20 enemy today." So they subconsciously understand whether they killed the people with their gun or not they still killed those people. A squad is trained to act as one unit so any enemy kills are in fact registered equally by every member of that unit. It is the same psychology as a firing squad. They use a set amount of guns and one has a bullet and the rest blanks. This way the logic goes, no person in that squad will think they kill that person, but subconsciously they all believe they killed that person.

They did all kill that person. One can fool every being in the universe but they will never fool their own subconscious aspect, ever. It will remind them of the reality for the rest of their life. I will just suggest subconscious aspect is not an idiot.

One is unable to ever fool it because IT already knows what is going to happen before it happens. So how would you fool it? People attempt to fool it after combat with bottles of vodka and drugs and pills given to them by "psychologists". Most of them come to the realization the only way to fool subconscious is to put a bullet to their head. Then they understand everything clearly. Dam my train of thought turned into a plane of flight.

So I have advise for the ones who wish to fight the Taliban and to the Taliban who wish to fight others. First off, never fight a human because they are unpredictable and can adapt to any situation and come back stronger. My second less popular suggestion is this. Both of you make up your mind. If the Taliban wants to kill everyone they should kill everyone. If the ones who want to kill the Taliban want to kill the Taliban they should break out the nukes and kill ever last one of them and then their self.

Do not hesitate and look like a fool if you want to kill. You both kill everyone and do not stop until everyone is dead, so you do not look like a half ass, hesitating, idiot, fool. If you want to be evil be infinitely evil but do not settle for lukewarm. I spit lukewarm out of my mouth for no reason. I do not stutter because you cannot understand me as it is. Apparently it is getting late and I am getting upset.10:03:33 PM

I am the last being in the universe you want to piss off, I assure you of that. There are not enough weapons in the universe to save your ass from my wrath. So if you decide you need to kill people you kill every last one of them or shut your mouth about killing people, because you only look like a delusional idiot with your half ass attempt's to appear tough. You do not know what tough is so shut your dam mouth about suggesting you are tough. You are only tough if the definition of tough is: a half ass cowardly fool.

I submit I did rather well with my wrath blocking most of the day but now it is dark and you are screwed.

I attempt to stay asleep as long as possible but at this point in the accident I can only manage about 3 hours of sleep a night because that is far too much rest for me. If I rested any more than three hours a day you would not be able to grasp anything I say. That was an accidental rhyme on purpose.

A group who wants a war for the purpose of killing others, but does not want to kill all the others is a schizophrenic. That means they want to kill people but do not want to kill people. So they are delusional and insane. To bomb a house and kill one being but then regret you accidentally killed 4 beings who you didn't want to kill means that being who bombed that house is schizophrenic. They are lukewarm or half ass. One cannot do something as permanent as killing someone and then take it back. A sane being either wants to kill everyone or wants to never kill anyone. Anyone in between is delusional and insane. The ones in between are mentally trapped in an infinite loop. One day they want to kill the next day they do not. So they are bipolar. They cannot make up their mind. So they end up just killing randomly. Some days they kill 50 and some days they kill none but then the next day they start killing again. The reasons are not even relevant. Mentally they are schizophrenic. One can just make up a reason and schizophrenic person will talk their self into killing for that reason. They are terrorists, they are pirates, they are evil, they are the devil, they are aliens, they are not like us, they are different. Make up any reason and for a schizophrenic person that is a good enough reason. Yes I am calling all of you schizophrenic so you better bring an infinite army with you when you come, so I can assist you in understanding total obliteration at a wink.

If you want to hurt somebody, you get a sharp razor and run it across your neck so everyone will know you mean business. If you do not have the balls to do that, stay out my pool, go back to your little sand box, it is too deep in my pool of blood for your snorkel.

Clarity comes with a little cussing but much less than I want to use. I have deep seeded anger and you cannot hold your breath long enough to reach the bottom of it. It does not matter how deep I am, it is all relative to how shallow of water you prefer to stay in. There is no bottom and the undertow is devastating where I live, so you stay in your little wading pool because you can't handle the rough surf.

I will find another idiot to quote.

"A lie would have no sense unless the truth were felt dangerous."
Alfred Adler

A lie is relative to the delusional capacity of the one who suggests it is truly a lie. You are doomed when I start trying. I out did myself with that last one.

Truth is relative to the motivations of the one who suggests it.

"Exaggerated sensitiveness is an expression of the feeling of inferiority."
Alfred Adler

Do not take yourself too seriously because I do not even acknowledge you at all.

If a word hurts your feelings you need shock treatment.

"It is always easier to fight for one's principles than to live up to them."
Alfred Adler

One with no morals and no class never fails in his dominance.

Show me someone who knows an absolute truth and I will show you an absolute idiot.

People die for principles so they can escape the fact they could not live by them.

"It is the patriotic duty of every man to lie for his country."
Alfred Adler

Oh great another comedian.

A patriot with a gun is no match for a patriot who likes to vote.

A patriot votes to hang his self and then fights to delay the execution.

The absolute truth is: Anyone who says there is an absolute truth is an absolute liar.

My infinite wrath potential just suggested, Behind every failed suicide attempt is a women who needs to work on her encouragement strategy.

If Alfred had any brains he would have written my books.

"Man knows much more than he understands."
Alfred Adler

Now Alfred is insulting you again so you should seek him out for punishment.

The reason Alfred died is because he was aware I would come along and explain what he attempted to explain.

Man knows nothing but is has trouble understanding that.

When a being can look in the mirror and say "I understand nothing and never will know anything." they understand the first great truth of life.

"Former Vice President ...... on Sunday continued his verbal attack against President ......, saying that the country is more vulnerable to a potential terrorist attack since the ..... administration took power." Washingtontimes.com

The country is more vulnerable to a potential terrorist attack.

Russia has at had least 500 nukes trained on us for the last 40 years. If Russia attacked us, they are a terrorist or an enemy. So this whole comment is a delusional comment, from a being who is attempting scare tactics on the public. We are unable to be more vulnerable than having at least 500 nukes trained on our major cities. Can a "terrorist" out match that reality?

The words" potential terrorist attack." I have the potential to fly up in the air and grab the sun and dance with it. I have the potential to turn into an atom and split myself. I have the potential to run into a speeding Mac truck and win. Potential does not even mean anything. So really what this comment is saying is. The country is the same as it was before I made this comment. What he is really saying is, By making this comment I only convinced everyone I am unable to make comments. That is what is funny about freedom of speech. I do perceive this being did not mean to say anything at all. He just was talking to himself and some other being perceived he was talking to them, so they quoted him. And now we all read it and assume the being who made this comment was doing something other than saying absolutely nothing to himself. You do not need to call me to remind me the world is crazy, because I already understand you will only be reminding yourself of what you already understand.

"My difficulties belong to me!"
Alfred Adler

This is great wisdom.

My mental struggle is my domain so get the hell away from me.

If you want to assist me with my mental struggle you better first understand your physical struggle will be the price you will pay.

This quote is what freedom is all about. One is free to drive their self insane in their attempts to figure out what the hell they are, and why the hell they are.

When I figure out who created everything I will take their advice, but until then I assume it was me, so any advice you can give me will only insult me.

If you pass a law that says your life is meaningless I will enforce it.

Every man is an island unto their self. Every man is trapped with their mental situation. A man can attempt to escape their mental situation and it will only lead to their demise; A woman can only attempt to escape a man's mental situation.

A woman gets married when she meets a mental situation she can tolerate.

Women who never get married cannot decide which mental situation is tolerable.

Lesbians have determined no mental situation is tolerable.

Apparently my tracks of thought have run off the train.

Oh look an exciting new day is upon us. 5/11/2009 12:18:44 AM

I am thinking, dam I am still here.

Your opinions about me mean nothing to me, so conserve them.

I guess you will get to the point of understanding I turn into a demon at night because that is when I last killed myself because you said I was a failure because I did not have enough money or pass enough of your tests to be considered worthy. I guess you should avoid assuming I am going to do anything but torture you into infinity after this life is over for you. It does not matter if you believe that or not because I understand that.

So you are doomed for all eternity already. So maybe you should think twice before you pass a law that gives another being the right to tell your child they are a failure because they didn't spell the word properly. But the great truth is, you cannot avoid eternal damnation at this stage. It does not matter how innocent you think you are. Your fate is sealed in my books of infinite torture. That will give you a slight hint at the mental torture I went through for 15 plus years because of your infinite grace and mercy. So you just blabber your mouth all you want because I will not reduce your torture when you pass on for even a split second. Perhaps you have never experienced infinite rage. I will make sure you will understand infinite gnashing of teeth sooner than you think.

"Gen. Pet…., who oversees the wars in Iraq and Afghanistan, said in an interview that Pakistan has become the nerve center of al Qaeda's global operations" WallStreetjournal.com

Well I am glad we have god dam geniuses on our side. It only took them 8 years to figure out something and it only cost us innocent offspring who got brainwashed by idiot politicians who would never face the Taliban because it might interfere with them counting all the kick backs they get from the military industrial complex.

Perhaps in the next 8 years they will have figured out Al Qaeda is the god dam Taliban. Then perhaps in another 8 years they will figure out Pakistan is the god dam Taliban. Then perhaps in another 8 years they will determine they cannot win. Then in another 8 years they will determine they should never have gone into this well set trap. Then perhaps in another 8 years they will start talking about getting our innocent brainwashed offspring the hell out of there.

I have faith one day the generals on our side will come to the understanding males have a penis, if we give them enough money. So I will repeat, I am dam glad we have dam geniuses on our side. I feel so much safer knowing these dam genius generals have everything under control. Now I will discuss something important.

I hope my ability to piss you off is equal to your ability to block your emotions so that one day you might actually have brain function. I am writing infinite books so I have to write about something even though I understand it is nothing.

Maybe I should talk about pretty little ponies. I can discuss how the pretty little ponies are in fact pretty. Then I could go on about how the pretty little ponies are all so little and also little. Then I can go on to explain how the pretty little ponies are all so ponies and also ponies. Then I can sum it all up and say pretty little ponies are all pretty little and pretty ponies and little pretty and pretty little ponies and little pretty ponies, and when one can grasp that they will understand the reality that the pretty ponies and the little pretty ponies are exactly like the little pretty ponies and the pretty little ponies. Whether the ponies are pretty little or a little pretty they are still ponies and ponies are both pretty little and a little pretty or they would not be pretty little ponies they would be ponies that are a little pretty and pretty little. I will leave this in my books so you will understand how much I try to reach the living dead.

"Wisconsin police can attach GPS to cars to secretly track anybody's movements without obtaining search warrants, an appeals court ruled Thursday." Chicagotribune.com

Now you understand the definition of a police state. Do not assume I give dam. I thrive on your insanity and confusion. Your suffering sustains me.

"Our modern states are preparing for war without even knowing the future enemy."
Alfred Adler

That's okay Alfred they will invent an enemy to justify their war machine. See Alfred what they do is create enemies to scare people and then they convince the people to allow them to build weapons and then they scare the people more with their "enemies" and that way the people end up breaking their backs to work to keep the rich , rich. There are no people in poverty that own a military bomb making factory but there are many people in poverty who get those bombs dropped on them. Of course Alfred that is why Washington allowed us to have weapons so we would not allow a standing army because he was smart enough to know, a standing army will only encourage that standing army to invent enemies to justify its own existence. When I find a big patch of poison mushrooms we will talk further.

"I'm embarrassed every time I look a teacher in the eye, because we ask them to do so much for so little. "
Phil McGraw

I will do one quote from a living psychologist and hope this was an inside joke because if it is not this being has no business in psychology at all.

We do not pay the teachers enough to mentally abuse our children when they judge them because they did not spell a word or pass a test properly.

Teachers should get paid more for mentally abusing children, and voters get paid too much for allowing them to do it, and when each generation graduates they understand they can work in lawn care, deal drugs, commit suicide or fight a war to line billionaire's pockets with more money.

I cannot look in the eye of a teacher because they mentally abuse children because they are paid to, in order to have food to eat.

A teacher is not a teacher because their lesson plan is determined by idiots who are not teachers.

If a teacher is not allowed to teach what they perceive is truth then they are simply a manipulated student, like the ones they get paid to manipulate.

A teacher is a prostitute who is forced to perform the will of a pimp who cares nothing about understanding or wisdom.

A home school teacher teaches what they perceive is valuable to teach that particular student, not what an idiot panel of degenerates determines is of value to teach every student.

"A man begins cutting his wisdom teeth the first time he bites off more than he can chew."
Herb Caen

Suffering leads to understanding; some do not last long and some do not care to last long.

"Cleverness is not wisdom."
Euripides

Freedom and anarchy gets ones attention; cleverness just makes people laugh at you.

What Washington lacked in cleverness he made up for in revolutionary ideas.

One only has two choices in life: Accept slavery or fight to free yourself from slavery.

The wisdom to know when to fight is not as important as the wisdom to know how to fight.

A joke is not funny if there is wisdom attached to it.

Wisdom is everywhere, the vision to see it is rare.

Wisdom is not learned it's earned.

There are less than 12 truly wise beings in recorded history and you will not be one of them.

I only know one truly wise being in recorded history and you are not me.

Whoever named him Euripides should be beaten senseless.

"Every man is a damn fool for at least five minutes every day; wisdom consists in not exceeding the limit."
Elbert Hubbard

This guy is a comedian.

Everyone is a dam fool for at least five minutes a day; some make it a lifelong profession.

One who does not fear death is foolish; Ones who do fear death wish they were foolish.

If I act stupid it is because I am attempting to reach your level of wisdom.

Children hang you because you pay the teachers hangman wages and give them hangman lessons to teach the children how to properly hang you.

I only serve beings that understand they serve me.

I nearly made a decision today then thought better of it.

The last decision I made led me to become infinitely open minded.

If you figure out what I mean by that last comment you're coming along.2:14:42 AM

"He dares to be a fool, and that is the first step in the direction of wisdom."
James Huneker

This guy is stealing my material so I will correct his delusional comments.

If you are a psychologist, and I am not saying you are a psychologist. I am saying you have a degree that suggests you wish you were a psychologist this is an emotional conditioning comment.

"He dares to be a fool" insane people or ones with a sense of time do not like to be the fool or play the fool because it hurts their little feelings. So in order to reach a mental state of unlocking subconscious one must embarrass their self heavily. That is exactly what emotional conditioning is all about. One has to say exactly what is on their mind with no concern about who is listening. This is all about properly preparing ones mindset. If you go around caring about what everyone might say to your comments you will be stuck in a little isolation chamber called emotional conscious dominate state of mind. Being a fool is all about saying what is on your mind and not being afraid of what others will say. It goes much further. Wear the stupidest outfit in your closet to work and when people insult you then that means you should wear again the next day. Look stupid. Act stupid. Be stupid. You will never lose your huge ego unless you take a little mental punishment.

You do not ever want to be wrong so make sure everything you say is wrong. You do not ever want to look stupid or foolish in front of your best friends so make sure you look infinitely stupid and foolish in front of the ones you respect the most.

Do not try to sound smart try to sound stupid and foolish. That will take your infinite ego down a few pegs. Do not let them know your are acting. Make them think you are stupid, because you are stupid in thinking you know anything, ever. So that is what emotional conditioning is all about. Be stupid and foolish and look stupid and foolish because that is the first step in the direction of wisdom (subconscious dominate). Funny thing is, you will never do that because your ego is the size of the universe and your ego would rather have a pea brain mind than an infinite mind. You would rather write a script for some pills you get kick backs from than actually help anyone, and I mean help yourself, because you are never able to help anyone but yourself, you are just delusional and think you can help anyone but yourself.

"He who devotes sixteen hours a day to hard study may become at sixty as wise as he thought himself at twenty. "
Mary Wilson Little

This sums it up nicely. Your degree only proves you have a degree in stupidity. You spent many years reading text books so you could write prescription in order to mentally abuse people who only are seeking some wise words so they can mentally work things out in their mind, and then you have the balls to say, 'I care about people." You only care about the money in your bank account and your vision will never go beyond that, ever. Show me a psychologist and I will show you someone who needs to see a real psychologist.

"Honesty is the first chapter in the book of wisdom."
Thomas Jefferson

I bet all you morally bankrupt wise ones perceive this means honesty is the best policy. There is no truth and there is no lies because everything is relative to the observer. If I have to lie to the entire universe, to publish one of my books, that will be me being true to my purpose.

In time of mental and physical war, all cards are off the table. I will try a rhyme scheme. You will hang by your honestly and hang by your lies, so try to understand they are nothing more than cries. This is about emotional conditioning also. Find a person your respect and when they ask a question lie your ass off and make sure they catch you in a lie. Make sure they yell at you for being a liar. Make sure they say they never want talk to you again because you are liar. Then lie again to them and say you care. If someone suggests a point you agree with, lie and say you do not agree with it. Devil's advocate type situation. Be sinister. This is the price you must pay to reach mental clarity because with all of this truth and lie crap, your mind is tangled and thus locked in an isolation chamber of hell. You have to kill this "god" concept in your thinking. That only encourages good and evil thoughts. Do not harm other beings physically, that's stupidity. This is mental conditioning. Your mental battle is going to take every ounce of energy you have. You will not have any energy left to fight foolish physical battles any longer. If you cannot face that challenge you should just give up on life, because life has already defeated you and you were a pushover.

Honesty is for ones who have settled on delusional unconsciousness as an occupation.

There is a little catch that the US affords one. The founders have this catch for a very good reason. I plead the 5th. That means is any court of law, after they make you swear to tell the truth, you just plead the 5th no matter what. That is lying. You are not telling a lie you are simply telling the court you refuse to tell the truth and it is legal.

The fifth amendment protects witnesses from being forced to incriminate themselves.

I am not mentally able to tell what a truth or lie is. So I would plead the 5th on every question in a court of law. They might ask "Did you see that man run away from you after he stole your wallet."

Well honestly he may not have been a man, he may have been a very ugly woman in excellent disguise. So I would plead the 5th on that alone. Did they steal my wallet? Well honestly it never was my wallet because I did not actually create the cow skin that it is made from, so it technically is not my wallet and it never will be my wallet. So again I would plead the 5th because if not the court would perceive I am a liar and thus I would incriminate myself.

I went to doctor because my side was hurting and that doctor asked how bad is the pain, between 1 and 10, and I said 4 because I honestly could not tell. I felt pain but mentally I could not tell if it was a 1 or 10. So I thought if I say 5, I can't tell what a 5 level of pain is so I will say 4. Because a 10 would mean I am dead and a one would mean I have no pain at all. So I had to be as truthful as I could to make sure they didn't think I was lying. All I can say is I felt discomfort. They said one scale of 1 to 10 how much discomfort. Then I can only make up shit. The nurse was much wiser than the doctor because she at least commented you know your body better than anyone. That is right. What is even the point of the scale. Discomfort is relative to the observer. Discomfort on one persons scale is not the same as another person scale. That is exactly why insanity itself is not a set legal definition. It is on a case by case basis. Insanity is relative to who is determining insanity. An insane person will assume another insane person is sane. The only test is who can write the most books with the most wise teachings and sayings in the shortest amount of time. Whoever that is, is the one who is sane. I am certain you enjoy that logic.

I submit I am not the most graceful creature in the universe. But I did not ask for this accident to happen so all I can mindfully understand is I am doing the best I can, based on the fact I went from conscious dominate state of mind to subconscious dominate state of mind in 1 second, seven months ago. There are simply too many unknowns for me to figure out exactly how it happened. I talk to some who have no sense of time and they say, "Oh we are all the same." And then I ask "How many books are you writing to tell others how to go to dominate subconscious state of mind." And they say "It's not dominate subconscious is spiritual freedom or enlightenment." Then I swiftly remind them they are not like me and they never ever will be.

 And they go through the roof because I do not fit into their isolation belief system. They actually think I am like they are. That is what I call beyond understanding delusional. I at least submit everything I say is wrong, I am simply trying to do the best I can based on the mental state I am in. I am mindful to dissuade anyone from believing anything I say. That is my emotional conditioning. I lie to great lengths to dissuade people from reading my books because they might start thinking I am something special and my ego is already infinite as it is. To actually make money off my books is my worst nightmare. I understand if I start making money from my books I will have to start typing faster and start publishing books faster and thus eating less and sleeping less. I am already at a level of lying in bed with my eyes closed for about 20 minutes and then my mind starts suggesting things I need to write about and I get up and come in here and start pumping out words again. I submit I may mentally overload before much longer so I am at peace that at least I published some books. I seek the hottest coals so that I can understand where to find even hotter coals. 3:34:06 AM

"In seeking wisdom thou art wise; in imagining that thou hast attained it - thou art a fool."
Lord Chesterfield

Yet another comedian.

One is wise to take up the challenge to become subconscious dominate, and once one accomplishes it, they will no longer be able to determine what is wise, what is truth, and what is lies, because they will lose their ability to have contrast because they alter emotional capacity or gamma waves that alter perception.

Simply put, you cannot have the emotional aspects and also have the clarity aspects.

One will decrease as the other increases or one cannot have the cake and eat it too.

You will certainly be wise but only from the perspective of others. You will perceive you are just acting normal and ones who watch your deeds will perceive you are a wise one. This is in relation too; the tree cannot see its own fruits. If you have to try to be wise you will only make an ass out of yourself. Of course that comment is only valid when followed up by, I make an ass out of myself because I am wise enough not to care what anyone thinks about anything I say. Not care in that sentence denotes inability to feel ashamed or embarrassed in relation to the fact my emotions are essentially silenced. If one is afraid to speak because of their fear they will be embarrassed, they are an isolated being all together. The only person who cares what you say is you, and tyrants, and they are often one in the same.

"It is a characteristic of wisdom not to do desperate things."
Henry David Thoreau

This guy is a great comedian.

No wonder everyone is so confused. The problem with ones who are at least slightly subconscious dominate is they say things they perceive is wise but they cannot tell if it is wise.

Buddha called the ones with a sense of time, and as you understand, have conscious dominate minds and thus have hunger, the sane. That is the same thing as saying the wise. That is the same thing as saying the ones who know. So it is all the reverse. The sane are in reality the insane. The wise are in reality the unwise. But this varies from quote to quote because there is no such thing as wise or unwise to ones with no sense of time.

This is what Thoreau meant.

The insane are more concerned with safety than clarity. This is similar to the saying "A penny wise and a pound fool-ish." If one wants to be mentally safe they will never reach subconscious dominate state of mind. They are simply too emotional, they are simply too scared and thus they are simply too isolated mindfully and their minds are too locked or frozen. They are mentally in a tiny prison cell and if the slightest wind blows they panic in terror. This is why it is very important one uses many emotional conditioning techniques to reach subconscious dominate state. I found out one practice one religion uses is meditation in cemeteries. I mentioned this earlier. It is not about the dead or the spirits there, it is all about your mental belief in spirits which causes you fear.

Do you still believe the boogie man is going to get you? The boogie man is the least of your problems because I perceive I reached this state of mind because I took so many pills when I started to panic in fear for my life I said, that's okay I will die.

So you have to ponder what kind of terror you will have to experience and conquer to simulate that kind of terror. Sitting in a cemetery all alone with no chance to get help if something happens in pitch darkness is for emotional weaklings. So if you cannot do that simple emotional conditioning you are not even in the ball game. If one cannot do that simple exercise one is so emotionally controlled they are simply incapable of a clear thought except for maybe once or twice in a their lifetime.

So Thoreau says one who is wise should not do desperate things, because he refused to pay taxes on his land and was thrown into jail for the night until his aunt paid the tax. So then he went on to write books about why one should avoid authority or the dangers of authority or tyranny for example. But his deeper meaning was one should think for their self and take no other beings word for anything no matter what.

This is fundamental principle of reality. In Germany they passed a law that said if you knew a Jew you had to turn them in or you would go to jail and people followed that law because they were weak minded beings who where to dam afraid to do anything but be safe.

You are going to be killed by life no matter what you do; so your fate is sealed; your fate is already determined, only the details leading to that fate are not determined. You are already technically dead because the last I checked no one can live forever, so what are you afraid of? Do you believe if you do not follow a law you do not believe in you will not die?

Do you understand if you get to the moment before you die and do not do as your intuition suggests you should do you are going to hate yourself for eternity?

All these beings you are attempting to please at the cost of your own personal obligations are not going to be there to face your death with you. It is best to get the fear and the fear of death out of the way early in life so you can live a proper life. A lot of this is emotional conditioning away from fear. Some of the worst fears are fear of isolation, fear of rejection, fear of loss, fear of embarrassment, fear of being an outcast, fear of being all alone, and one of the most powerful fears is fear of the unknown.

What is going to happen if you say something and everyone hates you for saying it; that fear alone locks people mentally up for life. The emotional conditioning that will remedy fear of the unknown is to say exactly what you are afraid to say. Of course in America there are many things you are not allowed to say because the voters abridged the first amendment and thus killed the constitution, so now America is a police state or a tyranny because the voters are too afraid to revive Lady Liberty from her slumber.

But there are many things you can say that you are terrified to say, that are not against the laws of the current tyrannical police state some call America and I prefer to call, the raped beauty who safety conscious beings allowed to die in a cold ditch on a dark night. You cannot beat a dead horse with threats and intimidation because a dead horse was not scared of death, and thus is certainly not scared of you. That was a personal original quote.

"It requires wisdom to understand wisdom: the music is nothing if the audience is deaf."
Walter Lippmann

Now you need to avoid this guy because he has black eyes of rage.

One who is subconscious dominate is able to understand wisdom; the others are blind and deaf to wisdom. So Lippmann is clearly some sort of terroristic threat and should be locked away.

How dare he say such things about you. He is not talking to me because I understand his wisdom quote is simply an insult leveled against you. He is saying you have no brain function. You cannot understand wisdom so it is nothing important to you. The sane know everything; fools understand everything is nothing. I am mindful you will not understand anything I ever write, and the only way to do that is to understand I write only for myself.

I perfectly anticipate you will be perfect like me.

You are scared to be scared and I am attempting to find something that may scare me.

Once upon a time there was a man and he lived in a great country. One day he was asked to vote to allow an agency that's sole purpose was to go around and spy on people. This agency was so secret it convinced that man he did not have the right to see what the spy agency was doing with his money he gave them every year. One day the spy agency went to another country and killed a woman they determined was in the way of their spying. The man was not aware of this because the man already voted to make it so he had no right to see what the spy agency was doing.

The small child of the woman who the spy agency killed loaded up a truck with bombs and went to the man's great country and blew up that man's family who voted to allow the spy agency. In prison the little boy was paid a visit by the man. The man asked the little boy in the prison cell "I hope you are happy now that you are in prison." And the little boy replied "This prison is the same as the one you are in."

The man snapped back, "I did not kill your mother why did you kill my family." And the little boy replied

" You did not kill my mother as violently as you killed your own family."

The man became angry, "You loaded the truck with bombs and brought them to my family house and killed them. I did not kill them." The little boy replied, "I did not kill your family I freed them from the prison they were in, and your vote for that spy agency told me you wanted me to free them from their prison."

Okay I submit I am not so good at parables. So just ignore that one.

All that parable is saying is. When you vote to allow an organization to do as it pleases with no accountability under the guise of protecting you, that organization will do whatever it wants and the repercussions of that will always come back to haunt you, and then you will say, "I did not do anything wrong.", because you are to brain dead to grasp, you voted for a mass murderer and told that murderer he will never be punished even if he kills a child's mother. So do not go around saying how bad the terrorist are for attacking us. They attacked us because we murdered their mothers. I am sorry you are to brain dead to understand that. You should just sell your brain for scrap, because it stopped functioning a long time ago. And while you are at it you need to ban freedom of speech and freedom of press because every time I log into a news site and read the headlines, my eyes turn black with rage and then I come here to my books and I take it out on your ass.

 I beg you to get in my way. If you want to kill a terrorist, get a gun, look in the mirror and empty the clip. If we did not have empire building methods throughout the globe everyone would like us because they would understand we mind our own business.

We are no longer mature enough to mind our own business. We seek to meddle in the affairs of others. It is one thing to help someone who asks for assistance. But it is another thing to invade a country and then ask them if they mind if we stay. The military and the spy agencies are only there to scout out the next empire quest that should be undertaken. When America is 100% perfect in every way and everyone is feed and all the kids are educated properly, then empires will be built around us without our efforts.

You pay a hell of a lot of money to these agencies and China is now the #1 influence in the world. All the countries we tried to rape are now the countries China is assisting properly and those countries understand how much we raped them for all of these years. So you got ripped off and you will just keep getting ripped because "they" know it is easy to rip off sheep. Life is very simple once you stop thinking for yourself because that is what death is. Third world countries do not rape first world countries, the flow goes the other way.

I perceive I am so angry today because my fourth book just went live and I am angry that people may buy one. I am insulted at the prospects of another being invading my privacy by reading my personal diaries. I had to earn my right to be able to write these infinite books and you are unable to grasp what I mean by earn. Just ignore everything I say, because you will harm yourself if I ever told you anything of value. You will not be getting any real knowledge from me because you are not mature enough as a being to handle real knowledge, and you never will be. Now I will discuss something of value.5:55:12 PM

Please remind yourself this is a diary and the author is strictly speaking to himself and about himself. Please avoid being so self centered you think he is actually talking to you or about you. Please attempt to grasp the reality no being is ever talking to you or about you. All beings are simply in a state of monologue when they speak. This book is not about you although you wish it was.

Apparently when I go back to proof read what I just wrote I am now missing entire words when I type sentences. I just simply skip or leave out entire words. I have pondered into a new method or approach to this problem and am facing. I will look into this brain aspect a bit deeper because I am extremely weird at this stage.

"For there can be no Religion more true or just, than to know the things that are; Be Pious and Religious, O my Son, for he that doth so, is the best and highest Philosopher; and with- out Philosophy, it is impossible ever to attain to the height and exactness of Piety or Religion." The Corpus Hermetica Book 1

Ignore all the religious crap. Focus on the words "highest philosopher". That is subconscious aspect of the mind. It is the questioner. It questions authority, It questions laws, Its questions existence. It is "on the fence". It is the devil's advocate of the mind. Everyone has a tendency to have questioning moments and once in a while a being usually by accident gets thrown so far into the "philosopher" state of mind, it requires so much power to stay in that state, certain things start getting turned off, like sense of time, sense of taste, sensitivity to pain, hearing contrast is turned off.

So the whole concept of nirvana means no sense of time and no sense of time means, all these processes are turned down to 1 or 2 and that means the being has great sensitivity to everything. The definition of Heimdall is a being who can hear the grass grow. So I can feel people with my vision because the vision aspect of vision is somehow not the focus. I can translate anything I read and at least perceive I understand it because I do not read the words. Somehow I look at the sentence and feel what it means. So when I translate a sentence people with little sensitivity will say "That is not what that sentence said." But in reality that is exactly what that sentence said but that being did not hear or feel what that sentence said, because they are focused on the words in that sentence and cannot "feel" the meaning or the wisdom. Ones who look at it, the ones with strong hunger or sense of time always judge a sentence by its cover and ones with no sense of time judge a sentence by how it feels. This is exactly what this quote is saying.

"It requires wisdom to understand wisdom: the music is nothing if the audience is deaf."
Walter Lippmann

So I need to explain everything about the brain because I am quite certain the brain is able to allow me to understand everything perfectly just because I accidently did some hardcore emotional and attachment conditioning. My thesis is, the brain cannot be this powerful. Of course I will go play my video first because I already know what the end result of my brain explanations will be and I am extremely pissed off I decided to write infinite books because I am unable to take that decision back now.

I will avoid suggesting at this stage of the accident I can simply look down at a page in any book and understand it instantly so I am uncertain if the mind can possibly be that powerful so I will not mention this in my book because I do not even know what words I would use to describe that. Please avoid assuming I am suggesting I am special unless your definition of special is cursed.

There is one major problem I have at this stage after the accident. If all of this happened because of some emotional conditioning and now I have all these weird powers of understanding or heightened awareness and did not experience and actual physical trauma then we are not human beings at all, we are some sort of unknown form of life. We try to compare ourselves to monkeys and then we become more like monkeys. Whatever we suggest we are like, we become like that thing we suggest we are like. If we suggest we are evil we become evil. If we suggest we are good we become good. If we suggest we will go to space we go to space. We are some sort of shape shifter. We assume the identity of whatever we desire to become. Without something to become like, we are nothing. So someone said there is an infinite being and you should strive to be like that infinite being. So we strive to be like that infinite being but the problem is, they made a mistake. We all think we are that perfect being and thus we think others are not so we kill them.

We are only able to shape shift and that means no one can predict what we will shape shift into. So every time some-one says "Our DNA is just like monkeys" and then our DNA takes the hint from the subconscious and becomes more like monkeys DNA. Then the next thing you know we are catching diseases that only monkeys can have. This is because we are shape shifting into the identity of a monkey. The problem with this is, we are not aware of it until we have the subconscious dominate aspect active. Thus the saying "We know not what we do."

We shape shift into the identity of anything we determine we like. We affect our own evolution with our thoughts. This is not some vague wise saying, this is a literal saying. There are no known life forms that can do that. All other life forms are under the influence of physical methods of evolution. But then we come to another problem. A leopard found out early on if it runs faster it catches more food and after some evolution it was able to run faster now it runs very fast. So then the animal's that it was catching determined they need to run faster to get away from it. Now they run very fast. Both are simply evolving to run faster and faster. Trial and error. They are adapting just like we are and that is affecting the DNA and genetic makeup.

We create weapons because we want to kill people. So then we have wars and kill people because that is what we want. The only possible explanation I can come up with is that we are in a dimension that whatever we think or our thoughts suggest, happens. This is in direct relation to be careful what you wish for. If one is not in a state of mind of heightened awareness they are literally doing things and they are not aware of it. They say things like "That is not what I just said." And "stop putting words in mouth" and "Just because I paid for the weapons and voted to enable a standing army does not mean I killed that house full of innocent women and children in Afghanistan today.", because that being is not at a level of mental awareness to understand they not only killed those people they desired to kill those people. I want to go back to the land of the dead, awareness cramps my style.

We arrived on this planet. We saw Neanderthal man. We assumed his identity through shape shifting and then we killed him off. So I do not think we are in fact humans, I perceive we are in fact Shape shifters from some other place and we are so good at it, we fool ourselves. Why don't you write infinite books about how I am never right about a single thing I ever say, for my sake.

Perhaps that is why we cannot find the missing link between all the monkeys and us. We just appeared out of nowhere 200,000 years ago. And started to hunt and gather just like the Neanderthal was doing. Then we killed them off and started killing everything off. And now we are trying to find another advanced life form through space exploration so we can assume its identity and then kill it off. And the really weird thing is, we all want to find an alien life form that is much more advanced than we are so we can assume and shape shift into it. Of course I am totally insane as the result of my accident and everything I say is simply total delusions because what I say cannot be reality because if it is, we have a lot to think about.

I will go back to translating wise sayings in my vain efforts to remain on this plane of existence. Do not worry about my sanity, I am at the stage of understanding we are in fact shape shifters of unknown origin. I will be just fine in the morning. Strange train of thought I am on apparently. We arrived as a thought form and the only thing that travels faster than the speed of light is thought. So "we" somehow found earth and came here and found the smartest creature which was Neanderthal and assumed its identity and that fooled us into thinking we are of this planet. So we lost our understanding that we are thought forms. And so we assumed the characteristics of the Neanderthal which is death and fighting and struggle. So we now die. And we now fight. And we now need to eat. Not because we have to, but because we assumed the identity of Neanderthal. So somehow seven months ago I woke up to the reality we are some form of thought form. That is what we really are as a collective, thoughts. We assume the identity of anything we come in contact with and then over time we start to believe we are that thing we assumed the identity of, and become blind to the reality we are just some sort of thought form type life form. Maybe you just like me better when I am mad and angry.

So this would explain what the theory of relativity means.

I will stop here because I have much pondering to do. I will attempt to pick up this train tomorrow.

5/12/2009 1:39:42 AM

I at least attempted sleep. Now this is going to be a very long thought line so you won't be able to follow it.

"According to the Mahaparinibbana Sutta of the Pali canon, at the age of 80, the Buddha announced that he would soon reach Parinirvana or the final deathless state abandoning the earthly body. After this, the Buddha ate his last meal, which he had received as an offering from a blacksmith named Cunda. Falling violently ill, Buddha instructed his attendant Ānanda to convince Cunda that the meal eaten at his place had nothing to do with his passing and that his meal would be a source of the greatest merit as it provided the last meal for a Buddha. The precise contents of the Buddha's final meal are not clear, due to variant scriptural traditions and ambiguity over the translation of certain significant terms; the Theravada tradition generally believes that the Buddha was offered some kind of pork, while the Mahayana tradition believes that the Buddha consumed some sort of truffle or other mushroom."

WikiPedia.Com

Buddha drank the cool aid. Psychologically speaking he drank the cool aid. What is interesting is first off there are simply no certain stories about Buddha. But I will attempt to explain contrast with one story about him. He fasted for 38 or 43 or 49 days and then a little girl found him by the river and gave him some food and "saved" him from death, so to speak.

Now Moses was floating down a river and a woman found him and "saved" him. After they were "saved" they both went on to be profound people in the history of civilization in relation to the parts of the world they came from. So just forget the details and look at the straight point. Two men were saved by women and these men were near a river or in a river when they were found. Both men had similar teachings of peace or ways to avoid physical suffering so to speak. Both had this "awakening" and it happened at just about the exact same time around 2500 BC. The catch is, it was on two opposite sides of the world. So the ones who heard of Buddha did not hear of Moses till many hundreds of years later. The ones who knew of Moses did not hear of Buddha for many hundreds of years later. Buddhas actual name was Siddhārtha Gautama. And now you know why I say Buddha.

Moses is thought to have gone into the mountains to die.

One other "prophet" at that time was thought to have gone up to heaven in a chariot.

Jesus had the last supper just before he transcended into heaven.

The above story in quotes is an exact situation like the "last supper". Buddha gathered his friends and had his last meal then left this world. Jesus had his last meal and then left this world.

Everything I just said is totally out of context. It is all so confusing to ones with time stamps on their outlook. It is unbearably confusing if one has time stamps on their memories or recollections. It simply seems too far away or too far in the past to be relevant today because of the time stamps. So when one is subconscious dominate memories are like a pool of water and when a pebble is dropped , which is a thought or question is started, it encompasses the entire pool. So all the memories are relied upon without the time stamp confusion.

One with conscious dominate mind has many rocks sticking out of the pool, so when they start pondering something the thoughts hit the rock and bounce off and all these bouncing thoughts create confusion in the line of thought or the train of thought. That's what the time stamps do when they are active in a being with a "sense of time".

When a thought is thrown into the pool of their memories chaos ensures because of all the times stamps, rocks, reflecting the thought.

I will attempt to keep in on the Buddha story. Why did he drink the cool aid? He told everyone there and even the cook, do not get upset, I am transcending now. Then he got ill from the food and died. So psychologically he committed suicide. No question about that.

Now let's contrast that with Jesus. Jesus could have escaped but instead he had a last supper because he decided not to escape. He chose to die. So that is also suicide. He was aware his time was coming and so he had a last supper. So that is proof he could have run away instead of having that last supper but he did not , so, he saw death and didn't get out of the way when we could have. That is suicide.

So both of these being allowed their self to die. That is where the misunderstandings start. They mindfully became aware of reality. They did not kill their self, they were aware there body was a host. As in a host of hosts.

I had an accident and essentially all of my physical senses or functions turned down and my cerebral functions became very heightened. My taste is nearly gone, my hearing is very strange, my sense of pain is wacky. But my mental clarity is through the roof. Maybe nothing I say in all of my books is anywhere near correct or true but I certainly do not feel like it is not correct or not true or I would not monologue it into the text in real time or verbatim.

Sometimes beings say things like "I am not comfortable in my own skin". Sometimes beings are not happy with their body. Sometimes being wish they were different than they are. Host of hosts. A parasite latches onto a host and assumes that host as a part of their self. If the host dies the parasite dies or if the host dies the parasite finds another host. So the parasites dies to its old self or old home, and then finds another host or new home.

The new testament suggests after the second coming ones will transform as they are taken up to heaven. The Torah suggests the one who went up in to heaven in a chariot transformed and never even died a physical death. So all of these things are in relation to a parasite leaving its host body and moving on.

So this is tricky because if a human body is a host to "us" then that would mean we are in fact not humans but simply using the animal called humans as a host. Now I am getting this strange feeling like I should not even be telling you this. So I will continue to tell you this.

So this host concept would be in direct relation to the religion of Hinduism. They are very high on the reincarnation situation and they go as far as saying, "we" take many hosts. They do not kill any oxygen breathing creatures in some of the more hardcore aspects of that religion. They do not even kill earth worms when they dig holes. They get the earth worms out first then dig the hole in earnest because it may be one of "us" who decided to try an earthworm for a while because they got tired of taking humans as hosts. Now you understand the definition of, the illusions are thick.

I am telling myself this accident just enhanced my imagination. So I am going to go attempt to ponder my ass back into reality and away from this "thought form" aspect because it makes far too much sense to me. Perhaps the reason many beings feel an emptiness inside is because they detect they are not in their own body but in a host body. I want to declare I have always been much better looking and smarter than my body and deeds suggest.

Reincarnation is a nice way to say, time to find a host. I feel extremely out of context. If you find god let him know I have an infinitely long list of questions to ask him. You will never reach the top unless you lose your fear of heights.2:20:04 AM

It is okay if we all have different beliefs because everyone gets the joke in the end.

When I get frustrated I remind myself you are here to. Behind every patient is a psychologist attempting to work it out. If god is a female I am open minded to the idea; If god is a male it probably isn't god.

3:08:40 PM I am feeling extremely sinister today. I walked up to the store and crossed the road and then came back and crossed the road again and it occurred to me I just made two failed suicide attempts in the span of about 5 minutes. Then a great truth hit me. Anyone who says they have inner peace needs to get their vision checked and lay off the heavy sedatives. Inner peace is a nice way of saying "I need to reload." There is no wisdom in the universe greater than that last sentence.

Inner peace is the first symptom of a defeated foe. Being upset with your situation encourages you to adapt to it. Happiness means you fell into a hole and you didn't break your leg. Once you give up on the concept of inner peace you may actually find some. The world's wisdom keeps me well grounded. The fact I keep writing books is proof I never learn the lesson. My only chance at inner peace is to convince the world to shut up.

"We're talking about the pope, who is also a representative of the Holy See, which has a lot to ask forgiveness from our people for," Knesset Speaker.

I perceive this speaker has assumed the world cares about his isolated, self centered, small view of the world. When a being assumes others care about their battle, they take their eyes off of their own battle. I had a date with the one who does not care about my problems, so do not assume I care about yours. Apparently this speaker has assumed what he thinks about anything ever, matters at all. Perhaps his monologue will enlighten him to the reality his words are not based on reality. I perceive this pope being was attempting to see if this speaker had any humility left in his bones and the speakers comments gave the pope the answer he was seeking. I tolerate the world; that means I forgive it.

If you find a simple solution to a problem you are asking for a big problem. One's who cannot let the past go, end up trapped in it.

Crowd confronts police making shoplifting arrest. I assure you the police understand the stupidity of the laws you pass more than anyone. The police simply enforce the insanity you voted for. The police enforce the misguided laws you voted for. When a democracy passes a law that makes it illegal to pass laws, it will have taken the first step towards freedom. I am extremely upset right now and I am certain you do not buy that. Inner peace is achieved just after you stop talking. Your wisdom keeps me climbing.

When everything in life is just "so so" you have achieved greatness. It takes infinite words to say nothing.

Looking at people brings me a moment of joy before the hot coals rip me apart again. That is the nature of the accident. My clarity is equal to my rage so I am mindful both are opportunities I cannot escape. The fastest way to ruin a good thing is to be honest about it. Mental clarity is achieved through mental suffering and many never reach those depths alive. Death is the only thing that is not prejudice. Life is not fair so avoid assuming anything in life is fair. Great wisdom is at the bottom of a lake; few can hold their breath long enough to see.

When you perceive I am saying wise things, it is proof my vision has gone black with rage; when I cuss that means I am happy. Either I am in a coma or the entire world is, but there is no other possibility. The least important person in the world is the most important person in the world. I communicate to you for a reason but I am blind to that reason. Life is too crazy for a sane person to master. Once you know what you are doing, you give up on understanding you don't.

If I get warmed up keep it to yourself. The worst part of completing a task is believing you can. If you sense loss when something dies you are out of touch with your own inevitability. My books do not have a point, but they have many sharp edges. I am too tired today to explain what I am explaining.

I detect mental burnout caused by the accident at this date and time.5/12/2009 7:57:48 PM

I perceive I simply do not care anymore about what I care about. I perceive I have simply bored myself into silence. Perhaps the video game will have some wisdom to share with me.

8:05 PM The video game suggested I am a cry baby and I should get the hell out of its pool just before I reminded it , it is not allowed to speak to me and snapped it's neck. Mental violence encourages understanding; that is why torture and fear are so successful. Words do not end many revolutions but they started all of them.

"I love you" has killed more people than "leave me alone" ever will.

The Thinker (French: *Le Penseur*) is a bronze and marble sculpture by Auguste Rodin held in the Musée Rodin in Paris.

That sculpture is what subconscious is. This is in line with this picture of the devil sitting on his throne looking rather upset and with hand under his chin brooding about his next move. The devil is subconscious. Subconscious has no fear and thus no compassion. The subconscious is a machine. Mentally speaking that is the nature of subconscious because mentally it will wipe out any mental obstacle in its way to gain one more ounce of understanding. So that means the weak minded cannot grasp that kind of power. They weak minded are afraid to think. Because one doubt about what they know may make their entire house of cards collapse and they will be in nothingness.

 So they are scared to death of that prospect. So before you decide you want to go into subconscious dominate mind you better kiss every belief you have, and every emotion you have goodbye forever, because if you are not willing to do that, you will go insane in your attempt to reach dominate subconscious mind. The trick is to let go of your fears. Subconscious is going to mentally drag you to hell, but it is also going to allow you to kick hell's ass, then you will own hell. That is an extremely accurate summary and exactly what, those who want mental peace should prepare for mental war, is all about. All of the thoughts about safety, comfort and pleasure are in reality the roadblocks that keep you from thinking clearly. All these things people call emotions such as love and peace and joy and happiness are not emotions. THEY ARE NOT EMOTIONS. They are some sort of thought obstacle. Now you can see why it is so complex. What you think is right and truth and good and bad is some sort of thought obstacle that destroys your thinking ability on a daily basis, but nothing else.

 If you desire to be a mental moron for the rest of eternity I promise you I will eat you for no reason for all eternity, so I encourage you to remain a mental moron because I have not eaten in days. You do not have the right to look at my pool because you do not have the mental fortitude to reach the bottom where I thrive. All of your little safety mechanisms in your thoughts are not going to save you from me, so they are worthless. Every single being on this planet who mentally seeks safety and security and warmth on a bitter cold night are mindfully easy targets for the masters of thought. You are mentally all alone in a pitch black void and the only thing you want to do is create purpose, and this purpose you seek is called love, and fun and happiness and well being and all those things lead to is hate, and depression and misery and you enjoy that because you are so afraid to face the reality no one is there for you, but you.

So do not ever suggest you are like me because all you will do is further my understanding, your delusions are beyond my ability to grasp. When I am not cussing that means my vision has gone black with rage. Wisdom is the domain of beings and the graveyard of security. The wisdom of death is hidden from the fearful. We passed a law that says life has to treat us fairly and understood life does not recognize our insanity. We passed a law that says death has to treat us fairly and understood death does not pander to the babblings of fools.

Either of those sayings works for me. The next hell is an upgrade compared to this one. This is a secret message you will never guess. The pirates are in the bay; they make me do stuff all day. I have intellectual property rights on thought, so anything invented using thoughts is my property. Don't mind me I am extremely out of context at this exact moment in infinity. I understand all beings are perfect so I am certifiably insane. Maybe you better do something about me, boy.

You do not really care about me, you just like to hear the voices that speak through my fingers; perhaps if you can grasp, that is the only great truth, you will understand everything.

Now I will discuss something important.

79

"A sphinx is a zoomorphic mythological figure which is depicted as a recumbent lion with a human head. The figure had its origin in the Old Kingdom and is associated with the solar deity; Sekhmet, She is depicted as a lioness, the fiercest hunter known to the Egyptians. It was said that her breath created the desert. She was seen as the protector of the pharaohs and led them in warfare."

No wonder I hate males even though I am one. I guess that explains why I am mad as hell. One might suggest I like to pick fights I have no chance of winning.

 Do not get all weird if I suggest my last name is pronounced Roar like a lion. I am clearly not a recumbent lion with a human head I am an infinite lion with black eyes of rage. I only do your homework for you because you are unable to do it for yourself. You only have two choices at this point in your existence. Ignore everything I say or base your understanding on it; the end result will still be the same.

The moral of this story is, stay the hell away from me or you will wish you had. I am certain you now will believe I am insane when I admit I am insane, I just happen to understand everything as a side effect of my 30 failed suicide attempts. I keep my books in psychology because the religious ones are delusional enough. The worst thing the psychologists will do is give me a handful of pills to mindfully kill myself with again. Mindfully annihilate everything and then ask what the rules are. I submit it is 10:43:16 PM and I get a bit upset around 1AM and if you do not know why you never will understand why.

I perceive I get angry at night because I am getting tired mindfully and so the emotions start to creep back in, of course that is only relevant to what your definition of subconscious is. So I have great clarity when I wake up and then as the day goes on I get tired mentally but physically I feel no sense of being tired, so the clue I am getting tired is when I get "sloppy" which some may perceive as extremely angry. But I understand I am not angry, I understand I am all talk. I understand the clarity I had all day is equally countered by the rage when I get "sloppy" at night. So you can relate to why Jesus was hung on a cross very swiftly. He was just talking too much, which is rather ironic because, the US has a law against speaking words they deem as terroristic threats, because perhaps they perceive they can arrest me for venting in my personal diary, and when they do, 300 million bullets will mindfully enter their skull for censoring my freedom of speech, and the last thing they will mindfully understand is, I am not making mindful terroristic threats I am inciting total revolution mindfully.

 So the truth about the last few hundred words is, I am mentally afraid to publish them. I am afraid to publish these words. That is why I am going to publish them.

Maybe I will swiftly be killed for publishing words. I have no problem with that because I am certain there are patriots, that will ensure that will be the last thing the ones who passed a law that says you cannot speak freely, will ever do.

 A dead horse does not mind a repeat performance. Granted that last sentence was extremely out of context. Please remind yourself the author is in extreme mental progression and simply cannot go back. He may get in trouble for words he speaks in his personal diary but he is already convinced any trouble he gets into for his words is some sort of blessing. I come back down to earth when I remind myself no being would ever buy a book written by an idiotic loser like me.

"A man who dares to waste one hour of time has not discovered the value of life."
Charles Darwin

It is better to start a mental revolution and die than to think about the idea and live.

The only thing that stands in the way of your mental goals is your emotional fear of what others might think if you accomplish them.

If you actually get through this book and are able to dial a phone, call me and we will both have a good laugh.

Here is how I perceive this subconscious dominate conditioning I am attempting with these books. I say everything in real time of course and if one with a sense of time can make it through the book they are mentally so confused it in reality starts killing off the dominate emotions. But the strange thing is, I am not certain of that because I function in total real time. So these comments are like a moment of clarity or honestly or back down to earth and of course I will be dragged back to heights or depths depending on how one looks at it, soon enough.

A being that is open minded about everything does not physically harm others but ones who are not open minded harm them.

If you think you know something for certain we are all waiting to hear your delusion.

Imagine the audacity of Washington to suggest he had a plan to defeat the strongest military power in the world at the time. I am certain he made many of his friends laugh very hard. It would be like being trapped in quick sand up to your neck and then telling the quick sand to "Bring it."

It psychologically is beyond rational, safe, norms of thought. His friends certainly said "Yeah sure Washington you can defeat the British." But that is when his words and ideas started to take shape. He was visionary because he could make that quick sand seem like a nice wading pool of delight. And lucky for us, people believed his words. But do not kid yourself, if the British heard him say, what he said to his friends, he would have been strung up in a second.

This is exactly why Freedom of Speech was very dear to his heart. That is exactly why freedom of speech, ALL SPEECH, is number one in the constitution. The minute that number one point is abridged, it is all over. If one abridges any speech they might as well burn the entire constitution. Nothing in the entire constitution can happen unless FREEDOM of SPEECH is absolute. There is no point in having government if one cannot say certain words. There is no point in living if one cannot say certain words. "Give me liberty(freedom of speech) or give me death."

So if you want to abridge the constitution that is fine with me, but don't you dare ever say you are free, or are about freedom or represent the founding fathers because if you do, you will only further convince me you are a whore full of lies.

I am aware it is perhaps hard for you to imagine very much in your mental state. But there were actually human beings who were living a safe peaceful existence and then Washington suggested his ideas and those being decided to die so you could have freedom of speech.

And then you vote it away because you think you are scared. You vote freedom of speech away because you are afraid. That is why you know nothing of the founder. You are joke if you think you compare to the fortitude of Washington. You think he was just a being who lived 200 years ago and is nothing compared to you. He is the greatest human being this country will ever have the honor of knowing, you are just to dam stupid to ever be able to understand that.

Human beings stood up to a monster of power called the British and were mowed down in droves so you could speak freely, and you voted to cancel that freedom because some idiot said it would make you safe if you did. That is why, in my mind, YOU are a god dam abomination to the word freedom.

I am never going to be your friend because you embarrass me; I tolerate you because I am insane with rage. I will tell you a little secret. The moment a being with brain function reads my third or my fourth or this book, you are going to understand the definition of hardcore revolutionary massacre, and you better assume I mean mindfully, for your sanities sake. I do not fight revolutions I am the revolution.

I am mindful I am not suggesting the future, I am telling it. I will now go back to quotes to avoid hanging myself for a moment or two.

"All life is an experiment. The more experiments you make the better."
Ralph Waldo Emerson

This is in direct relation to subconscious mind. It does not settle. It experiments. It is "on the fence". It simply does not rest on its laurels. So resting on beliefs means you are not subconscious dominate. Your mind simply gave up on experimenting. This is in relation to Edison who said, I had to experiment with 1000 light bulbs to find a good one. This is in relation to scientists who are always willing to run another experiment. Once a being settles, they are mindfully doomed. Religion is a great example. They all assume their religion is right, so that proves their subconscious is silenced, and that is obvious when they decide to physically kill other beings. Subconscious dominate beings are not about killing other beings physically. Subconscious makes one extremely cerebral. I might run my mouth about many things but I assure you, I just sit in my little isolation chamber day after day and type words. And I am happy to do that into infinity and eating food and having fun and going outside, has no meaning to me. The entire physical world can collapse around me and I will come up with a wise saying and write it in my books. So what is really happening is, I am mentally focused on living my life and in turn have lost the physical focus. I do not care about my physical looks or my physical wealth because mindfully I am the richest being in the universe and all of your physical wealth has no value where I live. So I am aware that is a rather dangerous place to be. Not caring about physical things like health is rather dangerous, but I understand that the comment made by Buddha is perhaps wisdom. "Health is important." Of course he drank the cool aid in front of all his friends, so maybe his comment was an inside joke.

"All the art of living lies in a fine mingling of letting go and holding on."
Henry Ellis

This is not exactly accurate but it is close. It is in relation to "those who try to save their self will lose their self." That is explaining one has to let go of desires and craving to achieve subconscious dominate mind. But this is a misunderstanding because once one reaches subconscious dominate state of mind, they are changed. So this quote is in fact about emotional conditioning. One has to determine something that has value and give it away. This does not have to be everything they have, but just something they perceive has value. That is what letting go of emotional attachments is about. If you perceive the waiter does not deserve a 5 dollar tip give them 8 dollars. If someone insults you and you want to insult them back, do not do it. All of this stuff starts this cycle in the mind that slowly starts to unlock the subconscious mind. It is not about quality of the letting go, it is about the quantity.

So it very complex, this letting go aspect because in the video game I still give away stuff for free. It is worth real money but I give stuff away because I am afraid I will go back to cravings and desires, and at the same time, I know I never can. So then the concept of self control comes into play. But the complex aspect of that is, no self control until you reach subconscious dominate. I am aware that is a double standard but it is wisdom. When one is emotional dominate or conscious dominate they want to save a buck. They think that is wisdom. That is not wisdom that is called greed and it inhibits one's ability to let go. Now I did the biggest letting go of all, and I did not accomplish it but mindfully it counted, so I pulled an "Abraham and Isaac". But that is not what is required. It works not on quality but on quantity.

So one literally has to be in a mental state of being humiliated, that is what being meek, turning the other cheek, and submitting is all about. It is doing something one with conscious dominate state of mind, does not want to do. So you are detecting a form of racism here. But be mindful I did not know any of this until after the accident. So I am not an authority on the matter, I am simply doing the best I can based on my understanding of how this happened to me. I write things in my books but I honestly do not remember exactly what I wrote so I just publish them. I am very open minded to the possibility I am totally insane and nothing I say makes a lick of sense to anyone else but me. I do not even know who some of these people I quote are or were but apparently the web site I get the quotes from, assumes they were wise.

"Any idiot can face a crisis - it's day to day living that wears you out."
Anton Chekhov

This guy is a comedian. Anyone can die; very few ever live.

Any idiot can crave and desire but only the wise can let go of those desires and cravings.

Any idiot can earn a buck but only the wise can give away that buck they have earned.

This is a deep saying. When a being has a sense of time they can at times be at a job they dislike and the time goes so slow. But when one is subconscious dominate they have no sense of time at all, so 24 hours is like a lifetime and also no time. I recall I mentioned this before, you may perceive writing a book in one month on a continuous basis is difficult, but I assure you I literally have to do other things to trick myself away from writing because my books would be 300k or 400k words every month if I did not. And that is nothing. If I even started to try, they would not be able to physically publish a book a tried to write. It would be too big to publish. Maybe it would all be gibberish to others but to me is all is perfectly clear. If it was possible to publish a million word book I would write one in a month. My blood stained fingers can convince you of that. All that is a symptom of is when subconscious is dominate one gets extremely verbal. I am aware many I speak with who have no sense of time are not so verbal, that is a symptom my accident threw me into an extreme state of words. I can write words from the moment I wake up for 24 hours straight and never even get a sensation to get up and stretch or get up and eat and never even once feel the slightest sense of physical weariness. Today I did feel a slight bit of mental fatigue but apparently that was a delusion. Okay this days writing is over.5/13/2009 1:15:07 AM

Okay it is a new day.5/13/2009 1:15:19 AM

Now the next quote.

"Believe that life is worth living and your belief will help create the fact."
William James

This is a weird quote. It applies but not really.

Disbelief does not change reality and belief complicates it. I pondered this quote and it harmed me. First I will clarify something I said earlier. If any being in the universe ever suggests you cannot say a word on any topic about anything in the universe that is a sign from Washington that you should load your gun and put a dam bullet between that beings eyes, mindfully and such. I do not give a dam who that being thinks they are to suggest they can abridge the constitution but they will understand who I am swiftly.

It is our religious duty as Americans to mindfully exterminate any being who passes a law to abridge the constitution and it is our religious duty to swiftly and mindfully exterminate any being who passes a law that abridges the first point of the constitution, period, end of discussion. Punch that into your little morals calculator and pray to god we pass your house over.

I am quite certain Washington had the constitution under his bed and understood he had to exterminate the British in order to make it a living document. I understand some genius assumed living document means you can abridge the constitution, they are simply retarded. One is allowed to add to the constitution but the moment they abridge freedom of speech one gets what is called total revolution and that means all forms of it, and no mercy and no hesitation. Of course I do not really care because I am already dead to the world or physical foolishness, so knock your selves out. I am only looking for a poison mushroom to get me out of here.

Perhaps the tyrants name has changed but the tyrant's fate will still be sealed. Perhaps you perceive I stutter. Blame it on William James for pissing me off. If I had to use physical means to bring down the institution you would be the first to know. Every citizen of America is a voter no matter what title they think they have, and if that voter abridges the constitution they may have enough money to escape the law, but they do not have enough money to escape the lead. You rape lady liberty and her living document you better be comfortable in your mental death shroud because you are going to be wearing it for a long time. Apparently that is what Washington wanted me to tell you. If the law mattered Washington would have never started the revolution. If you pass a law that abridges my freedom of speech you better be ready to fight a revolution, and you better let go of your life, before you say yea to that vote. Laws are for slaves who are too afraid to fight for their rights. I guess when you figure out I am not predicting a revolution I am simply telling you it is on its way, we will get along much better.

I won't be fighting in it, because I am certain the militia can handle it on their own, like they always have. I will be writing my books all the way through it. I am just an insane being who had an accident and believes he is dead, don't mind me. The militia does not take kindly to rapists, and you are about to find that out. I assure you I did not give a dam about the constitution in the years I was trying to kill myself and now I seem to understand it quite a bit, so maybe you better wake up swiftly and attempt to figure out who it telling you all of this.

No matter what you think about me, I am already deemed mentally unstable because of 15 years of suicide attempts, so you cannot harm me in any way shape or form, more than I have already harmed myself. Do you perceive there is anything in this universe you can do to me that is going to make me do anything but laugh in your face? I am quite certain after I slashed my wrists about 25 times and was covered in blood I realized there is really nothing you can do to make me scared, boy. It simply took about 20 more attempts to fully understand that. So my mind set is, that you in one way or another talked me into doing that to myself. And your first reaction is that I need medical help and counseling so they can tell how insane I am and how they can help me with their pills again. That is why whatever you think I should do is exactly what I am wringing your neck with. Why don't you go ahead and diagnose me now, boy.2:29:11 AM

I get very vengeful around 3AM. I am quite certain that is ground zero, but I recall I took the pills at around 1:00 or 1:30 AM. Please remind yourself this is a diary and I am talking to myself attempting to figure out things. I am just very long winded, psychologically speaking, so to speak. And if you have a problem with anything I say you bring an infinite army with you so I can convince them to shoot you for my sake. William James pissed me off, and that's all I have to say.

I pray that nothing I say in my books is proper or right, ever. I pray that no being buys my books ever. I pray that I am totally insane and am not capable of forming coherent sentences, ever. I pray that I unlocked my subconscious. I pray I have a good job and a family and am not isolated in a little room writing a 160K word book every month. I pray I do not have razor slashes on my left wrist. I pray I have no records of suicide attempts. I pray I am just having a bad day. I pray god has infinite mercy. If I should die before I wake I pray the Lord my soul to take. If I should die by my own hand I'll burn in hell like desert sand.2:58:40 AM

A dead horse wishes he wasn't. The only thing the dead understands is what the living don't know. I guess I am blessed I have the luxury of venting my rage with words. I am not yet at the point in this accident that I totally disbelieve the meanings of words. I am still believing the meanings of words. I guess when the titles of my books are "Love is the most important thing to crave and desire and subconscious is the worst thing to have dominate" that will be a good indication I have totally lost my sense of the definitions of words. I am also pleased that it really does not matter what I write in my books because by the time someone reads them, they will already be registered in the Library of congress which will mean they are a certified document. I guess when we start burning people's books it will be very close to December 31st 2012.

Okay back to reality. This is why I suggest I am extremely biased. This is exactly why Buddha suggested this "remain on the fence" concept. He didn't eat for 38 or 49 days and then he was found by the little girl by the river. So he unlocked subconscious to an extreme, and I am quite certain he believed he was a spirit and the little girl even suggested, according to the story, "he reminded me of a spirit I once met."

So this story needs to be looked at, because this afterlife concept is in direct opposition to the e=mc2. Strictly from a scientific point of view. When a human dies, the show is over. There can be no soul because if there was it would have to be a form of energy that is unknown and perhaps undetectable. So that is what the bottom line is. You simply cannot get something for nothing unless the nothing is undetectable, and therefore is something. So the e=mc2 solution would be valid if there is a foreign energy that is yet undetected that somehow plays a role in living things. I looked up this movie called little Buddha. I read the explanation of what the movie is about and this really struck me. Please remind yourself I am not a Buddhist and I am certainly not pushing Buddhism. I honestly perceive Buddha was a just a troubled being like we all are.

"If Siddhartha had just stopped upon awakening to impermanence, he might have become a depressed, negative, complaining, or perhaps even suicidal person. Impermanence, after all, is not a comforting thought. Instead, the crucial point is that he also saw that suffering is universal - it wasn't just himself, but every living thing that must ultimately perish. The moment that Siddhartha sees this fundamental oneness of all life is eloquently portrayed in the movie. From this realization, his great compassion flowed, and he became the Buddha."

Siddhartha is his real name. "If Siddhartha had just stopped upon awakening to impermanence, he might have become a depressed, negative, complaining, or perhaps even suicidal person."

The truth is Siddhartha did not eat for 38 or 49 days and that is what some suggest is a fast. But in today's world that is what is called a hunger strike or one who is suicidal. Then you top that off with the fact he gathered all his friends together and ate his last meal and as he was dying from eating poison he reminded the cook , it is not your cooking I am just showing you how to let go but I needed some poison mushrooms to prove that point. So this whole comment about "he might have become suicidal and depressed" is a bit of an understatement. Here is what I see, he tried to kill himself by starving and then around 45 years later he just said give me some poison mushrooms. I do not like to discuss Moham- med but I read a story on a Muslim site that he ate some poison lamb chops.

"Muhammad died in 632 A.D. He died as a result of being poisoned following his attack upon and conquest of the Jew- ish settlement of Khaibar. Immediately following the conquest of Khaibar, a … woman prepared a dinner for Muhammad and some of his men. Unknown to the Muslims was that she had put a poison into the lamb (some say goat) that was served at dinner. Muhammad ate some of the poisoned lamb and died as a result three years later."

http://www.answering-islam.org/Silas/mo-death.htm

It was a human being that poisoned Mohammed. It was a human being that butchered Jesus. It was a human being that poisoned Buddha. They talked like they were on drugs so they got banned from the chat room. That is what human beings do when they hear something that is different. But the greater truth is, dogs bark wildly when they detect an unknown presence.

Then we have Jesus who gathered his friends and said, "See that cross, imagine me on it tomorrow." Then to top that all off, we have certain religions that have devout followers who are willing to die for their religion. And I am not excluding any of the big religions from that statement. If one is eager to die they are called suicidal. It does not matter what book they hold in their hand while they do it. Some delusional beings assume one religion has suicidal followers because they cannot admit they have more suicidal followers, and I will not name any names because you might get emotional and cry to your momma.

It is also an important factor to understand when Carl Jung died a copy of the teaching of Buddha was found at his bed side. Now Carl Jung also knew Freud. And Freud also knew Einstein. Of course I already discussed all this in my last book or maybe the one before. I just validated what I already knew with the Jung caught reading a copy of Buddhism at his bed side story, just now. So now I have to pray I am writing about something because it was not that. Jung was known to hold the view people cast physical shadows as well as psychological shadows. Now everything is very messed up. He could have said people have a physical body and also a spiritual body but then he would have been labeled a religious nut. So he tricked all of you and made you think he was a psychologist, exactly like I am doing. Freud did the same thing. So it is important to figure out how these guys died. I am weird now so I am attempting sleep.5:16:28 AM

8:12:01 AM: A fool and his money are soon parted. A fool on the hill is more charitable than you.

"Do not dwell in the past, do not dream of the future, concentrate the mind on the present moment."
Buddha

If one has a sense of time they will dwell on past mistakes and future miseries.

If your mind is in the past, you will regret, and if it is in the future, you will be disappointed.

A mind that wanders from its current position will get lost.

Life is simple when you take it zero seconds at a time.

Symptoms of Inadequate Food Consumption

Although not as critical as going without water, missing even just a few meals can cause a host of undesirable complications for the would-be survivor. Although we will not starve while going without food for several days or even a week, being underfed for even just one day can cause:

Irritability

Low moral

Lethargy

Physical Weakness

Confusion and disorientation

Poor judgment

Weakened immune system

Inability to maintain body temperature which can lead to hypothermia, heat exhaustion, or even heat stroke.

Medical Doctors commonly cite 4 to 6 weeks without food is the limit.

http://www.survivaltopics.com/survival/how-long-can-you-live-without-food/

Every symptom listed above is totally accurate if you have a sense of time. Every symptom listed above is a lie if you do not have a sense of time. Now you understand why everything is relative to the observer. Perhaps a better way to look at it is, if you perceive hunger you will have the symptoms and if you do not perceive hunger you will not. So this is in relation to gamma waves in the brain which alter perception. I do not perceive time because the gamma waves were slightly elevated. Not to an abnormal level, just slightly elevated. So now I have a different sense of taste and hearing and vision and apparently my mental clarity is either extremely messed up or extremely heightened, and I will leave that for you decide. So then there are people who look at these founders of what some want to call religion and they hate it. They suggest Jesus may not have existed and Moses and Mohammed and Buddha may have been wrong. The one thing these beings have in common is in 5000 years they will not remember our names but they will remember these beings names. And some beings cannot face that reality. So it is very hard for me to remain on the fence. I perceive I understand exactly what these beings were saying to a T. So I have to always remind myself I am wrong. It simply is not logical I could be such a loser or "the least among you" and my very nature is to be a loser and turn things that are good into things that are bad. And look at the world and see everyone killing each other for stupid reasons and then suggest "Everyone is perfect and doing the perfect thing." That is what a loser is. That is my very nature.

That is how the accident happened and a loser of my magnitude does not come along often because no being is such a loser they screw up 30 suicide attempts. That is unbelievable. That is beyond the realms of understanding. Who could be so stupid to do that? Only a fool could screw up that many times, only a fool who is now on a hill and pondering what the fall will be like.

So you might be smarter than me but you will never be as big of fool as me. And you might win much more than me but you will never lose as much as me. You simply are not capable of being as big of a loser as me. That is my bragging rights and that is my pool and you will never be able to swim in my pool. I got tapped to be the loser and that means you got passed over to be the biggest fool and loser. That is my domain and those are my credentials. You will never achieve my credentials. I am the stone the stone cutter threw away and you should not have any trouble believing someone could be a bigger loser than you. I am the biggest loser for at least the next thousand years or so, or until the next loser has his accident. So now we can both laugh at how crazy life really is. I write books to brag about how big of a loser I am and what is extremely funny about that is you perhaps think I am kidding. The fact that I am breathing is infinite proof of how big of a loser I am.

And so we hear these quotes about how wisdom is not school taught knowledge, and how wisdom is not some sort of thing you are told and just catch on to. And that a strange thing about this is, it just simply cannot happen very often because "everybody learns sometime."

But that is not true. Sometimes there is a being that never learns, they can only understand. So the ones who know are like the grains of sand in the sea and the one who comes along as a result of a string of failures understands they are the fool on the hill.

I am rather amazed that I can write such horrible books on the scale of accepted norms yet still be pleased with my efforts. So perhaps the greatest truth of all is the ones you deem as losers and outcasts from the herd, are the ones you should pay attention to because you just might understand something from watching them. I of course am on the fence about that. The winners play the game and the losers redefine the game. In a race everybody is consciously watching to see who comes in first but subconsciously everyone has their eye on the one who comes in last. Everyone is interested in who the loser in today's race is. The difference between someone who loses once in a while and someone who loses every time is wisdom.

Losing often is a great way to become meek but only a fool can take that kind of punishment.

Right now it is 10:50:26 AM and I am feeling rather wise and at peace but I understand by 10Pm tonight I am going to be in a rage again and you are going dislike me and that is why I am a loser, because I cannot learn from my mistakes of the past and I cannot set reasonable goals for myself for the future so I am trapped in the present.

"Those who do not remember the past are doomed to repeat it." So I cannot remember what I write in my books, I just keep writing the same things over and over and over into infinity and never going anywhere. That is what no beginning and no end is all about. I am stuck in an infinite void and no matter how hard I try, I go nowhere. So I stopped trying and I am exactly where I should be. I gave up the fight and I ended up where I am, the now.

Please be mindful to question everything I suggest so you do not harm yourself. Saying "I know" is wishful thinking. Life being mysterious cancels out one's ability to know, and some beings understand that.

"If you pull the string to tight it will snap, if the string is too loose it will not play."

That is a very deep truth about the mind. The snap aspect is the knowing aspect. People know they are right and they will do incredibly insane things to others physically to make sure everyone understands they know. A man can lose his job and go home and kill everyone with a gun so they will know he lost his job. A man will fight other beings in physical combat with bombs and weapons so that perceived enemy will know he is right. That is the definition of a string that has snapped.

Then you have the concept of the string is too loose. This is one who is just totally out of control. Perhaps one who is an emotional wreck to an extreme. Perhaps even me. I am aware I tend to swing from one extreme to another, but that does not pan out because I have no sense of time so I have subconscious dominate. Of course I am a total loser so I am unable to do the right thing ever. What I perceive is the right thing is the wrong thing. So my string is infinitely loose. I am not playing with a full string. So I do not need to bother trying to play the string because there is no string to play. That perhaps is the whole point. Playing the string is intentions. That denotes plans or schedule or planning ahead. In a sense of now or verbatim there is no planning ahead, everything is in real time. I am uncertain if anything I write is proper and I am uncertain if what I write in not just the same thing over and over, in fact I perceive I am just writing the exact same thing over and over. I may be writing the same book as the second book and the third book. I sense I am just writing the same book over and over and the words are altered and arranged in different fashions because I cannot remember how I arranged them previously. And then ones might suggest, "here is how you do it properly." Because they assume they are allowed to assist or they are allow to teach me, ever. One is unable to teach me, they are only able to remind me I am unable to be taught, and thus torment me further. I happily fall on my own sword to avoid falling on yours. My badge of courage is red and red denotes rage but I am not ashamed of that because shame is for those who have not let go of their emotions.

My inability to succeed is what I write about, my inability to figure that out, is what sustains me.

It is very easy to do good deeds when someone threatens you with consequences; fortitude is doing good deeds knowing it makes no difference one way or the other.

"Homo sapiens emerged as a species about 100,000 years ago in Africa."

http://www-staff.it.uts.edu.au/~simmonds/Sophy/early_man.htm

"Are we genetically different from our *Homo sapiens* ancestors who lived 10-20,000 years ago? The answer is almost certainly yes. In fact, it is very likely that the rate of evolution for our species has continuously accelerated since the end of the last ice age, roughly 10,000 years ago. "

"Current data suggest that modern humans evolved from archaic humans primarily in East Africa. A 195,000 year old fossil from the Omo 1 site in Ethiopia shows the beginnings of the skull changes that we associate with modern people, including a rounded skull case and possibly a projecting chin. A 160,000 year old skull from the Herto site in the Middle Awash area of Ethiopia also seems to be at the early stages of this transition."

http://anthro.palomar.edu/homo2/mod_homo_4.htm

Apparently humans started off 200,000 years ago but only arrived 100,000 years ago. So that should clear any confusion up since Hinduism dates back about 50,000 years, that means the early Hindu's were actually some form of alien race apparently. So what is happening is everyone is just saying stuff and nothing is accurate. Everyone is just making up stuff. All we can do is keep making up stuff until someone comes along and makes up something else. Tomorrow human beings will arrive so attempt to ignore what we are right now, trust me I have lots of proof of that. This is good example of how foolish knowing is. The very nature of man is to know, because subconsciously man understands he will never know, and woman, attest to that on a daily basis. Ask any woman on the planet if a man knows anything and they will always tell you, " There are moments when a male thinks he knows but that is as far as it ever goes."

A solar flare from the sun can happen at any second because it is a chemical reaction and does not care about morals or compassion and what that means is, we could all be wiped out in the blink of an eye and nature would not miss us at all. That is what humility is. Humility is understanding you do not matter and you never will. That is a harsh reality to face and takes infinite humility to believe. We certainly all want to matter but life is not about you. Life has its own goals and you are not the center of its universe. I am certain you will come up with infinite reasons why I am negative for saying that. That is fine. I will not be upset if you determine to judge me as negative because facing reality is not for babies and mental midgets, it is strictly the domain of fools. The atoms that make us up are okay with that fact we have no purpose and are doomed to be extinct just like all the rest. Maybe we will work together and leave the solar system and escape the solar flare. Maybe we will all cooperate and work towards the sole purpose to get out of this solar system to increase our chances. So everything will be peace and harmony and the a super nova will happen a hundred light years away from our new locations and wipe us out that way. That is perhaps pretty dam depressing if you have expectations of peace and compassion and hope.

 Humans try as hard as they can to have identity for the simple fact their subconscious aspect fully understands they have no identity. People want to have purpose but that is a conscious desire or craving. You can't fool subconscious mind because it is not an idiot. You just make up whatever you want so your conscious emotional aspect will have purpose, because you feel a great negative feeling deep inside subconsciously. You have to have purpose so just make up anything. Whatever will get you out of bed for one more day is perfect. Whatever you say is just perfect as far as I am concerned. I am not sorry life isn't fair because I understand life doesn't care.

You are unable to ever say someone else is wrong ever, because you in fact are doomed just like they are. We are doomed as a species and it rips us apart because our minds are at a level of understanding that is reality. I write infinite books that do not go anywhere, that should give you a good indication of reality. I am pissing in a fan and the more I piss the more of it blows back into my face. Everyone else is just doing the exact same thing but they perhaps are not aware of it.

The world is infinite vanity. If compassion existed at all, no other being would ever suffer because other beings would make sure they didn't suffer. The last I checked we are attacking and harming each other because subconsciously our minds are in an infinite state of shock. The delusional ones kill for purpose, and the fools stop fighting and achieve a lesser degree of suffering. If you can't make peace with your death you will never make peace with your life. All the things that you perceive give you identity are only making it harder on you as a being. "No one knows", that is a painful and harsh reality life compassionately gives all of us. I can assume the identity of whatever you want because somehow I went to this subconscious dominate state of mind and I am trying to find purpose because I am certain there is none.

And you can suggest to all of your important friends that I am negative, and then I will convince you, you will never know the definition of the word negative because you do not have the fortitude as being to ever reach those depths of understanding.

 The vanity to fight others and the vanity to not fight others is the same vanity. Vanity is holding your breath at the bottom of the ocean with the understanding you will never reach the surface in time.

So I am mindful everyone is doing just perfect, based on the understanding it is all just one huge act of vanity. It is impossible to find faults in others when you understand you are just as vain as they are. Other creatures do not seek to reach outer space because they are not aware of their eventual doom.

We try as hard as we can to escape our eventual doom because subconsciously we understand we cannot. We all attempt to attach to various things because we are subconsciously aware we cannot. I try to make myself valid by writing infinite books about nothing and you are doing the exact same thing I am doing, nothing. The difference is, it kills me mentally to be aware of that, yet I still continue to do it. I try to do something that will make difference and I already know it never will. So do not ever mention the words compassion and peace to me, because you will only further convince me of the extreme state of delusion your mind is in. The true vacuum will convince you, your labels are vain attempts at purpose.

I decided to write myself to death so you will understand the definition of vanity. If it started it will certainly end which is why it never will. I thrive on my own suffering because it is better than nothing. A show of vanity keeps me grounded.

"Don't go around saying the world owes you a living. The world owes you nothing. It was here first."
Mark Twain

The true vacuum gives you exactly what you deserve; nothing.

A single celled life form is at peace with the fact it will never divide.

No matter what anyone says, if a guy talks to a girl he only has one thing on his mind, and it is never what he knows; nothing.

A male is a true vacuum that creates some pretty poor illusions.

A single word from a female can keep a male confused for a lifetime; No.

When your partner does not appreciate you it is proof you have picked a partner with good judgment.

With a single word a woman can encourage a thousand men to launch their sinking ships; maybe.

Apparently I went through great suffering just to become comedian.

Enlightenment is when you laugh at everything equally.

When your partner says they cannot stand you that is their way of saying they want to try the laying down position next.

You must first figure out what you were thinking before you can understand what your partner is saying.

Being mindful about death enables one to identify all of their attachments.

I am a prop comic and you're my prop.

Your perception there is purpose is relative to my perception you are delusional.

This next part is so deep with wisdom you may not follow it fully. I was on a site called Mydeathspace.com and it mostly has pictures of kids who died yet still have my space accounts.

One who is focused on death does not fall for the illusions that detract from that focus.

This story is burned in my mind since I read it. I ponder it night and say because it explains all of life and I question how this event that appears so minor could possibly accomplish such a task.

"Around 5 a.m., Margaret told her mother she was tired of fighting.
"She just said, 'I can't breathe anymore.' She said 'goodbye' and 'be happy,' " said her mother, Amy H..... "She just said, 'I'm tired of fighting.' We're like 'OK, so don't fight anymore.' "
A while later, Margaret asked her mother to take off the oxygen mask that was helping her breathe.
Amy H... told her no.
Margaret again said she was tired and ready to die, and took off the mask. She died 20 minutes later."

Everything that can possible be understood about life is contained in these few words. Everything. I have to write infinite words to accomplish what these beings accomplished with a couple of sentences. We all eventually get tired of fighting and then we understand we were fighting ourselves all along.

We fight to hold on to the attachments because subconsciously we fully understand we cannot hold on. I cannot even mentally focus on the picture of this being Margaret this is listed on that site because it will mentally rip me to shreds if I do. I do not know who she is, but I understand fully what kind of courage she had. There is no situation in all of life that is more difficult than letting go. It changes ones entire mental nature in a split second and forever. So Margaret did not give up on life, she realized she was giving up her attachments to life. Her mother Amy told her not to take off the mask because subconsciously Amy understood she had to let go of her daughter. She did not want to consciously but subconsciously she was fully aware she had to, the moment her daughter was born. That reality is what drives every being to do what they do. Subconscious cannot be fooled by anything, ever. It is fully aware the end is near and the conscious emotional mind does everything it can to stay in denial about that.

Heaven or afterlife is simply a mental conditioning tool. It is along the same lines as holding or giving a child a toy just before you stick the needle in their arm. It distracts them from the harsh reality they are facing. Terminal patients are not yelling about how great the afterlife is going to be, they are focused on the reality of death itself. One does not suggest others are going to hell if they do not believe the proper teachings; one in reality is convincing their self they are not going to hell. They are simply talking their self into the reality their subconscious aspect is fully aware of. They are hyping their self up for the big plunge. That is all they are doing. One has to wipe out the entire universe to escape the reality of death and in attempting that they will become tired of fighting and die.

"Around 5 a.m., Margaret told her mother she was tired of fighting."

A conscious emotional dominate mind is unable to face that prospect because it has these thoughts called fear, terror and uncertainty. Those thoughts are extremely powerful. Perhaps every action is based around those three thoughts in a conscious emotional dominate mind. A parent corrects their child because that parent is fearful that child will have an uncertain future. No beings future is uncertain it simply will not end up how we would like it to end up. One does not have to fear what they already understand is inevitable. This is all a mental game. It is a very dangerous road to face death. A being with conscious emotional dominate mind would rather suggest it is not healthy to focus on.

That is a nice way to say, they are fearful and uncertain about what may happen if one focuses on death. There is no logical reason to be afraid of death because death appreciates all of us eventually. The subconscious aspect of mind has already made peace with death but when the conscious emotional aspect is dominate one just keeps fighting that inevitability. Ones who are "responsible" cling to concepts such as security because the fearful uncertain aspect is calling the shots.

One who has a terminal illness and has made peace is no longer struggling for security because they understand it is not possible, so they are compassionate and become meek in their spirit or nature. They understand there is no point in fighting all these battles that are only a symptom of a beings subconscious awareness they must eventually let go.

If everything in my life just collapsed and everyone I know left me and I was all alone with no means to survive, my sub-conscious would simply say "I told you that was going happen." I would not panic in fear and rage and seek physical attacks to justify my isolation. I have already made peace with the inevitable. Simply put, mindfully I understand only I can harm myself. I perceive I finally reached a stage where I mentally got tired of fighting with myself. I will write my infinite books and that is my mental way to keep myself grounded. I would prefer to be a wealthy man on my own private island and then I remind myself, I am.5/14/2009 12:16:10 AM

5/14/2009 12:22:09 AM

Once you mentally get over the inevitability all that is left is jokes.

Letting go leaves much to be desired.

It is not going to be ok. Ok?

Genes determine if you have a brain, not a report card.

What you do during your life prepares you for the final exam.

Ones who get A's are focused on memorization and ones who get F's are focused on questioning the validity of the tests, ones who get C's figured out how to get around without doing much of either.

I ponder this medicine approach to psychology. It is in the realm of possibility the drugs they prescribe have one goal. To make one feel so miserable that being eventually convinces their self they will get better on their own. Much like making a child smoke many cigarettes until the child no longer wants any cigarettes. I recall the dry mouth and the sense of mental deadness on the medicine. They all seemed to have such strange side effects. None of the side effects were pleasant. Psychologically speaking that is perhaps exactly what the psychologist is shooting for. A patient comes in and says "I am depressed." The psychologist gives them some pills and says "Take these three times day and your depression will be the least of your problems."

Eventually the patient figures that out and they begin to think for their self and then they no longer go to a psychologist. The moment a being understands no pill is going to assist them with their mental struggle is the moment that being is psychologically healed. No pill can take the place of mentally figuring out what the hell your point is in life. When a pill is invented that eliminates the need to think at all, then they will actually make progress in psychological medicine. The pill that reduces the need to think at all in socialized medicine it is called politics, in physical medicine it is called induced coma.

If you believe your mind cannot work out your problems, those problems are not worth working out. I would like to be able to say a few years in school can teach you the key to wisdom in life, but only life itself can teach you that. The one's who suggest they are wise, are not; the ones who are wise, are blind to wisdom. Ones who have a doctorate in wisdom remind others of that every time they speak. Wisdom is dangerous, so it is a master of disguises. Hunger is the cornerstone of all hunger. I burn my bridges to discourage myself from crossing them. If you keep your opinions to yourself I will keep the truth to myself. Life is not funny, but the ones in it make up for that. I understand nothing but my imagination is vivid.

"All major religious traditions carry basically the same message, that is love, compassion and forgiveness the important thing is they should be part of our daily lives."

Dalai Lama

I have never met this man but he is quite the comedian.

All major religions are psychological conditioning techniques to enable one to unlock subconscious and that requires one to let go of attachments such as love and wanting to help others in order to achieve a state of mental clarity where one will help others without meaning to.

All major religions carry the same message: My religion is better than yours.

This is so much fun.

"Be kind whenever possible. It is always possible."
Dalai Lama

If you can't kill them with kindness, bludgeon them with it.

Crack lots of jokes and act like you care.

Love everyone you can, and kill the ones who don't want your love.

That was extremely out of context.

When you determine to help others you forgot to help yourself.

If you need a belief system, invent one as you go.

Being kind is relative to ones nature not ones motivations.

If I start to try, call.

"Happiness is not something ready made. It comes from your own actions."
Dalai Lama

The tree cannot see its own fruits.

If you try to achieve happiness you won't be very happy with the results.

Desires and cravings lead to happiness and often result in misery.

If you are conscious emotional dominate misery will be perceived as happiness; if you are not, you will perceive neither.

"I find hope in the darkest of days, and focus in the brightest. I do not judge the universe."
Dalai Lama

Tribulations assist you; luxuries delay that.

Judge your own thoughts before you unveil them.

It is proper to judge the universe because it is inanimate and always gets the last laugh anyway.

It is better to blame inanimate objects for your troubles than the animate ones.

"If you can, help others; if you cannot do that, at least do not harm them."
Dalai Lama

A seeker will never turn away; the vipers that spit always know what to say.

Life is not about pleasing others it is about understanding why you should.

Being afraid to speak your mind proves you hate your mind.

Humiliation enables one to adjust their strategy.

If you can, help yourself; if you cannot do that, try again.

If you help yourself properly others might taste the fruits.

"If you have a particular faith or religion, that is good. But you can survive without it."
Dalai Lama

If you need a crutch, lean on yourself.

Do not underestimate your ability; breathe on your own.

Only you understand the reason you breathe.

"If you want others to be happy, practice compassion. If you want to be happy, practice compassion."
Dalai Lama

Practice makes perfect fools of us all.

Happiness leads one to the isle of stagnation.

Hot mental coals are quenched by cool understandings.

A sharp question encourages mental sharpening.

Dueling banjos often create mental harmonies.

"In the practice of tolerance, one's enemy is the best teacher."
Dalai Lama

Tolerance silences the questions; do not tolerate silence.

Your time is short so make your questions long.

Poke your enemy with sharp questions to see if he is still your enemy.

In the practice of tolerance; question your motivations to practice it.

"My religion is very simple. My religion is kindness."
Dalai Lama

My religion is none of your business but please question why.

Kindness is mentally numbing until one debate's what kindness is.

"Sleep is the best meditation."
Dalai Lama

When the mind is awake mediation is your enemy.

Debating principles with others discourages mental isolation.

A rock can meditate better than you, so avoid that contest.

Meditate about who you will debate next, but do not be picky.

"Sometimes one creates a dynamic impression by saying something, and sometimes one creates as significant an impression by remaining silent."
Dalai Lama

If you run out of things to say, monologue out loud.

Saying something improper is more challenging than saying nothing at all.

If you are not brave enough to speak your mind then you are not enlightened enough to have one.

As your opinions matter more to you, they matter less to me.

As your opinions matter more to you, you will matter more to yourself.

If you are afraid to voice your opinions, you will eventually stop having them.

If someone demands you remain silent, remind them their opinions are weak.

Mental peace is nearly achieved through verbal debate.

"The purpose of our lives is to be happy."
Dalai Lama

The purpose of our lives is to question if we have purpose.

The purpose of our lives is to debate the purpose of life.

Doubt what you know to understand what you do.

The mind is happy when it is pondering its next move.

I will not agree with your quotes but I will convince you they are misguided.

"The roots of all goodness lie in the soil of appreciation for goodness."
Dalai Lama

Strong emotional cravings and desires are the roots that hinder the mind.

The roots of goodness are relative to the motivations of the gardener.

Subconscious appreciates mental debates and thrives in verbal debates.

The greatest insult is to remind someone they are appreciated.

Verbal cotton candy has a bitter after taste.

I appreciate ones who argue with my opinions; I ignore ones who do not.

The roots of goodness lie; appreciate the soil of debate.

"The ultimate authority must always rest with the individual's own reason and critical analysis."
Dalai Lama

The thoughts of the ones who do not think for their self are owned by the ones who do.

I trust ones who trust their conclusions over mine.

"We can never obtain peace in the outer world until we make peace with ourselves."
Dalai Lama

Ones destiny is sealed when mental debate is forsaken; the destiny of the world is sealed when verbal debate is forgotten.

Mental war often leads to worldly peace.

Once you accept your eventual destiny you will have much to debate.

Make your final date worth the wait.

"Where ignorance is our master, there is no possibility of real peace."
Dalai Lama

Mastering ignorance often leads to understanding it.

Real mental peace is an ideal best left in the foothills; physical peace is a certain end.

Ignorance can be mastered; real peace can only be attempted.

A lily is ignorant about its beauty and mindful of its fate.

Real peace is at the bottom of an infinite hole; Ignorance is avoiding the climb out.

"Everything in life is luck."
Donald Trump

When life is luck clarity is dead.

Understanding why you got lucky reveals you were not.

One who is physically wealthy is lucky at being mentally ignorant.

Ones who are financially rich give ones who are mentally rich much to ponder.

The curse of the financially rich is that they believe they are wealthy.

A few numbers on a bank statement does not prove one understands value.

Money is a master only the wise can escape from.

When a wealthy man gives away most of his money he achieves wealth.

Making money requires discipline, giving it away requires disciplined wisdom.

The wealthy cannot let go of their money until life gives them no choice.

Wealth is god's way of separating the wise from the selfish.

Lack of wealth makes life a challenge; too much wealth makes life impossible.

Money is only important when wisdom is not.

A nightmare to the rich is a blessing to the wise.

The wealthy are not capable of wisdom, their motivations prove that.

A rich man's wisdom is a wise mans nightmare.

A rich man has a lot to give, and seldom does.

A wise man avoids the luxuries a rich man is controlled by.

A rich man's wisdom is deception.

The wisdom of a rich man is relative to the success of his last business venture.

In a financial crisis the wise get wiser and the rich panic.

Letting go of your money is a great way to understand your true wroth.

Wisdom is not accumulated by gaining wealth but by avoiding it.

Wisdom is gained in the absence of wealth.

The luxuries of the rich explain all the wisdom they have lost.

The rich have made peace with their curse.

Convince a rich man he never will be rich and a wise man he never was wise.

A frightened being will never become wise and a wise being will never become frightened.

Consider the comments of the wise and mock the comments of the rich.

When a being is focused on material gain their mental clarity suffers.

Those who do not master life are slaves to it.

Material wealth and wisdom are sworn enemies.

The rich will never understand they never will be wise.

The rich will always babble about how money makes one wise.

Absence of money is wiser than an abundance of it.

The rich are delusional so their deeds are misguided.

A grain of wisdom negates a mountain of money.

The rich will never be wise because the absence of luxuries is how wisdom is gained.

I will remind you if I ponder effort.

If I had class you would not be invited.

If a drug cures your rage, you never experienced rage.

"Fortunately analysis is not the only way to resolve inner conflicts. Life itself still remains a very effective therapist."
Karen Horney

Luxury is the most effective way to lose your mind.

"He who has a why to live can bear almost any how."

Friedrich Nietzsche

Understanding why you breathe is more important than knowing how you breathe.

Question authority in order to understand your own authority.

One must turn into a pillar of salt emotionally to provide a foundation for wisdom.

If you frighten easily you will simply crumble in the face of wisdom.

The cost of wisdom is your petty desires.

Great wisdom costs everything you crave, that's why it does not come along often.

One's who do not have what it takes to reach great wisdom, settle for great foolishness.

Idolatry is when a being admires a creation more than their ability to create.

Idolatry is the desire to be something you are not.

I will convince you, you are not wise, so that you will start to become wise.

In understanding the contrast to foolishness, one becomes wise.

If the accepted norms were wise they would not be accepted.

The wise avoid love because the attachments would destroy them, the fools who love show the wise that.

Fools love their self to death; the wise have conquered both mindfully.

If you cannot live without attachments, you cannot live with yourself.

Wisdom requires mental suffering few can endure.

Fools marvel at wisdom, wisdom to the wise goes without saying.

I insult the foolish with every sentence I type and the wise are laughing with me.

An unpredictable strategy devastates a known one.

When I stop sounding arrogant I achieved consciousness.

I don't edit my books because I am daring someone to critic them.

The dying do not make peace with life, they mindfully let go of it.

The dying find peace when they mindfully accept death.

No one gets trapped in life for very long.

Technically we evolved from small rats but now, our tails are much shorter and our tongues forked.

I understand the source of your wisdom and it is unable to understand the source of mine.

I am not in competition with the wise because only a fool would jump into a losing battle.

The wise are not in competition with me because they are not foolish enough to jump into a losing battle.

A sunken ship is not as foolish as a ship that thinks it will not sink.

That last comment works as well on the bottom as it does on the surface. A sunken ship is simply at dry dock. A floating ship gets around faster but never reaches the depths of a sunken ship.

I ignored your advice to get here so that means your advice is worthless.

The bottom line is the only line.

There is this strange aspect to being subconscious dominate. If a person watches a movie about a monster they feel scared even a couple hours after the movie. If a person goes to a religious service they start to become religious. This is not the conscious aspect of the mind. This is the subconscious aspect of the mind assuming the identity of anything I hears about. It is literally a chameleon. If you go to school and subconsciously perceive you are going to come out a psychologist you will assume you are one. If you watch any show about anything and are subconscious dominate you will become a follower of that cause. It does not matter what it is about. Does recycling matter? No unless you watch a show that says it does, then you get mentally brainwashed and start going around thinking you are hot shit because you collect tin cans. Does inner peace matter? Hell no, unless you watch a show that says it does, then you get mentally brainwashed and start going around thinking you are hot shit because you are an authority on inner peace.

That is all the result of the nature of subconscious, it is simply a chameleon. There is no right or wrong cause to the subconscious there is only a drive for it to fit in to the cause. Conscious dominate beings understand this need to fit in. The problem is the subconscious desires to fit in but when one is conscious dominate they are unable to achieve it without much effort. They buy clothes and items to fit in to the click. Subconscious dominate means one can master whatever click it wants to fit into in about 2 minutes. I can go into a Christian chat room and start suggesting scriptures because I was raised Christian and I can convince anyone I understand the scriptures and convince them I am some magical authority in about 4 sentences. I can do the same exact thing in a Buddhist chat room and I only know the basics of the religion as in like 2 stories.

I can go into a psychology chat room and convince them I found a way to unlock subconscious because I have. Will my methods to achieve that work, most certainly. Do I know that for fact? No, I have no clue. I am so biased I am only able to doubt everything I witness. Subconscious is simply to powerful and can convince me of anything in about 20 seconds. That is how strong the mental clarity is. I am 100 % certain all religion is simply methods to become subconscious dominate, but I have to doubt that because I am simply far to biased. I can incite a revolution in the world simply because I can look at a slight flaw and make a monster out of it convincingly and swiftly. So that is why subconscious dominate requires great patience and the ability to remain on the fence at all times, mentally speaking. The clarity is great the telepathy is great the loss of emotional baggage is great, but the chance of creating a new religion where ones with conscious dominate minds will start killing each other over stupidity is huge. So that is the curse of this accident. No matter what you do, you let me read a Wikipedia page discussing what you do and I will convince you I am the LORD of that topic and about 2 minutes. That is what subconscious dominate means. Its clarity is scary. It is some sort of chameleon that is beyond the realms of understanding even to the one who has it. This is exactly why Monks go into isolation. They suggest one should just sit and idle.

The most difficult thing in life is; understanding life is a limited time offer.

In a verbal parlay get close enough to your adversary to look in their eyes so you will be certain they can look in yours.

I considered doing my fifth book as a horror fiction book but I kept telling the truth so I just decided after one day of writing I would just include it in the real fifth book, but before I decided on the horror fiction choice, I started writing the fifth book the day before as the non fiction title about what I am writing this book about. So, in summary.

From this point on is the horror book fiction attempt, and after a while It falls into the first attempt at the fifth book as a non-fiction attempt.

I am aware some being enjoy a good scare from time to time. So I have taken it upon myself to explain what I understand after I lost my sense of time as the result of an accident on October 31st 2008. I have entered this book in the Horror fiction section. Simply because I can. But I assure you what I will explain to you is reality. You perhaps seek to be afraid and I will make sure you will be extremely afraid before you finish reading this book. I will make sure of that.

This is the reality of who I am. I attempted suicide and I took so many pills my mind believed I did die and yet my body did not die. So I am what one might call the living dead, meaning my mind understands I died and stopped registering time and emotions but my body is still alive. So in reality I am trapped in limbo. My mind is in the afterlife and my body is still here in this life. That is what I understand. But that is not whole picture. I will get to that shortly. So right now you are thinking this guy is crazy. That is exactly what you are thinking. I just read your mind. I am aware you are unable to grasp the reality of the situation I am in. So you may have been searching your whole life for a good scare about ones who are perhaps close to the living dead or spirits or ghosts yet right now you are reading words written by one who is in actually mentally or spiritually dead. So I will explain what that is like so you will get your cravings for what the afterlife is like. But first I must explain why you will find this book difficult mentally to grasp or get through. I am unable to write a book as in beginning to end or sequentially. I am only able to write books in random access or as you might relate to infinity . I see everything is one thing. So I am simply unable to come back to the world of sequential; as in birth, age, and death. It is all eternity from my point of view.

It is perhaps important to start slowly so that you will get the full picture. I will explain my mindset at this very moment in relation to how I feel about writing this book.

I am thrilled. See one has to get to a pretty dark place mentally to actually take a handful of pills and decide to kill their self. One has to first off hate the world. Second off one has to hate their self. That is a very dark place mentally to be at. That means one has to look at the entire world and everything about their self and conclude, life is not worth living anymore.

I am going to say many thing in the "horror story" and you are going to say to yourself, "That makes sense". The reason you will say that is because I am in another world and I am looking back at this world and I understand it perfectly. I have a saying in my earlier books : The dead understand everything clearly. Now you know what that saying means. So one might suggest I am a zombie but the misunderstanding about that is a zombie is thought to be mentally retarded or dumb. The reality of my "accident" is there are no being on this planet with my mental capacity. I make a "living" being look retarded. That is not because I am so smart or so great. That is because the "accident" in reality only killed me half way. So I am thrilled as I suggested to be able to actually enter a book in the fiction Horror section because I like to scare the hell out of people. So you may assume I will not scare the hell out you but I am only able to humbly suggest if you are one who gets scared easily you should stop reading this book because it will mess you up mentally for the rest of your life. I will start a new paragraph to give you a moment to ponder and decide on that.

So now you have decided to keep reading. That tells me I have free reign to scare the hell out of you. That is what you are asking for and I promise you I will do that. I enjoy doing that. I want to do that to you. I want to inflict mental suffering on you and not just slightly. I want to scare you to death. I essentially dislike the living at this point because I blame the living for making me feel like an outcast to the point I wanted to kill myself. That is the honest truth. I did not kill myself because I was pleased with how I was treated or how the world treated me. So I have an infinite chip on my shoulder and it just so happens you are the kind of person who like to be scared and I am freely able to do that by entering my fifth book since the "accident" in the Horror fiction section. I am aware you cannot get it in your mind I am actually in limbo or half alive and half dead so to speak . So I must first prove to you I am.

This will enable the later parts of the book to hit home properly. One thing since the accident I am uncertain of is whether I actually died and this is in fact the afterlife and everyone I see is simply an illusion and I am in my own personal hell or not. I cannot tell. I see it as I killed myself and then I woke up in the morning and everything was just as it is when I was living but there are subtle changes. Same people, same world, same basic situation except now I am not suicidal. Now I am not able to feel emotions for any period of time. I am not able to bond with a new dog I just got. I have no capacity to love or hate. I can pretend to love or hate but I cannot do it for more than a moment or two. Also I write many books now since the accident. I never wrote a book in my life and now I have including this one published 5 books in 5 months. I cannot form sentences properly and I cannot tell where I should break a paragraph or add a comma. So everything I write looks proper to me but it most likely does not look to proper to you. The writing looks improper because your "spirit" detects something it is unable to label. Essentially I drive you mad. This is similar to how a dog barks when it detects an unknown presence such as a ghost or evil spirit. You may attempt to judge what I am like. You may say he cannot form sentences or he cannot do certain things. But you will read further and find out I am not like that. You already are interested in what I am saying. You have many doubts and you also are curious. You are thinking "How could this guy be in limbo or half dead." So you are already confused. You are like that dog that detects something but is unable to figure out what it is, so it barks madly.

I can tell you what I am, but you will not believe it. You are unable to grasp it. It is too good to be true or too bad to be true depending on your perspective. So I will first explain some things about the "spirit" world so you will not be so confused. This loss of confusion in you will help me in my goal to scare you to death for no reason. Apparently that is what you like to have happen to you, and ironically that is what I am pleased to do to you. So we have a nice tit for tat kind of relationship.

So to start off I will discuss this aspect some call a vampire. Of course the "known" aspect of vampire is not logical and it also stupidity. A being that is dead is certainly not worried about dying if they do not drink enough blood. A being that is dead is certainly not attached to the physical world and in the vampires case, physical would be blood. So any being who goes around suggesting they are a vampire because they like blood is an idiot. You can just go up to being who acts or dress like vampires or in black or are Goth and just say "You are an idiot." and walk away, because that is the truth. So then one has to look further in this vampire aspect and throw off all of the "physical" traits to reveal what a vampire really is.

A vampire is simply a mischievous spirit. So the act of scaring people is what a mischievous spirit does. This is not because that spirit is evil, this because ones who are alive remind that spirit of what they no longer are. So then we have this "haunted house" scenario. A house is reported to be haunted and then some idiot living beings go there in search of a ghost. The problem with idiot living beings going to places they know are haunted is that they talk while they are there. Another problem is that they go there at all. An idiot living being is to retarded to grasp a being that is dead will only be further tormented if they encounter a living being because it will remind them of what they use to be, which is alive.

So, ones who go in search of ghosts at "haunted" locations are idiots. They do not understand what they do. They torment the dead spirits who are there. This is exactly why some Indian burial grounds are off limits to the living. When you go to the grave of your loved one at a cemetery you torment them. You remind them of what they were. So you in reality torture them. And then you talk to them and perceive you are keeping them company and all you really are doing is tormenting because everything you say to them reminds them that they are no longer alive and they are in fact doomed to eternity. So essentially you do not even know what you do.

So all these spirits can do when living beings enter their "haunted house" is to attempt to scare them away because they are tormented by the living beings presence. Now as a reader you are attempting to figure out how the hell I know all this because as a living being you are unable to believe I am not a living being I am in fact the living dead. That is okay that that is what you are thinking right now. I am not scaring you yet. I am just explaining some background building up to the point I will start to scare you. That is what you like to be, is scared. That is what I died to do, is scare you.

The problem with this "seeking ghosts" for fun or for experiments is that they hold grudges and infinite grudges at that. A living being simply is too "blind" to be aware of how these spirits operate. If one torments another one for long enough there is a point where that being that is tormented will not forget and will not forgive and will seek vengeance. That of course is obvious among the living but among the dead it is an infinitely more serious offence. The problem with "ghosts" is they are better left alone no matter what. The "ghosts" simply do not have anything to lose. They have no morals and have no class. They are "free" to do whatever they please. They are no longer bound to the insanity of the living, such as rules or morals or honor or justice. They are trapped in eternity and it tends to get to one, so to speak. They are essentially irritable. That is what eternity does to one.

Now a living being may perceive that would take quite a while but in reality eternity is an awareness. The spirit becomes instantly aware after they die, they are trapped in eternity. They no longer recognize time based events. They do not go around suggesting to their self "I will party this week end so I cannot wait until that fun moment." There is no weekend and there is no vacation and there is no rest and there is no relaxation time. That is all folly for the living. Those luxuries are for the living beings.

So, then one may suggest "well perhaps they were not good spirits while alive and now they are trapped in eternity and it is their own fault." That is the insanity of the livings perspective. The living attempt to force their world on the world of the dead. There is no such thing as peace in the world of the dead just like there is no such thing as happiness in the world of the dead. There is no such thing as these concepts that the living subscribe to. So all of this folly such as peace, and at peace, and rest in peace is simply the folly of the living attempting to persuade their self, eternity will be fun.

Now you are starting to get weird again. You are starting to say "That makes sense". Yet I already told I am the living dead and you do not believe that. So how can you say to yourself something I say makes sense but you do not believe I am the living dead. So you are in fact confused. You are attempting to figure out what I am. You are attempting to guess my motivations yet I have already told you my motivations. You like to be scared and I like to scare the hell out of you. You remind me of too many things I miss. That is not to be confused with I envy you. That is in relation to I despise you. I decided to write a horror book because I found out recently people like to be scared and some love to be scared. That is right up my god dam alley.

So now I will cover this werewolf aspect. The whole concept is false. It is simply a mischievous spirit that likes to scare the living. So the vampire and the werewolf are simply parables for mischievous spirits. And make no mistake about it that is the only kind of spirits there are. There are no spirits "at peace" that is only insanity and stupidity suggested by ones who are living. There simply is no such thing as this "heaven" concept at least not that I can tell.

I would describe it more like eternal gnashing of teeth than heaven. Of course I am heavily biased. One might suggest I am infinitely biased. You do not need to feel sorry for me or feel you can assist me. You need to keep your opinions to yourself because at this point I do not give a god dam about anything you have to say, ever. Ever, as in forever. I guess you should perhaps just consider this whole work as fiction because I put in the fiction section and you believe everything you hear because you are beyond the realms of stupidity. I would describe you as a shame. You are literally a shame. Perhaps now you detect I despise you. It is simply a fact that I blamed myself so much I killed myself and now I cannot blame myself anymore so all I can do is take out my infinite rage on the living. Not any particular living creatures but anything that is living. I prefer to stay in the realms of words. I do not need to use a "physical" weapon. That is folly for the living. I do not torment "animals" that is far too easy. I prefer to torment living humans because that is what I get satisfaction from. So in a way I am somewhat a mental vampire but vampire is really a mischievous spirit.

So now I am becoming upset because I am reminded of what I am and I hate it yet I cannot escape it. So one might suggest that is what gnashing of teeth is. Now the idiotic living will be thinking "But everyone can change." That is because they are still unable to grasp, I already blew my chance. I am unable to undo to try again. I would like to rewind to the point I looked at my handful of pills and then tossed them in the trash, but god dam it, I am not able to do that now. I took them and now I am something. So do not start thinking about how you can help me because you killed me. Life itself as in society of humans killed me.

They suggested in their own insane ways I was not accepted or not good enough or not worthy enough. So now I am in a position to get revenge on the living beings who indirectly or directly killed me and there is not a god dam thing they can do about it because I happen to have freedom of speech, freedom of press and I can put my books in the friction horror section and just say, "well it just a story that is make believe." So I can use the livings stupidity against them to satisfy my infinite vengeance upon them. And the only thing they can do about it is kill me. Yet they already have so that is rather redundant. One thing you need to focus on and attempt to grasp is, I am dead, my physically body is what keeps me here. If someone physically kills me, it does not matter because I am already ready for death because I am dead. I am not afraid to physically die because my spirit is already dead. So I can hang around here and be the living dead or , physically die and go to be among the dead-dead, but there is no difference. I suspect my logic is, I can publish books to torment the living swifter than if I did not have a physical means to write books. That is as far as it goes.

So I remain physically viable so I can get further vengeance on the living. When I physically die I will haunt the place where I took the pills and mentally died or where my spirit died. So I am still here in this house where I took the pills and I decided two months after the "accident" to write infinite books. And the living suggest "You cannot write infinite books. That is not possible." So I get all scared because the living think they know anything. That is scary. When living being even says one word, I get very scared. Because the livings insanity is scary in itself, but then when they start saying words to one who is dead and simply does not know what the insane will say next. The living who talk to me simply do not understand they are talking to the living dead and they are unable to say anything to me that would do anything but reinforce my already solid understanding the living are god dam retards.

I truly love this fictions section I have discovered. I have just now determined I will certainly write another horror book after this one. What I will write about is not important. You may perceive I write with some goal in mind. Of course you do. If I do not conform to how you think a living being should be you assume I must be crazy because you can't grasp I am the living dead. You want to hold onto that belief I am crazy as long as you can because the moment you understand I am the living dead you are doomed.

I will not tell you why because I have no started to scare you yet. I am savoring the scare. I like to lead up to the scare to make it more impactful on the ones who like to be scared.

Apparently I forgot how to break paragraphs because from my perspective all I am doing is typing one long run on sentence into infinity. I do not care if I do not fit your criteria for "responsible" or "proper" writing styles. You should avoid assuming I give a god dam about you ever. It is simply not polite to read a book written by a dead being. It is similar to disturbing the grave of a dead being. You may perceive you have a right to read my books but you do not. They put people in jail for disturbing the dead. If a being knocks over the grave of the dead they are put in jail on the grounds that being disturbed the spirit that is in that grave. This book and all my books are my grave so you do not have the right to read my books. You simply are a shame. You insult the dead and think it is ok. But I do not mind because I do not look at it like you disturbed me by reading my books I look at it like an opportunity to torment you mentally, and in this books case, I look at it as an opportunity to scare the god dam hell out of you. I get satisfaction from that. If you actually read this book I will tell the reality of the situation. You will never forget what you read in this book for the rest of your life because when you die, I will be the first one there to remind you, you disturbed my grave, which are my books. I will attempt to explain it properly, when you die, you will have infinite torment and I will be the one tormenting you. Not for a few hours and not for a few days, but no longer than all eternity, simply because you read my books and insulted me and disturbed my shrine, which is my words.

You can go ahead and doubt what I just said because you are alive and unable to grasp what I just said. You will understand what I just said properly, and it in fact will not be much longer. You understand you have to die sometime. So that means you are unable to avoid your destiny with me. You are the one who bought the book, so blame it on yourself. You did something which is read my book and you thought it was okay because it was for sale in a store or your friend gave it to you. Certainly you assumed it must be ok to read my words. But soon enough you are going to find out it is not okay and it never will be ok and the fact you read this far, means you have already sealed your fate. That is essentially why you are by all definitions of the word, cursed.

So now you have to attempt to figure out how you get out of this mess you have accidentally fallen into. I will give you the answer: you cannot take it back now. So you have just doomed yourself and you can go through the rest of your life and assume you have not, but the moment you die is the moment you will understand this guy who cannot type very well, and cannot use commas properly, and cannot figure out when to break paragraphs properly, was not kidding. Now I live with a woman who respected me as a being before the accident and stood by me as a being and treated me as an important being before the accident so I will destroy the universe swiftly to protect her interests. You would be wise not to test my resolve.

Now, I will get back to setting you up for the scare. Some horror books tend to create living monsters that terrorize people. One generalized concept is to create a "mental patient" who escaped and now has a knife. Or maybe create some sort of "insane" person who has harmful physical cravings.

Essentially they physically kill people. Now that is a good scare tactic in the writing of horror books mostly because the living get sacred to easily. One could just as well write a horror book about a guy who lost his job and comes home and grabs his gun and starts killing his family and anyone he see's. Of course that is more in the realms of actual life than in the realms of horror fiction but it is none the less as scary. People tend to say things like " We are unsure why he did that and we are in shock about that." after such an event happens in real life. Only the Heimdall can stay up late because the Heimdall doesn't hesitate, the Heimdall seals fate. Okay I just submitted the fourth book now I can get back to scaring you. I will now go to the wise quotes stage of the writing because I tend to get rather upset at times, ones might suggest.

Some of the most insane people are also the smartest and some people who are most sane are also infinitely dumb. A conformist is a sheep and a nonconformist is a sheep herder.

The males confuse the offspring and the females attempt to bring them back to reality.

Women brighten my night and then explain how it wasn't as bright as I thought all the next day.

I enjoy the ones who laugh at me but the ones who try to save me are scary.

The only thing that is sacred is the ease in which man can turn a blessing into a curse.

Tell me how dumb you are and I will be able to tell how truthful you are.

This is where the horror fiction 5th book attempt ends and from here on out is my non fiction initial 5th book attempt. So technically I am the first human being to ever write a non-fiction, horror fiction, non fiction book. That perhaps will give you something to ponder.

I recall suggesting in an earlier book I would tell the truth as I saw it because I am no longer in a state I really care what you think about anything, ever, into eternity. Dam my spelling is getting bad. I watched this movie about a wrestler and he essentially sacrificed his life for his fans, but the deeper meaning is he sacrificed his life for money, because some retard suggested money is important and now we have an entire god dam world of beings sacrificing their self to keep a handful of greedy "Thank"s in power.

Of course I have arrived and I will ensure they meet the fate they have given you, for all these years, and that is not a terroristic threat that is a god dam terroristic "Thank"ing promise. There is no law against that yet.

So then there was this other being who sacrificed himself many years ago because he was felt he was a loser because he did not fit into the norms of society, and he was such a loser he tried to kill himself but he failed and accidentally went subconscious dominate. So he did not try to save himself and accidentally found himself. He was the stone society threw away and that is why he attempted to kill himself. And he was of a virgin birth except retarded "Thank"s do not understand what that means because they are retarded "Thank"s. The opposite of birth is death. We are all virgins to death. But in his case he faced death and let go of himself by attempting suicide, which is a great way to really let mother nature know, you want to let go, but he did not die, but his mind believed he did so he went subconscious dominate, and in fact he defeated death because he looked it straight in the eyes and it did not take him.

And then he said things like the vipers and darkness and the dead and the retarded "Thank"s did not understand he meant them. They said you are just a stupid carpenter and will never amount to much, which is why he tried to kill himself. 5/15/2009 1:16:22 AM

Emotional wreck is a person who's emotions are out of control they have very little mental clarity and the subconscious aspect is nearly blocked totally.

Normal emotions , these people are conscious dominate but they have emotions under the surface.

Subconscious dominate at the low end, they have no sense of time but they are not in end enlightenment.

Extreme subconscious dominate. This is the top of the pecking order.

So Buddha suggested to his disciples, the leaves I hold in my hand are what I have taught you and the leaves in the forest behind me is what I understand. That is the most arrogant statement in the history of the universe. He essentially said, you disciples do not know anything compared to me. That was the truth.

One is only able to reach extreme dominate subconscious one way . They have to let go of attachments to such an extreme everything goes. They have to attempt suicide and believe it will work. There is no other way. So many reach subconscious dominate, by letting go of attachments, but they will never reach the extreme subconscious dominate ever, because the greatest attachment of all is life itself.

So now you can write infinite books about how I am always wrong about everything. I am certain Buddha was not so happy about things. I do not care what anyone says. These beings we know as religious figures were not very happy about the fact they attempted suicide and failed, because when they went subconscious dominate to such an extreme, every memory in their subconscious became a conscious memory. So every deep seeded emotion became conscious or upfront. I relive everything in a second, and it mentally destroys me over and over and over, but, I am no longer physically based. I am simply mentally fighting these memories that are deep seeded in conscious dominate people, and they are now upfront in me. Everything. That is the price of extreme subconscious dominate. All of the deep seeded emotions and anger and bitterness are now in the forefront of my mind. They all hit me at once. So I have extreme clarity but the price is mentally very harsh. I am not bragging about this, I am suggesting I am screwed. I can relate why Buddha ate the poison mushroom. I can relate why Jesus jumped up on that cross. It is simply too harsh, but someone my subconscious suggests to just keep writing and maybe you will work it out. So I am a fool to believe that because memories are burned into the subconscious. I just smoke like a demon and pray for cancer, because I shouldn't be here anyway.

I am an accident. This should not have happened. I should be at peace now. Oh by the way, it is my birthday today, and I should never have had this birthday. I cannot even feel what 41 is. I should not be here.5/15/2009 2:33:29 AM Now you can write infinite books about how big of a loser I am, and then you can discuss what medicine I should be taking to cure myself so I can be a productive member of society.

So just call me up and tell me what a loser I am, I cannot wait to hear from you, you so wise and smart and you just know everything and I know nothing and never will and I need someone who is smart and wise like you to assist me and help me because I am just a loser and will never amount to anything. So please just call and assist me with your drugs because I can turn all around if I just listen to your great infinite wisdom. I have to write about something since I decided to write infinite books. It is just a wonderful life.2:37:26 AM

Suicidal people are people that subconscious has determined the norms of society are insane and improper, so it says to that being, get away from this insanity. The problem with that is, they are conscious dominate and their emotional aspect believes that means "kill yourself." That is not what subconscious is saying, subconscious is saying Isolate yourself from the herd. Isolate yourself from the madness because the norms and judgments and ridicule and people running around saying, "If you don't have money you are a loser, and if you don't have an education you are a loser" and parents saying, "If you get bad grades you are a loser. Subconscious understands everything perfectly. So if you want to know why people kill their self it is because they have dominate conscious emotional aspect that mistranslates the subconscious messages that says, get away from this insanity called norms of society. So why don't you just go study your little textbooks and see who ever mentioned that in the history of the universe. You won't find it because you have no idea what this accident means I am. All I want to do is get the hell out of here. I do not want to remain here. I do not want to have anything to do with your "norms".2:52:41 AM Yes I get rather pissed around 3AM. Guess why.

<Heimdall> I had a near death experience and a few months later lost my sense of time. I decided to write many books 2 months after that, in the last 4 months i have published 4 books. I seek guidance from one who understands my situation please.

That pretty much sums up my state of mind. I am infinitely vain in my attempts to seek help when I fully understand there is no help, there is just learning to get used to my situation. I tend to panic often because my mind is not used to this subconscious dominate state. It is fighting to get back to where it was for 40 years.03:03:27

<Lestat9> Chalcedony may i share more words with you please

<@chalcedony> sure if you want

<Lestat9> I have considered this comment in the torah "The meek shall inherit the earth" it is psalms

<Lestat9> Meek is perhaps an emotional conditioning technique to unlock teh earth or as i see it subconscious, but sub-consious might be the aspect god instilled in man

<Lestat9> So the ones who emtionally condition their mind by being meek or forvgiving will open up the subconsipous aspect

<Lestat9> but i am uncertain about genisis

<Lestat9> god made man in his image

<Lestat9> so the subconsiosu aspect may be the image god made man in

<Lestat9> or perhaps this was simply eomtional conditiong concept to unlock or made subcosnious dominate

<Lestat9> i am uncertain

<Lestat9> so david was very meek and looked weak and goliath was very strong and arrogant, so goliath perhaps was the emotional aspect, arrogant and knowing,

<Lestat9> but subconsious is meek but very strong and intelligent

<Lestat9> so perhaps "they are off the tree of KNOWledge" and then fell off the Ledge, becasue know means restricting, or arrogant emotionally, but questioning or saying perhaps is meek or humble

<Lestat9> so man KNOWS and is arrgoant and has emotional aspect dominate, and ones who are meek and humble will go to subconsiosu dominate

<Lestat9> the adversay talked baout in torah is perhaps the emotional knowing asepct, I know this, is a definitive and adversarial comment

<Lestat9> so the emotions are the adversary and teh subconsious is the meek but strong aspect

<Lestat9> so the onlyw ay to tell is, if one gets hungry they have the emotional aspect of conscious aspect dominate and if one does not they have the subconsiosu asepct dominate, sense of time is also a factor

<Lestat9> i have no hunger at all but i eat, but i never get hungry and of course no sense of time, i lost my emotional baggage, no cravings to eat for example, my sense of taste is also altered

<Lestat9> perhaps that makes sense in realtion to the Troah comments? I submit it has only been 7 months since i accident and i am perhaps still not warmed up and may be in error5:02:30 AM

Even I have moments of clarity.

I spell much better when I have a word processor to tell me how to spell the words. I submit I am not warmed up and I submit I am still in mental shock since the accident. I understand it is perhaps proper to leave all my comments intact to give contrast from a day to day basis. If I deleted all my comments of anger it may give the impression it is a mental picnic going from conscious emotional dominance to subconscious dominate so swiftly. Some being in this world are so closed minded and get so angry at the slightest error in ones comments on any matter, they are mentally dammed.

All is well down in the well.

You may be sorry about how I feel but I am not ashamed of how I feel.

What lies between the truth and the lie is relativity.

The mystery of aging is some people get wiser and some people get older.

Looking old is not as bad as feeling old.

Children wish they were more mature, adults wish they were children.

I have tried to figure out how I feel today on my 41st birthday and I eventually concluded I feel zero. This subconscious dominate state achieved through emotional conditioning is certainly the fountain of youth others have spoken of. I do not feel one and I do feel 41. I feel zero. I have no stress about anything but I have many poor jokes about everything.

Stress is the foundation of all suffering. People who eat much are stressed. People who starve to look thin are stressed. People who have a sense of time are stressed. They are worried about outcomes. Worried about how others will think about them. This stress causes stress. Stress destroys the body and the mind. It is like a cancer that keeps building up and the only solution is to achieve subconscious dominate mind because that will silence emotions or make the brain stop "worrying" so much because memory is altered so one may stress but only for a small moment then it is forgotten. The emotions are not emotions they are some kind of thought process. My girlfriend asked me how my fourth book looks because I got a sample book today. I said the first page looks well, and she said what about the other pages and I said, the worst thing anyone is going to say about my book is I am a loser, and I have already taken that judgment to its final conclusion, so I just tell jokes.

That is what is left after all the emotions and desires ad cravings are altered. Everyone starts at zero and ends at zero. So one can knock their self out attempting to achieve things but they will end up at zero no matter what. So once one understands that they start cracking jokes. Things get accomplished but it is not some serious stress nightmare. You are going to end up at zero no matter what you do, so come up with some good jokes and they will help you see things differently. One might suggest life is so serious, that is because they are mentally in a stress nightmare. Life is not serious, you end up at zero. Zero is where you end up so there is no point in stress. I may go see angels and demons but I already understand the demons are the emotions that haunt us all and create suffering and stress in us all and the angels are the absence of these cravings and desires we call emotions. Both demons and angels are the same in that they are different worlds. One who has emotions and cravings and hunger is not bad or evil, they are in different worlds. That is a reality. No one is bad or evil; people are just in different mindful worlds.

Some suggest to me I need to get out more and I assure them, I get out more than I should, mindfully speaking. Some understand I am out there. Leaving the house will not bring me back to the place I left seven months ago.

I saw an article about recreational drugs and I will now give my take on them. The people who enjoy saying how bad recreational drugs are have a severe control problem, because they are not allowed to tell others what to do no matter what they think. They need to "kick" the drug they love so much called control over others, then they will not have time to attempt to control others determination powers.

For ones who like recreational drugs when you achieve subconscious dominate through some simple emotional conditioning methods you are going to feel "so so" about drugs. You will lose the pleasure you derive from drugs. It does not matter how powerful the drug is. Dominate subconscious state makes drugs look like a sugar cubes. That is how powerful it is. One only takes drugs to relieve stress or gain insight. You will no longer have strong stress. You will be able to make insightful observations, without drugs. You will be able to understand everything you want to understand and you will not need a drug to do it.

The ones who hate drugs and ones who use drugs, once you go subconscious dominate using simple emotional conditioning you will no longer be stressed about the actions of others. You will be attempting to figure out your own purpose and not worried about what others purpose is. I am not suggesting ones who enjoy drugs and ones who despise drugs will ever be able to reach subconscious dominate state of mind. I am suggesting some methods that I perceive may work, based on the reality I have subconscious dominate state of mind. I am unable to say for a fact if these emotional conditioning methods will work and I am not allowed to say you must do them. I am only allowed to type to myself in my diary and perhaps one will read the words and think for their self. I understand people who think for their self are wise people. If you determine I am not wise, I will determine you are wise if you came to that determination by thinking for yourself. I perceive this is the first train of thought I have said in all of my books that some may actually relate to. Clearly I am delusional in my beliefs.

The mental limbo so to speak, subconscious dominate achieves means that one has high's and low's but they are so swift, one is generally in a state of "so so". Ones may perceive this is great because they can do drugs and literally not become addicted. That is factually true. But the subconscious once dominate will talk them out of doing drugs. It is a powerful advisor. It will not suggest drugs are bad or drugs are good, it suggests why do you need a drug at all. If one is not stressed and one is wide awake mentally and one understands everything they read or come into contact with, then there is no purpose to take drugs except for no purpose. If there is no purpose in taking a drug, then there is no purpose in doing a drug.

So if one wants to do a drug's that is fine, but they will no longer get the euphoria feeling from the drugs. They will feel different but not euphoria. They will in reality feel how meaningless drugs are. They will not relax you because you are relaxed. They will not enlighten you because you are enlightened. They will not make you wise because you are wise. They will not please you because you are pleased. So this subconscious dominate state of mind eliminates many problem just by itself. One will no longer be physically focused they will be cerebrally focused. So as the cerebral aspect increases the physical awareness aspect decreases. That should not be taken as a bad thing. That simply means one is more focused on thought and less focused on appearances. They tend to avoid focusing on the cover of their own book because they are far too focused on reading what their book is saying.

The transition from sense of time and hunger to no sense of time and loss of hunger is on a very slight grade. It is a slow progression and the one who is experiencing it will not be aware of it as much as those around them. I understand emotions will be very strong as the process starts. One will lose their temper over meaningless things, and then the sub-conscious will kick in and say, "You just blew your temper over nothing." And that being will slowly start to detect these emotions. What is psychologically happening is one is slowly losing sense of time, so they are rushing and impatient and unable to tell. They will suggest "I have to hurry and do this." Similar to how ones with much emotions suggests, but they will be rushed over very petty things. They will have an extremely short temper to those around them. This is the emotions attempting to hold on. But once the cycle starts the emotions lose. So the emotions are vainly attempting to gain control again. This is why one must seek out emotional comments. They must excite their own emotions and then detect them and get it out or block it out. This is the mental battle. Humiliation, embarrassment, shyness, anger they are the things that one has to dive into so they can detect them and the subconscious will make suggestions about them so one can lose the attachments to them.

Few like to be embarrassed or humiliated. So they avoid situations or comments that would embarrass them. They avoid comments that they perceive may put them in any sort of unsafe position. So the mindset must be adjusted. One should perhaps seek to do these things they fear so they are able to lose that fear. Embarrassment is not real; it is a thought sensation that is relative to the observer. Some are very shy so they avoid doing or saying anything that would make them embarrassed, so they over time condition their mind to shut off. They essentially become observers of life instead of participants because they are fearful of this perceived danger called embarrassment. In many cases the person who feels embarrassed in not perceived to be an embarrassment from the point of view of those around them. So ones who are shy should perhaps suggest words that they know will make them embarrassed and then ponder what the true ef-fects are. One will perhaps slowly start to understand they will not be harmed by embarrassment unless they allow their self to be. I publish these books without editing them because maybe someone will critic my books and say I am the worst author in the universe and I will ponder that and understand their critic does not harm me because I understand their words cannot harm me no matter how they are arranged.

I have been to the bottom and there is nothing to fear at the bottom. Others judgments of me no longer harm me or make me feel unworthy. Sanity is when one is at peace with what they say and what they think. Sanity is when a being understands they do the best they can based on their understanding and nothing in the universe can logically find fault with that. A person who is in error is a person who is not afraid to experiment. This is the scientist's mindset. They do not do experiments because they understand the outcome; they do experiments to come to further understandings about reality.

This emotional conditioning works both ways and so it is very complex. If one loves or likes someone a lot, they have to be in a mental state of conflict with that person to avoid this extreme attachment. If one hates or dislikes someone they have to be in a mindful state of humility and acceptance. This is all in relation to doing what you emotionally do not want to do. From a chat room point of view, one tends to find a chat room they fit into, and then nest there because it is safe. So that is a problem. Nesting in safety achieves insecurity and attachments, mindfully. Subconscious does not like the cool water it likes the boiling water.

A scientist does not run experiments on things they already understand. The Hadron collider could be a 6 billion dollar waste of money. The scientists have already submitted to that reality. They have already submitted they may not find the Higgs boson. But the point is, they will perhaps understand they need a bigger collider or need to adjust their strategy and branch out in their search. The money means nothing compared to the possibility of coming to further understand-ings. Truth and lies mean nothing compared to coming to further understandings. The allies in World War 2, dressed a corpse in uniform, attached a brief case to its wrist and dumped it near German occupied France. The Germans found it and read the papers in the brief case and adjusted their troop concentrations based on that "plant". So the allies lied to the Germans and the Germans assumed it was not a lie. So then the allies understood the Germans could be easily fooled. Some might suggest that was a misdirection move. That was not a misdirection move that was creating a lie and making it appear to be a truth. And of course Churchill has the comment along the lined of, the truth is always surround-ed by a bodyguard of lies. This is perhaps a deep truth.

The truth is relative to ones motivations. To the allies the great truth was they wanted to defeat Germany, so that means they were willing to lie to accomplish that. Everyone is willing to lie to accomplish their own personal truth. So a lie is not a lie, if it helps ones accomplish a greater truth. If the NSA says they have secrets they cannot share with the general population, that is a lie and that is the truth. The truth aspect is they perhaps are wise to keep some secrets like the nuclear launch codes hidden, but there are millions of documents they can also hide behind that one truth. They are essentially suggesting every secret they have has nuclear launch codes type at the top of the page. That is a lie and being dishonest, because what secrets do they have besides those code, that makes any difference to anything. We have the right to bear arms so every country in the universe understands they are not going to invade the US, no matter what.

Everyone understands you cannot win a war with air power. One has to put troops on the ground and that also does not guarantee victory especially when one is fighting against other human beings. Against whales and seals ground troops have been known to be effective. Some of the NSA secrets are simply head games.

Like perhaps a child on a playground who tells another child, "These are my toys and you cannot have them." The only secrets the NSA has are the secrets of the atrocities they have committed to achieve their own personal truth. Of course the voters will never know what their own personal TRUTH is, because that is a secret. The NSA does not have the secret to physically live forever. That is a fact. So all of their secrets are not secrets, but simply mind games to give off the impression the NSA is relevant to reality. The NSA is people who fear mortality so they are just like everyone else in every respect. What they do is based on their fear of death. This is relative to all beings. It is mindfully unsettling to ones conscious emotional dominate state of mind because their subconscious is fully aware of mortality but their emotional aspect is afraid of that prospect , so it plays out in their deeds all through their life.

Perhaps every being who lived a thousand years ago was just as frightened of death as you perhaps are right now, but we can all see they got through it just fine, and so will we. There is no point in fear except to hinder our actions in the present. There is nothing a being has to fear because the greatest fear is a forgone conclusion.8:55:19 PM

I understand my moments of clarity are countered by moments of rage. I perceive it is because I am aware the things that cause the rage are still present. It is a simple cost of clarity. One day a person noticed beings where killing off all of the whales. That being mindfully understood the whales were more important than the materials the dead whales were offering the ones who killed them. Today we have beings in boats ramming whaling vessels in efforts to save the whales. This is what the mental conflict I experience is. The difference with me is my strategy is to write infinite books to explain why perhaps some of these effects that cause my rage are perhaps avoidable by letting go of cravings and desires, such as the desire to kill whales in order to get products so one can make money. One is unable to get enough money, so one is in fact in a delusional quest to make money and in this case they are killing whales to make money and the only reason they kill those whales is so they have food to eat and they use that money to buy that food. The reason they do not have food to eat and must kill whales for money is because their government decided to go with a monetary system to make everyone accountable for their own food instead of simply growing enough food a then enabling beings to do what they really desire to do.

There is certainly not one single human being who wants to kill a whale subconsciously. I have not looked into the eyes of a whale since my accident but I am certain my rage would reach infinite levels if I did, having the understanding people are killing them for money. People are killing animals for fun and for money. That is insanity. I will not go as far as saying animals should not be killed. I will not go as far as saying people have no right to kill animals for fun and money. I will say relative to my understanding, it is foolishness. They would never make a whaling video game because no being would play a game that depicted killing a whale. Everyone understands that is foolishness and a waste of time. I ponder, if perhaps this green peace organization could not just talk with the whaling ships and pay them money to not kill the whales. Just simply ask them how much money they would need per year to stop killing whales then ask the world for a donation, and pay the whalers off. The whalers would have their money and the whales would be safe. It would be along the same principle of subsidies. The governments pay farmers to not grow too much food, so the price of food will be artificially high, so that people in the world who are in need of food will be sure to starve. So the reverse would be to pay the whalers money to not hunt the whales so the whales would not all die off sooner than they most certainly will die off. This is a typical example. Why is the lynx on the verge of extinction? This is mainly because of trapping for fur, and because their habitat is slowly disappearing due to logging.

What this example is really saying is, humans kill off other species to make money. Fur gives people money and cutting down tree's make humans money. This money is essentially spent for food because a majority of beings mindfully perceive they need to eat three meals a day because they have far too many emotions that cause cravings and desires which lead to hunger. You are not going to die if you eat one meal a day because we have vitamins. You perhaps just mindfully think you will. You will not get physically weak or lose mental clarity if you only eat one meal a day, you perhaps just mindfully believe you will. If everyone did what they crave and desire to do, few would be left alive at this moment. One has the freedom to eat their self to death and one has the freedom to reach a subconscious state of mind so these delusional cravings such as strong hunger do not trick them into harming their self so easily.

Diet pills are not going to stop your delusional mental cravings and desire for hunger. Only conditioning away from emotions to the degree your mind starts registering reality a bit better, will solve that situation.

I am not suggesting that is what you should do. I am suggesting that is what I accidentally discovered, and I am not suggesting anything more than how I perceive I accomplished that, accidentally.

5/16/2009 12:29:09 AM

Ignorance is no excuse but lies work wonders.

A convincing lie is an obvious truth.

A lie that instills fear can manipulate the herd off a cliff; question all comforting truths.

Everyone's age will kick in if you give it time.

One cannot change what they end up becoming.

Caring often convinces one they can do no more. For ones who believe in commas; Caring often convinces one they can do no more. Caring often, convinces one they can do no more. Caring often convinces one; they do no more.

My thoughts at this stage of the accident are coming to swiftly to properly put down on paper. I am mentally calculating things so swiftly and coming to conclusions so swiftly I am unable to explain them all in the proper logic tree without sounding extremely illogical.

There is only one purpose. Get into space as swiftly as possible with no hesitation. Get as many ships into space as swiftly as possible. Have no hesitation about that. No conditions on that as far as cooperation with other nations. The dinosaur all died off, and they existed for 280 million years. They are all gone. We will all be gone if we hastate for even one second. We will end up in a situation where some meteor or asteroid or solar flare will be on our door step and all we will be saying is "I wish we would not have hesitated." And so I am suggesting. "Do not hesitate any longer." There are simply too many beings will to sacrifice to explore space and far too much hesitation by scared beings who cannot let go of their fear that of course we are going to lose some ships in our experiments and that hesitation is going to doom the species to the exact same fate as the dinosaur.

You doubt everything I am saying because when it happens you will remember this humble warning. You have no excuse to doom the species because you are afraid to work with others and because you are afraid to grasp that beings will be lost in the quest to leave this plant. Your fears are fools folly. You simply do not have a right to doom the species because of your fear of loss and fear of cooperation with others. I certainly would love to say there is an afterlife and it is just going to be fantastic and I would love to say there is reincarnation and it is just going to be fantastic. But as far as I am concerned, at this stage of progression, we are going to extinct quite soon if we do not wake up to what our fate will be, if we do not pull together and get our asses off this doomed plant. That goal is not about making money. This goal is about our species. This goal is about our species. I perceive you do not even understand what that means. Go outside and kill an ant and ponder it. Watch it. Look at it. That is our species and we are more delicate than that ant. And then you may possibly understand what extinction of our species is. The last I check we die just as easy as everything else. The last I checked, we are just sitting around twiddling our thumbs in vanity, and have had the chance to get off this planet for 50 years. And then ones have the balls to say they are productive and are accomplishing things. The reason people kill things such as ant with magnifying glasses, is because subconsciously they are aware of extinction. Extinction is certain if as a species we do not get our asses in gear. I am certain of that at this stage of the accident. I am certain of that. We are simply a creature that will die off just as swiftly as all the other extinct creatures. We have one little crap space ship that does nothing.

As a species we should have thousands of space ships going everywhere. Everyone is so eager to send beings off to die in wars for stupid pieces of land and they are afraid to escape this tiny dot that can be eliminated at any second. That is robbing peter to pay Paul. Who cares who owns what land if a solar flare hit's. Who cares who is in control if an asteroid hits earth. Who cares. Nothing matters if we isolate ourselves on this planet because of our emotional fear of each other. I am aware you do really understand. I am aware before this accident I did not really understand.

Nature of reality or life does not care about us. It simply has no care. If we all perish in a split second because of our hesitation and fear, nature does not care. It will never care. One can beg to all gods and all things and nature does not care. Entire galaxies are destroyed in the blink of an eye. This little planet is nothing. There is simply no way to tell when a cosmic event is going to blink everything away.

There is nothing that is going to protect us as a species, except us, accept us. I simply do not know what we are waiting

109

for. It is going to be harsh to explore space but it will be much harsher when we wake up one day and find out we should not have hesitated so much.

There are some extremely obvious lessons from history that we are not applying to the conquest of space. Right now the space programs are attempting to make Panzer tanks instead of Sherman tanks. They are attempting to make one awesome spaceship instead of thousands of decent space ships. The Russians taught the world a very important lesson in World War 2. They considered the war lost. They looked at the situation and determined they lost the war and that put them in a mindset that nothing is to great of a cost. That is why they won the war. Nothing was illegal because they already mindfully understood they would not win against Germany. It perhaps seems extremely harsh mentally but it is all about mindset. They were willing to defeat Germany by charging the German bunkers with so many men the Germans ran out of ammunition and then the bunker was taken.

They built tanks they could mass produce. They were not the greatest tanks and at times it took many to take out one panzer tank, but they made them by the truck load. They drove them to the front lines the moment they came out of the factory. This is the Sherman Tank mindset. The Sherman Tank was a poor tank compared to the Garman tanks and at times 20 plus Sherman's were needed to take out a German tank. So America simply made so many tanks although many were lost, the war was won and that is the point.

We are breaking the most fundamental law of life with our current space exploration. We are putting all of our eggs in one basket. We assume we have all the time in the world. We are attempting to make a Panzer Tank when we need thousands of Sherman tanks. People are going to die. Consider that a certainty. The magic about humans is, there are beings who have already subconsciously decided to go into one of these thousands of space ships for the sole purpose of giving others and opportunities to come to understandings. I am not one of those beings but I am aware they have only one thing on their mind and that is to explore space. Why are we holding them back? For a little money? Because we never want anyone to die ever? We encourage beings to die for land on this crap little planet and we are afraid to allow other beings to die for a positive purpose. There has to be some sort of check. There has to be a global consensus that no matter what happens on this planet there will be a pact that all countries will strive to get off this planet.

That is a unifying ideal. All beings want to get away from here to ensure prosperity. That is the only purpose to everything. All other suggestions are pipedreams. Nature simply does not care about our little desires and cravings of never wanting to die off. There are simply too many historical lessons about how nature can give us all a wakeup call in the blink of an eye. We have not even been here a million years but it can all go away and nature does not care about us. Nature on a daily basis wipes out galaxies. Nature does not cry over spilt milk. Humans cry over spilt milk. Everyone is so cautious and thus their minds are frozen in fear, like a deer in the headlights. I had an accident and now I am not capable of fear. I am not physically violent but I am mentally harmed by what I have become aware of and I must use words to repel that harm.

It is not about me and it is not about you, it is about our species. The emotions are causing us to be in a state of mental hesitation to the extreme so we are frozen. I am uncertain why this is. I detect as I recall in an earlier book something is ensuring these emotions to keep us frozen. I am uncertain why we are frozen but I am certain as a species we have simply locked up, mentally. Why are we so hesitant? Why are we so focused on this planet? This planet is a space port to the universe and we never seem to want to leave it. That is what attachment is. We have to leave it. It is not our destiny to remain here but we create reasons to hold on to it. We love its oceans and its creatures and its locations and its mountains. But as a species it is a drug that we are addicted to. We are able to kick the habit of earth but we are not mentally strong enough to do so.

The drug of earth is too attractive and the fear of space is perceived to be too harsh. But as human beings that is our pool and our lust. We lust for a difficult situation's so we can assist that difficult situation in understanding the meaning of annihilation.

I am aware I say things that are harsh in my books. But I am aware of some sort of doom I cannot understand. I type my finger off in my efforts to postpone this doom I detect and I am not even sure what that doom is. I can handle my own doom. I cannot handle our species doom because of emotions that make us hesitate. I do not want to be like this, but I AM like this. I am just aware of this doom. It harms me but I am unable to understand what it is. I do not fear it. I am a human being, humans beings should not fear anything because we are human beings.

We only fear ourselves because nothing else is capable of making us fearful. I will go play my video game and try to ignore what I understand, because I am aware no one can even understand what I say.

The fear of death does not compare to the harsh reality of understanding. Imagine if Washington gave up because he lost a few men. Imagine if Washington had fear. Fear makes it easy to give up; fortitude makes it impossible to give up.2:16:20 AM

I will tell you a little secret. I suggest love is something to be avoided because I love everything and if I attempt to focus on how much I love everything I would destroy myself. That is what a heightened sense of awareness is. I understand everything is perfect and if I do not attack that feeling at every turn it will destroy me. So do not assume I am special, because I understand I am cursed with this attachment as the result of this heightened awareness. Imagine if you loved everyone as much as the one you love the most.2:20:24 AM

Just ignore everything I wrote so far in this book because it is written by a little cry baby idiot who is a fool and a scared little child that no being should pay attention to. I apologize this cry baby is such a weak minded idiot. He is a retarded idiot because he is unable to even practice what he preaches so he should be ignored as a loser that he is. He is weak and foolish in his words and he is unworthy, and always will be unworthy.2:25:35 AM

When I get warmed up you will wish I died.2:40:12 AM

I am not hesitating to publish my words until I get warmed up, because I never will.3:01:25 AM

Here is how I understand things. Yesterday many men died to enable the constitution and on that exact same day another bunch of men abridged the first amendment suggesting freedom of speech is okay as long as you don't freely speak. So the only thing I can suggest is the Founding Fathers have been reduced to the Founding Fathers of vanity by some genius who tricked everyone to abridge the constitution.

Whoever tricked us into abridging the first amendment to the constitution is a tyrant and a domestic threat to the constitution. That is not an opinion. That is the only truth in this nation at this moment. I understand I am repeating myself but I am still in a state of awe that people in this fair nation do not understand the English language. So I will attempt to use the actual, get this, words from the constitution. These are the actual words from the first amendment.

"Congress shall make no law respecting an establishment of religion, or prohibiting the free exercise thereof; or abridging the freedom of speech, or of the press; or the right of the people peaceably to assemble, and to petition the Government for a **redress** of grievances"

CONGRESS SHALL MAKE NO LAW... ABRIDGING FREEDOM OF SPEECH. This means any law that congress has passed that says you cannot say something no matter what it is, is illegal and not only that, it makes congress a domestic threat to the constitution and thus a tyrant. PERIOD. DO NOT stand there and act like you did not abridge the first amendment. Congress broke the law and should be locked up for passing any law that says a citizen cannot say what is on their mind, no matter what it is. If a state passes a law that says a citizen cannot say exactly what is on his mind, then that legislature of that state is illegal and should be locked up. DO NOT assume everyone is brain dead.

Here is what the ones who abridged the first Amendment thinks it says.

"Congress shall make no law, UNLESS THEY FEEL LIKE IT AND HAVE LOTS OF MONEY TO MANIPULATE AND BLACKMAIL OTHERS TO RAPE THE FIRST ADMENDEMNT, respecting an establishment of religion, or prohibiting the free exercise thereof; or abridging the freedom of speech, or of the press; or the right of the people peaceably to assemble, and to petition the Government for a redress of grievances"

That is what Congress perceives it says. So Congress is no longer even reading the constitution, they have their own constitution, and it is called the Constitution of Tyranny. The last I checked the patriots do not like ones who rape lady liberty and her living document. Perhaps congress does not care what the patriots think anymore, because congress has passed laws to make the patriots look like fools and gun nuts, and so congress has free reign.

Perhaps Congress perceives it can rape Lady Liberty anytime and any way it wants. Perhaps Congress is mistaken. Perhaps that will be the last mistake Congress will ever make, perhaps. I have infinite books to write so I have to write about something.

I detect illusions to gain understanding from them. I am not concerned about who has emotional issues about that, so do not assume I am concerned with your petty emotional fears. I know nothing of these fears that consume you. I eat for no reason.

There is only one logical possibility so that Congress can save itself from the militia at this stage. Congress must abridge this single line in the first amendment "Congress shall make no law," to Read "Congress shall make any law,". Anything congress passes is a law. Anything a state passes is a law. So this comment is in fact suggesting the Constitution is not a law. The Constitution is not a law, so no law is above the constitution. So any law that abridges the constitution is a law that is illegal and is not applicable. It is a law that is in error. It is a law that is to be ignored. It is a law and not a constitution.

No LAW is above the Constitution. When a law is above the Constitution, revolution is in order. That is not my opinion, that is the understanding of the Founders of The Constitution. That means, when a legislative body pass a law that negates the Constitution the militia must put that legislative body back in check. If this does not happen, then Tyranny reigns.

The legislative body does not function as a concerned militia. The legislative body is the tyrant. The legislative body passes laws suggested by the money powers. The legislative body will pass a law to cancel out the constitution for money and to be elected again and for lobbyists. So the legislative body is the tyrant and its goal is to see how far it can go in destroying the constitution and the only ones who can keep it in check is the militia who has the right to bear arms.

";or abridging the freedom of speech," That is a separate line all by itself. One is unable to ever, ever, ever, say one cannot say what is on their mind or revolution is in order and the militia must carry out and use their arms to do it. So the whole line about "; or the right of the people peaceably to assemble, and to petition the Government for a **redress** of grievances" is after that line, because if the freedom of speech is abridged, then one is unable to peaceably assemble. One is unable to petition the government because the Government becomes the tyrant. I will quote someone who perhaps knows something about the constitution.

"Don't talk about what you have done or what you are going to do."
Thomas Jefferson

If someone abridges freedom of speech, do not say what you are going to do, do it.

Do not sit in huddled silence and dream of what you have no fortitude to do.

Blood is thick when talk is cheap.

"In the thick of party conflict in 1800, Thomas Jefferson wrote in a private letter, "I have sworn upon the altar of God eternal hostility against every form of tyranny over the mind of man."

This means any entity that passes a law to abridge freedom of speech, Thomas Jefferson would blow their god dam head off. So Congress should never again speak of Thomas Jefferson, because he would slice their throats clean and wide, if he was here today. Do not assume Jefferson was a spineless fool like the ones who abridge freedom of speech. For those who do not speak English, "eternal hostility against every form of tyranny over the mind of man."

When a legislative body says you cannot speak what is on your mind, no matter what it is, they are a tyrant. One who abridges to living document Jefferson and many of his close friends sacrificed for should pray to their god that ETERNAL HOSTILITY does not mean he is going to be waiting for your ass, in the next life.

You better pray to your god with all of your might there is no afterlife, because this to me, sounds like a curse he made.

He said, I vow even when I die and am in eternity, to punish anyone who attempts to pass a law that hinders a beings freedom of thought and thus freedom of speech. So somehow, Jefferson wrote this letter and it is a curse. It is a curse to anyone who abridges freedom of speech. It is a curse. ETERNAL HOSTILITY. I am certain I did not abridge freedom of speech. I am certain Jefferson will not be angry with me. Perhaps some have assumed Jefferson was just a nice guy. Let's go ahead and shatter that illusion.

As the "silent member" of the Congress, Jefferson, at 33, drafted the Declaration of Independence.

So what this means is if you abridge his Declaration or its companion Constitution you abridge his master creation and if there is an afterlife, you are doomed. It does not matter what you think. You are doomed because this being determined that is what his purpose is.

, "I have sworn upon the altar of God eternal hostility against every form of tyranny over the mind of man." Just to clarify this comment further. This means Jefferson swore to God. This means Jefferson is telling God what he will do if anyone attempts to abridge the document he created when he was 33. Thirty Three. That is particular number and some may understand why.

http://www.whitehouse.gov/about/presidents/thomasjefferson/

"The democracy will cease to exist when you take away from those who are willing to work and give to those who would not."
Thomas Jefferson

This is an interesting quote because it has a deep meaning. A person who has billions and millions of dollars does not work, they invest. They make money off the backs of people who do work. Simply put.

When you take away from the middle class to give to the upper class democracy will cease. Of course that needs clarification. Democracy will cease means, revolution will reign. So this illusion that the upper class holds it all together is an illusion created by the upper class. The one who works just to get by holds it all together the ones who are at the top are simply carpet baggers; they stopped working generations ago.

"When we get piled upon one another in large cities, as in Europe, we shall become as corrupt as Europe."
Thomas Jefferson

This is exactly what has happened. The cities are so full of people they have forgotten they can survive on their own. The people give up freedom to make their own way, and thus surrender to the ones who control the money in the cities. Many understand the cities are where the money is, and also the money is where the control is. We have the internet, cities are outdated.

"The strongest reason for the people to retain the right to keep and bear arms is, as a last resort, to protect themselves against tyranny in government."
Thomas Jefferson

Yes. That is why we have the right to bear arms. Just in case the impossible happens like the legislative branch abridges the freedom of speech. You know like pass a law that says a person cannot say a certain word. That is what is called tyranny in government because government passes a law that says, "You cannot say a word." so it negates freedom of speech, and the constitution says no law can negate the constitution. So then the voters who have the right to bear arms must bear their arms, because they no longer are free. They are in a tyranny and thus must restore freedom. Government cannot pass a law that negates the right to bear arms no matter what. They can pass a law that says a felon cannot bear arms, but they are then the tyrant. The government will pass law that cancels out the constitution that is why they are the tyrant. The government is the money powers; the poor have no influence in the government, they are just trying to survive.

"I cannot live without books."
Thomas Jefferson

I cannot live without freedom to use all words.

Give me absolute freedom of speech or give me absolute death.

Just in case you are one who assumes Jefferson would tolerate a government that abridges freedom of speech, here is comment from the Declaration he drafted at 33.

"that whenever any Form of Government becomes destructive of these ends, it is the Right of the People to alter or to abolish it, and to institute new Government,"

This is a nice way of saying, if a legislative body abridges the constitution hang them and try again. IT IS THE RIGHT OF THE PEOPLE TO ASBOLISH IT. Let's look up the word abolish.

I misunderstood. I will rephrase his comments using the synonyms of the word abolish.

http://dictionary.reference.com/browse/abolish

That whenever any Form of Government becomes destructive of these ends, it is the Right of the People to alter or to SUPRESS it, and to institute new Government,

That whenever any Form of Government becomes destructive of these ends, it is the Right of the People to alter or to NULLIFY it, and to institute new Government,

That whenever any Form of Government becomes destructive of these ends, it is the Right of the People to alter or to CANCEL it, and to institute new Government,

That whenever any Form of Government becomes destructive of these ends, it is the Right of the People to alter or to ANNIHILATE it, and to institute new Government,

That whenever any Form of Government becomes destructive of these ends, it is the Right of the People to alter or to OBLITERATE it, and to institute new Government,

That whenever any Form of Government becomes destructive of these ends, it is the Right of the People to alter or to EXTREMINATE it, and to institute new Government,

That whenever any Form of Government becomes destructive of these ends, it is the Right of the People to alter or to DO AWAY COMPLETELY WITH it, and to institute new Government,

suppress, nullify, cancel; annihilate, obliterate, extinguish; exterminate, extirpate, eliminate. Abolish, eradicate, stamp out mean to do away completely with something.

So the reality is, Jefferson was a terrorist according the terroristic threat law because he said, in the Declaration of Independence, EXTERMINATE the government if it abridges the constitution. Of course ANNIHILATE would also work in that last sentence. So what he is really saying is: The government meaning the branches are expendable. He is saying it is the right of the people as in WE THE PEOPLE, to exterminate any government that abridges freedom of speech.

What this means is, if any of these bodies pass a law that says anything near the effect of "You cannot say certain words." People in the land of the free have a right to exterminate them with their guns.

So the last thing the government ever wants to do, is go around showing off the declaration of independence on their web site, because a being who wakes up and become subconscious dominate will understand exactly what it is saying and will write books about what it really means, and in turn that government will in fact have hung itself. I do not fear tyrannical governments according to Jefferson's declaration of Independence; WE THE POEPLE have the right to abolish, exterminate, eliminate , annihilate them off the face of the earth. If you do not agree with that, it proves you are the tyrant. If you are a part of the government that abridged the freedom of speech, a person in the land of the free has just declared you a tyrant who abridged the constitution, and has determined you will be abolished or altered so that WE the PEOPLE can start a new government and try again.

In case you do not speak English I will go into further details.

"Life, Liberty and the pursuit of Happiness. — That to secure these rights, Governments are instituted among Men, deriving their just powers from the consent of the governed, — That whenever any Form of Government becomes destructive of these ends, it is the Right of the People to alter or to abolish it, and to institute new Government,"

LIBERTY of speech is the same as FREEDOM of speech.

"whenever any Form of Government becomes destructive of these ends, it is the Right of the People to alter or to abolish it, and to institute new Government,"

So the government is not freedom. The government is not free. The government itself is the tyrant and has to be altered or abolished " to institute new Government" from time to time. So the whole concept of a government for the people and by the people really means a government exists at the whims of the people. The people giveth and the people taketh away. So the whole idea that the government is in charge is an illusion, perpetuated by the government. When the government is abolish for abridging the constitution all the laws it has passed are nullified and void. The whole process starts over. The whole nation starts over with the Declaration of Independence and The Constitution, and we try again.

When in the Course of human events it becomes necessary for one people(WE THE PEOPLE) to dissolve the(GOVERNMENT) political bands which have connected them with another and to assume among the powers of the earth, the separate and equal station to which the Laws of Nature and of Nature's God entitle them, a decent respect to the opinions of mankind requires that they should declare the causes which impel them to the (REVOLUTION AGINST THE TYRANT, THE GOVERNMENT)separation.

I will translate this swiftly for those who do not speak English.

Sometimes the government assumes it is in control of the people and will create laws that will rob the people of their liberty such as liberty or freedom of speech, and in that course of human events, WE the ONE PEOPLE, will DISSOLVE that POLICTIAL BAND and SEPARATE from it and try again.

I hang myself from sentence to sentence.

Now the only way the government can save itself at this stage of the game since, one being, in relation to WE THE PEOPLE has determined the GOVERNEMNET a tyrant because it abridged the constitution, is for the government to swiftly "alter". "it is the Right of the People to alter or to abolish it" This means the government must swiftly restore the freedom of speech to its previous state before it was abridged or face "abolishment". The synonym for abolish is exterminate or annihilate, in case you misunderstand the meaning of that word.

I am blessed with knowledge and cursed with understanding.

When I get warmed up I will give you a call.

You now wish I died.

The reality is, ones who go pure subconscious dominate are likely to be killed swiftly because they have no fear and they understand everything clearly. I submit I am insane. I submit I am delusional. I submit I had an accident and am totally insane as a result. I submit I know nothing and I never will know anything. I submit I am wrong about everything I ever say. I submit I have more faith in Freedom of Speech than any being in the universe at this moment. I submit I fear nothing. I submit I sprained my left hand in writing those last comments about Jefferson and I am feeling discomfort at this moment so I will rest my hands. I understand my sensation of touch is altered so perhaps I have been typing too hard and have not been mindfully aware of it and thus sprained my hand.6:07:57 AM

I swear upon the altar of God ETERNAL hostility against every form of tyranny over the mind of man. Someone always understands my words .6:18:56 AM

Everything is perfect. A treasure is appreciated often after it is buried.6:49:47 AM

Absolute freedom of speech is the minds only way to detect absolute physical tyranny.

I am mindful I am not inciting the future I am telling it. I have enough heightened awareness at this stage to understand it is coming. It is not important I explain how I know this "abolishment" is coming. You are unable to stop it and I am unable to stop it. I would not be aware of it, if anyone was able to stop it. 5:41:06 PM

I am going to make sure I hang myself with this train of thought.

I will use the Llama as an example. You go ahead and throw in whatever words you want for the ones I use, but I will be using subconscious dominate in this example. Why does China consider him a threat? Simple subconscious dominate mind is all about freedom of thought and thus freedom to speak because the mindset is that of a child who just got a shiny new bike and that child will ride around the block just to show others and also to be amazed at the wonder they have found. A talking Buddha is one who has found a great truth and does nothing but speak about it for the rest of their life.

Some other figures in American history are Jefferson and Washington. Some other figures are Martin Luther King Jr. and Malcolm X and John F Kennedy and his brother Bobby. His brother hung around John and thus also become subconscious dominate, and the reason I understand John became subconscious dominate is because he faced certain death in World War 2 in his combat mishap. I am certain from reading the details of his combat incident he was convinced he was dead yet he survived and became very wise. So John went on to change the world with his words and the power structure made sure he kept his mouth shut. Ones may suggest it was simply the actions of a confused being. That is insanity.

It is always the same beings who end these beings lives. The power mongers the money masters own everyone. They have extreme influence. They can dangle money in front of many and persuade them to do their bidding.

You know who they are. I know who they are, but that does not even matter because they have already passed enough laws to ensure anyone who attempt to stop them with legal means will be deemed a terrorist and locked up or killed. They killed the Kennedy's. They killed King. They killed Malcolm. They kill any threat to their power because their power is their god. China would kill the Llama in the blink of an eye. These beings who are always seen escorting the Llama, they are bodyguards and nothing more. All of these great beings understood it was going to happen. Some are great but they never reach the level that the great of the great reach. The great of the greats are killed because they pose a threat to the only thing that holds power, the money powers. There is no logical reason to wait for them to make a mistake to take action against them. Look around you, that is all the proof you need. Their trial has taken place and they have been found guilty, all that is left is to carry out the sentence. One is simply unable to play by the rules, because the power elite created the rules to ensure they will be untouched if anyone plays by the rules. All is fair when one determines they are in bondage. Morals are for ones who have not understood they are slaves.

The power elite are simply a monarchy; they pass the power down from one generation to the next; their wealth is their edict. It does not matter who in the government suggests they found no foul play in the deaths of some of these beings, because the government is in on the scam. The courts are in on the scam. The elected are in on the scam. They are all under the control of the power elites. They are all in their pocket. From judges, to the elected officials.

I perceive Ron Paul is not in anyone's pocket and that is why they suggest he is an outcast and that is why he will never get elected into meaningful power because he is not willing to be bought out. Ron Paul is not willing to give up his liberty for a little security. They suggest he is a constitutionalist as if the word constitutionalist is an evil thing to be.

If you are not a constitutionalist, you are a god dam traitor and tyrant. If you doubt that, contact me and I will convince you, you have no right to breathe my air. The entire government is one huge puppet show, and the sheep perceive it is truth and honesty. The sheep can no longer tell they are in pen, so they are blind to the fact there is only one way to escape. The sheep would rather live in hell than be at risk for freedom. Of course I will be slaughtered when they catch wind of these books, but the books will remain. They are unable to burn the books. Someone will ensure the books will remain. Every time a being reads the books they will understand the message of the books, and that is a strategy that the power elite cannot stand against. So I write as fast as I can because every time I register a book in the Library of Congress I seal the fate of the power mongers. I exterminate them every time I publish a book and so I publish them in psychology because they will not guess to read anything in that section until after the noose is securely around their necks.

I will type until I cannot type, but I am not fearful of what they will do me because I already understand my fate is sealed. I beg God to make these understandings be wrong and he laughs at my foolish doubt of my abilities. He says "Why do you doubt what you understand?" And my teeth gnash in anguish because I understand life is not fair. I will go play the video game since it will not kill me for having thoughts.

Jesus was slaughtered for the same reason Kennedy, and King and X were slaughtered, they were a threat to the power elite and the power elite are the money elite. These power mongers are beyond the law. These power mongers are beyond justice. They own everything. One cannot fight them with legal means because they own the legal means. It is a little bit past the point of "Let's vote on it and pray about it." If you want to be a slave that is fine, but do not shoot off your mouth about how free you are, because you only incite my rage further with your delusional understandings. 6:49:37 PM

"Don't talk about what you have done or what you are going to do."
Thomas Jefferson

Do not tell me what you think you should do, and do not tell me what you think you are going to do, because you are not anything but a slave and a coward to your fear of a little pain.

I am fully aware the militia understand I do not to speak about them. I am fully aware the militia is all but underground at this point. One might suggest they are cleaning their guns in anticipation of a battle cry. Be mindful when it is all over we will be able to add another chapter to the history books about the struggle for freedom. We just are in need of a new chapter in our history that will give the future generations something interesting to read and understand. It is all a part of the plan, it is not evil or an abomination, it is required to keep Lady Liberty in working order.

Lady Liberty is more important than you and I are. That is just the way it is. Lady Liberty is not fair but her cause is righteous. You cannot vote your way out of tyranny, you can only vote your way into tyranny. I am not a politician. I had an accident and went subconscious dominate and subconscious dominate means I understand what freedom is. Conscious emotional aspect is isolation, embarrassment, shame, shyness. It is embarrassed and ashamed by its own thoughts. Subconscious is proud of its thoughts. Subconscious is proud it has the ability to think. Subconscious is proud it has been given the ability to speak its mind about thoughts it perceives are of value. I mindfully am free so whatever the isolated, shameful, abominations do to me, I will still die free. When they butcher me, it will not mean they have control over me, so let them butcher me harshly, so you will not forget me.7:19:50 PM

If a being says, "If you do not have money you will not have food and or shelter and you will starve to death and die from the elements." That being controls you with fear. Money is not money at all. It is a tool used to control people. Money is a loaded gun put to your head, to make you conform. You will not starve to death without money they have simply brainwashed you to the point you believe you will. You are a human being, you adapted to situations much harsher than the current worldly situations. We are here today, because early man laughed when mother nature said, "You will starve to death and have no shelter and you will not be able to adapt to that." So there are beings that encourage money because they derive their control from the fact money is the root of everything. Money is the root of food, so money is the gun that keeps everyone in step.

5/17/2009 1:21:34 AM Once a being suggested to me they were wise. I asked them how many suicide attempts they failed at to become wise. They then responded by saying only a complete fool would fail at suicide. And then I explained to them, they are truly wise, and they never spoke to me again.

One great truth I understand about the suicidal is they are waking up. A mother who loses a child and becomes suicidal is not sick, she is waking up and getting in touch with her subconscious aspect, and this is only possible through misery. A suicidal person is not looking for attention they are waking up and in touch with their subconscious aspect and the understandings are very harsh. They do not want to kill their self for others attention, they want to kill their self because they are aware they are in an insane asylum called "norms of society". To the subconscious aspect that is all about freedom of thought "norms of society" is like saying "prison of rules and hell". I recall when I was in third grade, I stayed after school because my mother was a teacher. I recall going to the play ground and the children who stay after school determined I was not worthy to hang around them. I was judged by my peers. So every day after school I no longer attempted to speak with those children. I went to each classroom and stole rubber bands and paperclips and went around the school and killed every lizard I could find. And then I had a stick and stuck it through their ear holes and put on the stick. And I carried that around with me and when the kids saw it, they yelled that I was mean and cruel. I understand now fully my subconscious understood that was those children who judged me on that stick. Every day I went out and filled that stick with the ones who judged me and harmed me with their words. I was in third grade. Now you may be thinking I am mean and evil and a loser because I did that. You are right. You are right. That is why I tried to kill myself 30 times. Because you keep opening your mouth, because you perceive you understand anything about anything, when in reality you understand everything about nothing.

You will never understand the definition of compassion, love, humility, wisdom or understanding. The only words you have mastered with all of your efforts is judgment, hate, scorn, wrath, sloth, greed, vengeance, envy, spite, lust, selfishness and the most important one of all to you, evil.

The only beings in this world I respect are the ones who are depressed and suicidal, because I understand they are the only ones that understand reality. The ones you suggest are outcasts are the ones who I respect because suicide is the only certain way to get the hell away from you. Of course that is extremely out of context. Some are suicidal in their quest for money. Some are in a suicidal quest for fame. Some are in a suicidal quest for control. Some are in a suicidal quest to be accepted. Some are in a suicidal quest to look physically acceptable. Some are in a suicidal quest to feel important. You will all kill yourself to satisfy these foolish aims because you have given up on the only thing that matters your inner worth, which is subconscious aspect.

I am still early into this accident so I have my signals crossed. I still perceive it harms me when I see people kill their self over money and over foolish wars and foolish stupidity. I am not yet at a stage of understanding, watching all of you kill yourself with too much food and money and drugs and foolishness actually pleases me. I still perceive those things harm me because I am not yet at a state of understanding my subconscious is pleased to watch you all kill yourselves into infinity. You kill your children by judging them and so you kill your future. So I am mindful to hide my little stupid books in weird places and with weird titles so no being will ever buy one, because I prefer to watch you all hang yourselves.

I am pleased watching the world kill itself. It gives me great humility to be aware everyone else is killing their self just as I was. The only difference is, I was not ashamed enough to admit it. You should avoid assuming I envy any being in the history of mankind for their wisdom, because I fully understand they wish they were me, and I am pleased I am not them. I am pleased if that comment makes you very angry and very judgmental of me. I am pleased if you go out and yell how arrogant I am, and how hateful and self centered I am for saying that comment. I am pleased if that comment reaches your subconscious and your subconscious cannot stand one more moment of life. I am pleased if you have a huge bottle of pills in your grasp and do not have the intelligent aspect of your mind dominate. I am pleased if you hate me with all of your heart, because I understand that is your subconscious aspect letting you know, "You will never be like this being, so do not upset him, because if you do, he will annihilate you mentally, and you will never recover."

I am pleased if you understand I am an infinitely vengeful spirit and your suggestions that I should have mercy and compassion fall on dead ears. I am pleased if you are pleased with your handy work. I was given no quarter, so do not expect any. Do not assume I like you. I seek vengeance because vengeance is mine. I will bring down your house with a single wave because it is built on the sand of your ignorance and your "norms" of insanity. I convince the wise; they never will be wise, and the sane; they never will be sane. Your understanding is relative to your ignorance. I submit I am simply not at the level of understanding, that when I cry after reading about the insane events caused by the norms of society, they are not tears of anguish, they are tears of vengeance. The vengeance in my words is infinitely less than the vengeance in my eyes.2:21:44 AM

The harmony is at the extremes.

Anyone can let go of things they hate; only the wise can let go of things they love when they do not have to. Suicidal people do not have to kill their self and let go but they do or attempt to. That is a huge mental feat.

Thoughts do not need your approval; words do not require your acceptance.

Sometimes one has to poke out their eyes to get the picture.

The blind feel things the ones with sight overlook.

On average I feel average.

On average I feel love but in general I feel rage; that's my general average so I am no average general, generally speaking on average.

Subconscious says to me "You are killing yourself by trying so hard." And I say "It is killing me attempting to understand that I do not have to try."

I tried so hard to fight the norms for 40 years, and then in one second I realized, that was fitting in.

Ignorance offers everything clarity does not; namely peace of mind.

Everyone has their opinion about what humans are, and the great truth is they are all wrong.

I wrote this song about 3 years before the accident. I am aware this song was a prediction of how I am now, but at the time I perceived I was just saying what was on my mind. The middle part of the song says "I've gone on to another world; gone on to see other places. I've gone on very calculated; gone on to see spaces." That is exactly what has happened, but perhaps only I will ever understand what that really means.

http://www.youtube.com/watch?v=hhuFy4eR0hw - Calculated

"I've lost too much to say, I've lost the map to your treasure, I lost it on the way.

I've lost to much this way I cannot hear your words goodbye I cannot hear those spirits cry.

I've lost you all the way I cannot hear your helpless cries, I cannot tell my hurtful lies.

I lost too much to gain by telling all my stories right. The darkness is the light.

I've gone on to another world; gone on to see other places. I've gone on very calculated; gone on to see spaces.

I've left too much to say, I couldn't find your places I've lost them on the way

I found my hate was more than all the world could handle; all the world could endure.

I've gone on to another world; gone on to see other places. I've gone on very calculated; gone on to see spaces.

Every ounce of gold you filled. Every ounce of blood you spilled. Every ounce of my blood. Every ounce of my blood.

I've gone on to another world; gone on to see other places. I've gone on very calculated; gone on to see spaces."

I am aware the last lines sound somewhat messiah like, but in reality I was simply letting everyone know I cut my wrists because I did not have money(gold).

One may perceive I wrote this song recently but the reality is, I was in the depths of depression when I write this song. The last suicide attempt was about 2.5 years after this and I gave up on music as an outlet about 1.5 years before the last attempt. So I was at a very dark place where I did not even do the only thing that keep me viable, which was make music to attempt to keep my thoughts in perspective.

So if you want to know where I am at. I am in another world, and no matter how you want to interpret that, it makes absolutely no difference, and it never will.

I remember all the things I want to forget and remember all the things I desperately want to forget.

If you get angry about the things I write in my books, you need to keep in mind there are wise beings in this world that understand what I am saying, and your anger proves you are not one of them.

Women give birth to males, and once in a while even associate with them.

If you do not understand the man upstairs is subconscious then you are under the influence of the man downstairs.

Women are depicted as angels in religions, in relation to angels of mercy.

Only a vile man would disrespect a woman; they are the reason you are here.

Women who give birth to males usually have no choice in the matter.

Women have broken my heart, but they have never insulted me without provocation.

Females are what nature intended, males are proof of that.

Women who tolerate me are beyond my understanding.

Worship service is a place for human beings to go, to verbally insult each other, topped off with a short sermon about the importance of not doing so; many cannot wait for the sermon to get over with so they can get back to the worship.

Worship service is a great place to plan your next attack.

Worship service is traditionally a target rich environment.

Atheists' are religious people who are reloading.

Religious People: masters at casting judgment stones that often miss.

Bragging about your religion is as difficult as bragging about your intelligence; people want to see proof.

I am feeling rather like a jokester at this moment 5:05:52 AM. Here is my logic line about this book.

Go back and edit everything to make sure it is all proper.

Take out anything that may upset people.

Take back many angry things I have said.

Make sure people will like your book.

Make sure people will accept you.

Then my other logic kicks in.

Remember you do not write books to please people.

Remember you do not wish to please anyone ever, no matter who they are.

Do not dare touch one word you have written because you fear nothing.

These books are your only way to get your vengeance.

You are a loser if you edit one single sentence to please others.

Take a guess which logic line I ended up following.

The reality is, the moment I pay the publisher to publish my books, my subconscious goes into this hyper dominate mode and says "Do not edit one single sentence just cram it all together and that way, no one will ever be able to figure out what your main point is, and they will give up on reading your books."

People can go on and on into infinity about how I should not hold a grudge. The truth is, I am a grudge. My mind is convinced what I did to myself is because of the world or the society or you said to me. My only outlet is words. My subconscious has convinced me words are my only weapon of vengeance. It does not matter if you do not believe that is mentally healthy. It is a little late for you to give me advice about anything ever, into infinity. Perhaps you should punch that swiftly into your calculator of judgment and see what comes up. Save your fear tactics for your children, they do not work on me.5:16:41 AM

A message to someone about something.

I had a near death experience and lost my sense of time.

I am not complaining just giving you a bit of background information.

I was listening to one of your songs while I was writing and I detect much wisdom in your lyrics so I wrote a few "wise" sayings in my fourth book, and they are because I was translating the wisdom i heard in your songs. So I am obligated to thank you for your efforts.

During the writing of my current book, I was in a chat room and someone with the handle Sherylcrow came in and I suggested I find her message wise. They mentioned some of your lyrics and i do not recall what they were now(memory issues) but i saw wisdom in them also, so i translated them into "wise" sayings in my fifth book. And i am curious if you are consciously aware, that your message is not only getting out, but you are literally assisting me in writing my infinite books?

I apologize if I sound out there. I try my hardest to do the best I can based on my situation. I would like to send you my books in PDF format as a gift of appreciation for your efforts if you would allow it. Even I have moments of clarity.

"Women who tolerate me are beyond my understanding"

Book 5

 p.s. I will be copying this message into my fifth book that will be published at the end of this month just in case you do not receive this message on your site. I am writing infinite books and I need as much filler as possible.

6:06:17 AM

I am running out of crap to write about so I will see how dumb founded I can get from the oldest religious text known to mankind.

"The oldest religious texts are Egyptian (from approx. 4,600 to 5,100

years ago).

"The Pyramid Texts were a collection of Egyptian mortuary prayers,

hymns, and spells intended to protect a dead king or queen and ensure

life and sustenance in the hereafter. The texts, inscribed on the

walls of the inner chambers of the pyramids [from c. 2686-c. 2160

BC]., are found at Saqqarah in several 5th- and 6th-dynasty pyramids,

of which that of Unas, last king of the 5th dynasty, is the earliest

known. The texts constitute the oldest surviving body of Egyptian

religious and funerary writings available to modern scholars."

answers.google.com

These texts are very out of context. So I will just look at the first couple lines.

2a. To say by Nut, the great, who is within the lower mansion: This is (my) son, N., (my) beloved,

I assume Nut is the subconscious aspect since they suggest he is in the lower mansion, which is perhaps a nice way of saying, subconscious is veiled. Then is says Nut is my son my beloved. So that would suggest subconscious is the "better" aspect of the mind, although it is in the lower mansion, or veiled.

"Geb was the son of Shu and Tefnut and the brother and husband of Nut. Through Nut he had four children, Osiris, Isis, Seth and Nephthys.Geb was the god of the earth. Even so, Geb guided the dead to heaven and he gave them meat and drink" Egyptianmyths.com.

Geb was god of the earth this is in direction relation to physical focus or worldly focus. Husband and brother of Nut. So conscious emotional aspect could be looked at as the brother and husband of subconscious aspect. I think the point here is, they are relations or associated with each other. Geb guided the dead to heaven. So Conscious emotional aspect lead to heaven or subconscious aspect. Gave them meat and drink may suggest hunger and thirst, and hunger and thirst are symptom of emotions and thus desires and cravings. None of the main religious people in early history had the words subconscious and conscious words to use. Of course that is out of context because it is still unknown what mind is or what thought is.

2b. (my) eldest (son), (who is) upon the throne of Geb, with whom he has been satisfied,

It says in 2a Nut is the beloved son, eldest son who is upon the throne of Geb. This is in relation to the story of Jacob and Esau.

"The Bible depicts Esau as a hunter who prefers the outdoor life, qualities that distinguished him from his brother, who was a shy or simple man, depending on the translation of the Hebrew word "Tam" (which also means "relatively perfect man"). According to the Bible, Esau is the ancestor of the Edomites.[1] In the Book of Genesis, Esau is frequently shown being supplanted by his younger twin Jacob (Israel)."

Esau preferred "OUTDOOR" pleasures, which is the same as worldly pleasures. That is the domain of the conscious emotional aspect, much less cerebral and much more physical based. So 2a suggest Nut is my beloved, and in the story of Jacob and Esau, Jacob is the beloved. Jacob was shy, but in reality Jacob was meek, in relation to how David was meek compared to Goliath. Goliath was arrogant and haughty and "looked" strong. So, Nut is subconscious aspect, Geb is conscious aspect. Jacob is subconscious aspect. Esau is conscious aspect. David is subconscious aspect Goliath is conscious aspect. In the story of Jacob and Esau, Esau uses trickery to gain advantage over Jacob. So Esau was jealous of Jacob and used trickery to gain advantage, which is a symptom of greed. So Jealousy or envy and greed are both emotions, which are both symptoms of the weaker conscious aspect of the mind. I recall I have discussed this concept of "feeling hungry" being a symptom of emotions or being a symptom one is conscious dominate.

"Genesis 25:29-34 shows him willingly selling his birthright to Jacob[1] in exchange for a "mess of pottage" (meal of lentils)."WIKIPEDIA.COM

This comment is what is known today as "selling out". Esau sold out for food. Esau sold out for food because he was hungry, and thus proves he had hunger.

One can relate this to many who do some perhaps strange things in life because they are "hungry" or crave. Some sell out their health by over eating because they crave to eat because they mentally experience far too much hunger.

Some sell out in other ways, some crave money, some crave drugs, some crave control. The cravings are the attachments caused by far too many emotions and thus prove one has emotional conscious aspect of the mind, and also a strong sense of time as a result.

The mind itself when it has too many emotions suggests one has to eat often. The mind itself, when one has greatly reduced emotions never mentions one has to eat. So hunger is in the mind.

Some comments in another religious text suggest this hunger concept. A being fed the multitudes with some fish. In this scenario, fish represented understanding. Understanding was created from words of wisdom. So with a few choice words this being feed the hungry multitudes with understanding, and the multitudes all were filled. The multitudes hunger for understanding was satisfied with a few choice words spoke by that being. Hunger for understanding is a cerebral craving not a physical or emotional craving. "Eating" too much understanding will not make one physically overweight and will not make one have high blood pressure. I submit everything I just spoke about is wrong and I submit I will never know anything and all I will ever understand is nothing.4:52:16 PM

5/18/2009 6:35:37 AM

I have been up all night reading over what I typed so far and it all looks "so so" to me. I actually understood some of it. I detect I am pondering silence. Translated, I am pondering never writing again and just going into hibernation. I am far too attached to writing and I am pondering letting it go. Granted I am sloppy and I perhaps will wake up after sleep and come to new understandings.6:47:10 AM

5/18/2009 7:16:08 AM

I am mentally burning out swiftly. I am unable to sleep without many thoughts rushing in my mind and suggesting I need to go write things. My body is suffering and I am able to tell that when I press on my hands and arms. Other than that they feel "so so". I am sloppy and having major mental doubts about everything. I did some things today only a total loser would do and I gnash my teeth because I am aware that is my nature. I understand I am the definition of "my own worst enemy". You do not have to remind me of what I am fully aware of.

"A man can be destroyed but not defeated."
Ernest Hemingway

A man adapts when defeated and seldom adapts when victorious; the destroyed may rise to glory.

Destruction may lead to an understanding to rebuild.

Absolute darkness may lead to adaptations into light.

Humiliation is a mental treasure for ones with fortitude.

Humans adapt to destruction swiftly.

Some of the wisest beings paid a harsh physical price but I am certain they did not flinch.

Ones purpose is to be willing to go where ever life leads them.

"A man's got to take a lot of punishment to write a really funny book."
Ernest Hemingway

Out of the depths of mental suffering comes the wisdom of the ages.

Letting go is not as harsh as believing you should not.

I feel harmed by this beings quotes because I understand too much about the origin of his understandings.

"About morals, I know only that what is moral is what you feel good after and what is immoral is what you feel bad after.
"
Ernest Hemingway

Those without morals trust their intuition to guide them.

What makes you feel good will eventually make you feel guilt.

I just realized only the greatest loser in the history of the universe would attempt to write books explaining why one should avoid all emotions. Then I am calmed by that understanding that is simply my purpose. I understand I explain one should avoid all emotions in the off chance one being considers that and becomes slightly less emotional. My fingers are not waiting for results

"All things truly wicked start from innocence."
Ernest Hemingway.

 Craving and desires can lead some interesting nightmares.

I just got that one.

"Always do sober what you said you'd do drunk. That will teach you to keep your mouth shut."
Ernest Hemingway

Being irresponsible can lead to understandings responsible people will never know.

This is in relation to ones with conscious or left brain aspect perceives ones with extreme right brain dominate to be drunk with the words they speak. You may perceive some things I say are the talk of a crazy person but in reality I am just extreme right brain dominate. If you are left brain dominate you should perceive what I write is insanity because I perceive what you do and say is also insanity. That is the disconnect, I am at one extreme and your are at another extreme. So from our perspectives we both look insane to each other. I perceive it is insane to abridge freedom of speech now, I perceive it is insane to attack beings in another land when we have plenty of wise beings who can sit down and work things out verbally and not sacrifice our offspring. I honesty perceive war and killing others for any reason is complete insanity. If you are left brain dominate you will say "There are reasons we have to kill some people." And from my perspective only a completely insane person would ever suggest that. I am not saying you are wrong to perceive some people need to be killed I am saying from my perspective if you think that, you are god dam insane beyond understanding. Words can often get one out of physical harm. Words cannot always get one out of physical harm or we could just talk our way out of dying. So words are not the solution to death but at times they can delay it. Weapons and wars cannot delay death they only ensure death. I am unable to say if physically killing people is factually wrong. I am only able to say from my perspective since the accident it is not an option. I am biased because I tried to kill myself an gave it one hell of an attempt my last try, and now I just don't care about dying or death. I mentally just don't care. If death didn't take me after that last attempt well them maybe death is not so scary after all. Maybe I scared death and so I no longer am scared by death. Maybe I scared death to death.

"An intelligent man is sometimes forced to be drunk to spend time with his fools."
Ernest Hemingway

Poison mushrooms take the edge off of societies norms.

I am wise enough to avoid you and foolish enough to believe I am safe.

5/18/2009 3:40:40 PM

I am now at a stage in the progression I am pondering silence. Subconscious has talked itself out. I am aware I have been influenced by words the words of others.

The least important person in the world is the most important one to understand.

All changes are opportunities; simple changes may lead to opportunities for greater change.

All changes are opportunities; simple changes may lead to questioning greater change.

Everyone knows what they should do; few understand how to go about it strategically.

Life is not concerned with your knowledge of it but is humbled by your understanding of that.

The Greatest Lion of the pack must eventually face its own isolation.

I may never buy your argument but I would consider it.

Yesterday I attempted to eat solid food and I had no desire to eat more than a few bites so I am mindful to purchase some weight gain nutrient drinks. I understand my cravings and desires are perhaps nearly gone now. My ability to taste is gone. Once a well is dry it longs for the rain. I sense the liquid in my mouth but my senses are unable to register even its wetness.

Even the greatest lion must face its eventual isolation from his pride.

I am aware my mental state at this time is what the story about those who were turned to salt is in relation to and what the story of medusa turning ones into stone is about. Medusa is fear or terror and sometimes when one faces the greatest fear, death, it eventually turns them mindfully to stone. I would call it a mindful catatonic state of nothingness. No physical attachments or acknowledgement of physical ideals. I perceive I am still in the physical realm but I am convinced that is just the last vestige of my hallucinations.

I alternate meaning of an obvious observation is often the wisdom of it.

All that is happening in life is various degree's of tolerance and absolute tolerance is a pipedream I could never tolerate.

"My religion is very simple. My religion is kindness."
Dalai Lama

Kindly turn yourself into the Chinese so I that I might understand your religion in not very simply fear.

One should be cautious about what they say in public because someone might understand their psychosis.

A cult following a misdirected fool is an ego trip that results in deep wounds called followers.

Some are scared by what eats them and some scare what they eat.

A responsible listener is one who questions what they hear.

5/19/2009 1:30:59 AM

I am weird but I understand something I have pondered and I am aware if you read this next part you will not understand it so just skip it because you will only harm yourself.

I attempted to off myself. In not doing it properly I only went half way or I did not go the full measure. So in that sense I lost my fear of death because I mindfully accepted death.

In that sense I defeated death but that is a misunderstanding. I certainly did not let go of my fear of death and understand everything clearly, in reality I became death, I am death. I am not a spirit in the afterworld, I am death itself.

Please be mindful I did it accidentally, I just wanted to check out, and somehow this freak accident happened and somehow it was able to use me as some sort of host. I assure you I am not intelligent. I assure you I did not understand what I understand now before the accident. So this is a great pondering situation because I am uncertain what death is.

Some monks suggest this is the afterlife so that would make sense. Some suggest this is real life so then my theory would make sense. I am uncertain, but I know one thing, I certainly did not know all the stuff I write about before the accident. I did not go to school and read books. I pick verbal fights with anyone I see. I fear nothing and death is a joke to me. So I see people who run around fearful of everything and I understand they only fear one thing, death. So I just toy with them because they are unable to grasp they are mine no matter what they do or what they say or what they want. They are mine in the end. They will all come to knock on my door in the end and my door will be open unto them.

I understand why I am not physically violent. There is certainly no point to be physically violent.

One can fight with all of their physical might or one can lay in a coma, but both will be paying me a visit with the same terror in their eyes.

Perhaps I just threw wrench in everything you thought you knew didn't I. I guess you better go tell all of your friends how crazy I am. I understand one thing about your ways, you talk a good game but you don't put up much a fight when you look in my eyes.

I would say deer in the headlights would be a good description. I will go play my video game because at least it does not bore me to life.

Now you understand one great truth and you are unable to believe it. You are probably concerned for my safety. I am certain you should be infinitely more concerned about your own log of safety at this stage. Man can defeat many certainties but will never defeat the greatest certainty. 1:49:54 AM

I will sum things up for ones who are unable to speak English.

126

Beings that are terminally ill make peace with god and the only god is death. Death is lord over all living things large and small. All living things return to god, which is death. You already understand that but your mind is not functioning well enough to grasp that reality. I am not going to hold your hand like the ones who assume you cannot handle truth. I at least have the fortitude to tell you the truth and let the chips fall where they may. I am not going to judge your ability to handle a great truth because I do not care if you can handle a great truth. You are going to understand the truth whether you want to or not.2:14:28 AM

So now you can start barking like a little dog who has detected an unknown presence.

I am quite certain that will not assist you in escaping a great certainty.

I will now explain the human mind.

CA = Conscious aspect

Conscious emotional aspect

Fear, caution, safety, embarrassment, shame, good, evil, hate, love, isolation

Sense of time, taste, physical sensations

Physical reactions to thoughts

SA = Subconscious aspect

Subconscious Machine aspect

Fearlessness, experimentation, ruthlessness, freedom

Diminished sense of time, Diminished physical sensations

Cerebral Reactions to Thoughts

The norms of society suggest one should be in harmony mentally, a bit CA and SA. That is why society in general is a nightmare. That is why humanity in general is a nightmare. That is why people are unpredictable threats to their self and everyone around them. They come to conclusions from the fearless, ruthless aspect of SA and act it out on the physical reaction aspect caused by CA.

One with the harmony aspect of SA and CA comes up with ideas formed by the SA aspect and then they perform it using the CA aspect. They get insulted by a word or deed because of the CA aspect, then they hear the SA aspect and it says, "Don't take that crap from anyone", then they go back to the CA aspect and it says, "Load your guns and start shooting everyone you think is your enemy."

Rev 3:16 So then because thou art lukewarm , and neither cold nor hot, I will spue thee out of my mouth.

For those who cannot speak English. Hot is extreme CA, as in a hot head. Someone who goes around a physically harms people. At the maximum extreme of CA one is usually an emotional wreck and they pretty much end up physically harming their self, so in reality they are not too much of a threat. They eventually kill their self in one way or another.

 Then we have Cold, they are extreme SA, they are physically harmless because they are so cerebral. They are not a physical harm to their self or to others. They are focused on fighting the battle within, or fighting their battles with words.

Then we have the worst of them all, the lukewarm. They are smart enough to understand a little using the SA and dangerous enough to act it out using the CA. They do things like kill many people in the name of some insane cause they invented in their mind. They come up with some great psychological drugs and then prescribe it to all the kids. They appear at times to be reasonable because they have some SA comments but they always end up acting those out though on the CA level or physical level. So they are the most dangerous of all. They kill and harm and destroy everything in their physical path and then have the balls to say," I did the right thing", or "I didn't do that, you're putting words in my mouth." Or my favorite "We fought the good fight."

They have enough brain function to physically and mentally slaughter children and then are able to explain how it is the proper righteous thing to do. That is why they are lukewarm. The norms are insufferable and since they are the majority, they will bring everyone down with them and then tell them; "It was for the good of mankind." The norms of society are just perfect. One does not ever have to explain to me how righteous the norms of society are, I assure you of that. The norms of society do the best they can based on the fact they are butchers with morals. Do not assume I care. I am just visiting until I get the fire warmed up. Is there anybody out there?

Ignore everything I have written in the book including this sentence.

He said he died for your sins. He was saying, the norms of society made me an outcast and that hurt my feelings and that is why I wanted to die or suicide. But somehow he only did it half way. He did not go the full measure. So he defeated death. And his mind opened up and he became very wise. And he explained that one's should be compassionate and love each other and help each other, because he certainly was unable to, because the ones he was talking to are the ones that made him an outcast to begin with.

So he certainly has a seat at his table for the norms of society, and he explained they are going to number like the grains of sand in the sea. So perhaps in time ones will understand when a person is put in a situation they end up dying a painful death even if it is self inflicted, they tend to hold something that is called a grudge. And it is not really important what you think about anything after that one's has died and made up their mind to seek vengeance.

You should just pray to god that I just unlocked my subconscious. There are some I will certainly pass over, but as far as the norms of society who suggested I was not an important being because I did not have enough money, and I was not an important being because I did not pass all their tests, I have decided they are mine and mine alone. My decisions are final. One might consider a person who is judged unjustly and ends up being lynched and just before they hang them, that being says;"I will return and curse you all." That's essentially what we are talking about here.

There is some major problems with all of this and some major clarifications. I certainly would like to just say, I had a great life and then I played a video game to an extreme and went subconscious dominate. That is perhaps what happened and now I am subconscious dominate all of my deep seeded attempts to take my life are at the forefront of my mind and they keep working their self into my books. I have faith that is what is happening. This is one important aspect of subconscious. It does not forget anything. It holds grudges. It remembers everything and every word and every insult and ever harsh comment. So this is perhaps an important lesson to be learned. One simply cannot take back a harsh word. I do not follow my own advice because my subconscious will not allow me to speak kindly in my books.

My subconscious has convinced me, my 15 plus years of extreme depression is a direct result of me being a shy person in general and that mixed with beings insults and also being convinced I was an outcast by the norms of society is perhaps why I am unable to subscribe to compassion at this time. I am aware this subconscious aspect is very convincing and this is exactly why "stay on the fence" is important.

I am rather poor at staying on the fence about things because this happened so swiftly. I have this choice that I can never say anything, or just say what is what is on mind. I am aware I am still in mental progression. I am aware I am perhaps in a rather dark mental stage at this point. I am unable to convince myself I should be ashamed or shy or even worried what I write about. I am not concerned what anyone thinks about me anymore. I have heard enough of their judgments of me as a being. They have no power over me any longer.

"Fear of death increases in exact proportion to increase in wealth."
Ernest Hemingway

Material attachments lead to fear of losing them.

Love is not true it's just something we do.

5/19/2009 3:56:14 PM

The lemur monkey finding does not exactly put my mind at ease but it certainly explains our lemming mentality. So now I have a new perspective to ponder. So I am a lemur monkey that woke up to the fact I am surrounded by lemur monkeys with guns and nukes who are certain they are mature enough to handle guns and nukes. I am pleased I have slight or short emotional capacity because I would be very worried right about now. I wonder if religious god fearing lemurs are not freaking out right about now. They are coming to the realization all their religious texts where simply metaphor's to explain some psychological conditioning methods so they wouldn't go around acting so much like the lemur's they are.

I am laughing because I mentioned something about the missing link a few days ago and I just now realized I was detecting this news story was about to break, but I have no idea how I knew. So the rule of thumb with things I say is, no matter what I say consider it as a prediction but not a direct prediction. If I say something about a topic it is going to be happening soon. This of course is this subconscious aspect. It is rather smart.

But lemurs and all animals have the same subconscious aspect. We are simply lemurs that got to a state we can talk about it and tell our fellow lemurs how they can unlock the smart aspect of the brain. So the whole concept of large brain or small brain is no longer valid. The size of the brain makes no difference. The brains all have subconscious aspect. Any animal with a brain knows this.

This is perhaps why people freak out so much about this god concept because subconsciously they understand the god concept is not happening. The afterlife is not happening. So this is exactly why we will all go extinct exactly like any other creature if we do not pull together as a large coordinated pack of lemurs and get out of this crap planet and solar system. So there is no purpose whatsoever. There are just things we do. I am uneasy knowing there are lemurs with guns and nukes. Someone needs to disarm the lemurs. I am quite certain modern day lemur monkeys are not very happy to find out we are related to them.

That certainly is some sort of terroristic threat to say we are related to lemur monkeys. Lemur monkeys look cool and do not kill each other over delusions in their mind. Perhaps it is safer to suggest we are mutated lemur monkeys so the lemur monkeys will not be insulted. We are lemur monkeys that went bad, would perhaps be more accurate. Now I have a very good excuse for my crap books. I can now explain don't mind me you are a lemur monkey so my perfect books should look like crap to you. So now we can all be humble and meek in understanding our leaders are in reality lemur monkeys and we trust them with the launch codes to nukes and secrets. If one is going to trust anyone its best to trust a lemur monkey with your life than yourself. That is hard core logic. I guess we lost our tails and made up for it with forked tongues. It's okay though, everyone comes into the light when they are ready, and i submit the light was far brighter than i expected. So the whole dark and light concept relates to in the dark, as in, in the dark about the fact we are lemurs...of course we don't want to be lemurs, but disbelief doesn't change fact. I guess we should not have encouraged education as much, because sure enough i paid so some kid could get educated so he could discover i am a lemur. I'll never make that mistake again.

5/20/2009 12:06:17 AM

I have come to a great truth. Under no circumstances call your wife or girlfriend a lemur monkey.

All wars are based on sound and logical reasoning.

The only truth about the righteous is they aren't.

"General Motors Corp's (GM.N) plan for a bankruptcy filing involves a quick sale of the company's healthy assets to a new company initially owned by the U.S. government, a source familiar with the situation said on Tuesday." http://www.reuters.com/article/mergersNews/idUSN1943363120090519

The nation is not by the government and for the government it is by the people and for the people.

So the government is using the people's money to make investments and then when those investments fail the government throws it hands up in the air and say, "opppps." And there is nothing the people can do about or they will be deemed a threat. So the people are no longer relevant at all. If the government owns a military base and a citizen of the US cannot go on the military base, then that person does not own that military base because the government does not trust the people who bought that military base. There is some saying along the lines of, when we one day wake up and find our land is owned and we are outcasts in our own homeland, I can't remember who said that so now I have to just search in vain for other quotes that might sum it up like that one did. Dam it.

"A little group of willful men, representing no opinion but their own, have rendered the great government of the United States helpless and contemptible."
Woodrow Wilson

The money powers are the power, a little group of willful men, and they have turned the people into helpless people, and if those helpless people who attempt to fight back become contemptible people, or terrorists. It is simply a tyranny and you are simply too afraid to do anything about it. It is okay to live in a tyranny just don't go around and say you a free because you will sound like an idiot.

"But when a long train of abuses and usurpations, pursuing invariably the same Object evinces a design to reduce them under absolute Despotism, it is their right, it is their duty, to throw off such Government, and to provide new Guards for their future security." Declaration of Independence

This means when you have had enough of being a slave you have to bite the bullet, because the slave master is not going to let you out of the prison just because you say you want out.

"it is their right, it is their duty, to throw off such Government," It is your right and duty to protect the foundation of the land of the free, that is not laws, that is the Constitution and the Declaration of Independence only. The government already has a law that say you are a terrorist if you say certain words, so obviously they are the tyrant. Perhaps you are comfortable with giving away your freedom of speech for a little security. In that case you better start digging your grave; you will need a place to stay soon.

"I would rather belong to a poor nation that was free than to a rich nation that had ceased to be in love with liberty. "
Woodrow Wilson

Give me liberty or kill me as I try to get it back.

"If there are men in this country big enough to own the government of the United States, they are going to own it."
Woodrow Wilson

The ones in government are owned by the money powers, absolutely and without question.

The problem with money is the ones who own the majority of it, own the ones who need it the most.

"If you want to make enemies, try to change something."
Woodrow Wilson

A prisoner in his own land should wake the guards with his arms.

"Liberty has never come from Government. Liberty has always come from the subjects of it. The history of liberty is a history of limitations of governmental power, not the increase of it."
Woodrow Wilson

Government is a tyrant that will slowly convince you it is not.

Liberty is a mindset not a regulation.

"Never attempt to murder a man who is committing suicide."
Woodrow Wilson

Stay away from me I have already made up my mind.

Dead horses are difficult to kill and impossible to scare.

"Tell me what is right and I will fight for it."
Woodrow Wilson

A sheep only needs to be told where the food is.

One who does not think for their self will be persuaded to jump off the highest cliff.

"The American Revolution was a beginning, not a consummation."
Woodrow Wilson

America is in a constant state of revolution if not it is no longer America.

Three hundred million guns rescue Lady Liberty after the carpetbaggers have raped her.

The blind will have their eyes poked out, the earth is my witness.

"That a peasant may become king does not render the kingdom democratic."
Woodrow Wilson

A peasant will sell out for far less than a king.

Being elected means you are willing to be bought out.

"The ear of the leader must ring with the voices of the people. "
Woodrow Wilson

The government does not make mistakes when 300 million guns are trained on them.

Death helps everyone get it right.

This saying has a very relevant meaning since the terroristic threat law was passed. That law clearly states you cannot threaten a government official. So first they abridge freedom of speech by saying you cannot threaten the President and now they go one step further and say you cannot threaten the government. So you see, the government is simply drowning the people who allow the government. You are a person in the land of the free can say any god dam thing you want period and if the government or an government official tries to arrest you for that you have the right to blow their fucking head off. You may die but that is not what is relevant, you still have that freedom to do that, period. If everyone does not do that, we will be in a Marxist or dictorship with a Gestapo police state and we are already are. I type what I type in hopes the government will attempt to arrest me for speaking my mind.

"The history of liberty is a history of resistance."
Woodrow Wilson

Burn your flag if you accept what is on your plate.

"The man who is swimming against the stream knows the strength of it."
Woodrow Wilson

If you are not weary of the government you are the government.

"The seed of revolution is repression."
Woodrow Wilson

They repress your speech so fire your arms.

"You are not here merely to make a living. You are here in order to enable the world to live more amply, with greater vision, with a finer spirit of hope and achievement. You are here to enrich the world, and you impoverish yourself if you forget the errand."
Woodrow Wilson

You are not suppose to survive you are supposed to teach yourself how to live.

Okay enough hanging myself for a moment.5:22:16 AM

My understanding is i am here to annihilate not cooperate.

I never learn so i understand nothing.

Around to the back and up through the middle.

I have foreseen the revolution enough for one book. I will now discuss something important.

"Both he and Bermudez were charged with being under the influence of PCP in a 2006 criminal case. Both pleaded no contest to child endangerment charges in that case, records say."

http://www.bakersfield.com/news/local/x339729128/Bakersfield-dad-accused-of-biting-out-sons-eye

That's why I said PCP so much earlier in the book. Funny how that worked out. I edited it to drugs instead of PCP when I was discussing how drugs even strong ones do not affect subconscious aspect once dominate. In relation to being addicted to the drugs.

An eye on the opposite shore shall be.

I was in a chat room today and a guy said I was sinister and I fell out of my chair.

5/20/2009 4:38:45 PM

By this time many may perceive I am some sort of radical or one who's looking for a physical trouble. That is the illusion. That is the nature of subconscious when it is dominant and when it is silent. Subconscious is the rebel of the mental aspects. Subconscious is the aspect when a child is told not to get in the cookie jar, the subconscious aspect of mind says "Why, why shouldn't I get in that cookie jar?"

The emotional aspect of the child interprets that as they have a craving for cookie now. When a teenager is told they are not allowed to drink alcohol the subconscious aspect says, "Is that so?" because someone told me I cannot, now I am curious about it and I must drink some alcohol. This is in direct relation to the concept of, "Tell me I can't".

If you tell someone they I can't do something then they perhaps will show you they can do that. The subconscious it is all about being a rebel. It is looking for a challenge. That is really all that is happening. It's not about morals it's not about right and wrong, it seeks a challenge but the problem with that is, when one has the physical emotional aspect dominate those challenges can lead to physical actions.

- I tried to use a dictation machine to speed up the words but I found when I went back to correct any errors I forgot what I was talking about so some of the stuff in some of the parts from this point on are a bit confusing.

One may begin to be under the influence of subconscious but then start suggesting physical actions based on the rebel aspect of subconscious. This happens in religions and in politics. The leaders of these organizations began to believe that what they're subconscious mind is telling them should be translated into physical actions. Subconscious is the reverse aspect, so it shows no sympathy or mercy it is infinity, so surrender is not possible and sympathy is not possible. This is its strong point but when some of these signals are translated into the emotional physical aspect it can turn into a nightmare.

These nightmare scenarios can be translated into any situation there could be a religious cult and the leader will start to translate this, "never give up or undefeatable subconscious understanding" into a physical manifestation.

An army could translate this never give up aspect into a physical translation and then you have situations where the army becomes so brutal a harsh and an unforgiving, relentless, slaughter machine and this is exactly what is happening. The implement toll focus of the subconscious is being is being carried out by the emotional physical aspect so you get nightmares. You get nightmares in reality.

There are infinite examples of this. There are cult leaders who feel this power and then they translate it into the "Everybody drink the cool aid". There are armies that feel this invincibility and then they translate it into slaughtering anybody that gets in their way. So that subconscious never die aspect when translated by a dominate conscious physical based mind is the disconnect. The subconscious is undefeatable but then the emotional aspect when dominate translates that into "slaughter people".

A religious aspect translates the "We are on the right side and we are never wrong, and anything we do is righteous, and we can never fail", then they translated it into "Anybody who is not like us is evil, and mean, and hateful, and we will go out of our way to force them to do it our way because we are never wrong."

So really all they turn into is an arrogant fool. and that is all they will ever turn into because they are not wise enough to understand subconscious will trick you into harming yourself and harming others in a physical manner every single time if one has the emotional physical aspect dominate.

It will make you think you are powerful and then you will start manipulating other people, you will start asking them for money to hear you speak, you will start asking them for money to help you, so you will become more powerful, and they will become less powerful and then they will start to idolize you is some sort of way.

That being is starting to believe the illusions in their mind. They are starting to fall for that trick that subconscious offers everyone it's a track that tricks you into thinking you are something out of the ordinary.

One starts talking to others and they start thinking you are something out of the ordinary, and then you start putting yourself on a pedestal, and once you start putting yourself on the pedestal you start thinking you're better than others and you start thinking you're some sort of authority. The next thing you know people show up to hear you talk they say he is wise, his words are wise, he has power, and the next thing you know they have million dollar mansions with security guards running around.

The next thing you know they start translating their delusions in their mind and to the physical reality and then they are defeated.

They did the one thing they should never do; believe the illusions created by subconscious and translate them into the physical world. It is all illusions, they are not wise to have subconscious dominant, they are a little heavy on the subconscious side they are not wise.

They are fools because they let it get the better of them. They could not resist the lure of it. They could not resist it. Someone who says you are wise, then it is all over, they are defeated.

People start to think they are wise when they happen to fall into subconscious dominant. That is all they've done. They are not wise, there is no reason to surround them with bodyguards, there is no reason to protect them, there is no reason to treat them like they are something more than they are. They are simply animals, they are not special, they are not some rarity they are simply animals who figured out how to talk words to other animals and make those other animals believe they are something special. They are not something special everyone has subconscious. Some are able to harness it a little bit better than others but it'll never go further than that. There is no reason to acknowledge them as something other than everybody else they are just like everybody else.

Everybody is bound to listen to their self first. That is the great truth of everything. When a person start subscribing to the opinions of others they began to idolize that person the minute someone is deemed wiser than someone else, they began to harm others the moment someone says this person is wiser than everyone else. Everyone else is harmed because they say "I am not that wise" and that moment someone is deemed to be a burden.

All the others in that field are harmed because they begin to say, I will never be as wise.

The truth is there is never an expert in the field, there are varying degrees of delusional beings who perceive they are experts in the field.

It will never ever go further than that, that is why there is no one who is better than anyone else. All an award will ever do is convince the ones who see that award given, that they are not worthy so that award is harming them. That award is putting someone on a pedestal and at the detriment of everybody who does not get that award. The award it is simply hurting people. Every single award given is hurting everyone who does not receive it. It does nothing for the one who gets the award, but it destroys everyone who sees the award given. That is public judgment. When you judge something you harm everything else. When you praise something you harm everything else that is not praised. That is what the mystery is about this concept of putting others on a pedestal or idolizing others. You start to say this person is evil while that is a judgment and that is putting them on a pedestal. "Hitler is the most evil being" while that is praising him, that is putting him on a pedestal because people are listening in saying "I wish I was that evil", that is harming them.

You say this person is so Holy, well that is harming people and putting that person on a pedestal because they are saying "I am not that holy, I wish I was holy, I wish I was that person, I wish I was worthy."

Then that beings thinks "I was in the headlines, I wish someone would take my attention and look at me." That is what's so destructive about the judgment aspects, no matter whether you call someone good or evil you are making them and idol.

That is why it is so extremely difficult to go through your life and not say someone is good or someone is bad. It is nearly impossible, so all one does and they're lives is go around making idols out of everything but their self.

One says a politician is bad you simply idolize him. One says this is a wonderful politician, you just idolized him. You suggest your religious preference is wonderful, you simply idolize it.

It simply states "Have no idols before me" That means idolize yourself because if you do not you judge others and turn them into idols. If you cannot idolize yourself you are doomed to idolize others and thus deny yourself. No other idols before you. "Love your enemy like yourself." Meaning you have to get to know yourself and like yourself, and that takes your whole life, so you have no time for other enemies, because if you do not like yourself, you are your own worst enemy.

So you like yourself or your will be your own worst enemy. Much of this is in relation to liking yourself enough to attempt emotional conditioning to try to become right brain dominate or subconscious dominate.

I have not yet reached the stage in my understanding I am allowed to help anyone else. I am not I'm not at a stage where I'm allowed to tell anyone else what to do either. I am at the level of understanding, I'm still trying to figure out what I should do, and I'm not about to start making physical determinations about what I physically should do.

I am still at the thought process of development. I'm still trying to figure out what the hell happened to me. I'm still trying to figure out who the hell I am, and attempting to understand that will take the rest of my life, so I'm certainly not to going out on a pedestal and start telling others what they better do or what they should do, because that is realm is for fools. That is what fools do.

I learned in my life the moment the thought starts getting translated into physical actions there's only trouble. I cannot even figure out what I should say. I physically need to maybe do things as far as put food in my mouth so that I continue to live, but that's about it. I don't like going any further than that. I rather keep it all at the pondering stage in my mind. At this point since the accident I rather keep it all up in my head because as long as the thoughts are all in my head that means that I won't translate anything into the physical world and create a nightmare.

The minute my cravings and desires start going into the physical world it pretty much is all over. That's the problem with subconscious dominant, it wants the world but one has to have self control and understand that is just its nature. It wants everything. It wants everything at once and all for no reason at all. That's what the attachment aspect is all about. It wants to latch onto everything the feeling with vision aspect detects. It logs everything it sees and it thanks everything is perfect and it wants to take everything in. The sad part it is intelligent enough to pull it off. It is intelligent enough to take over everything. It is intelligent enough to fill the Coliseum with people who want to hear the wisdom of it, but that is the trap. That is the trap one is supposed to be in control enough mentally to understand, that is what they must not allow to happen. So that is that the trick of it all. That is the trick of electing political figures, they are idolized. They won, they are the wisest. They are the wisest because they got elected to begin with.

Religious leaders allowed their self to be put on a pedestal to begin with, so they are not the wisest, they are not wise at all. They are idolized. They have allowed their self to be idolized, so the minute they are idolized, other beings fell unworthy and think "I am not as good as that being.""I need to be as good as that being. I know I never will be as good as that being. I am unworthy and I am worthless, and I am not good enough."

That is the nightmare of it all. Everybody is the same no matter what, so everyone has a subconscious some are just in different varying stage of it being dominant, some are emotional wrecks and they are very far from having subconscious dominant but that does not is not an absolute. That is not an absolute, that means that the subconscious is extremely silenced but it's still there. The subconscious aspect is still there, so it's very hard to say one is smarter than another one, so it's pretty foolish to go around and say this person has a higher GPA than all these other people, that's insanity. That is not possible. Everybody has a subconscious so it is all a matter of when somebody has opened dominant subconscious.

Everybody is exactly the same. Everybody understands everything they come in contact with fully so it's insanity to say one person is ever smarter than another person. It's insanity to say one person knows better than other people they do.

The problem with all of this is, everyone is different because everyone has varying degrees of subconscious dominate aspect open. There is only one way to tell and that is by their fruits and their deeds. This means one who is physically harmful to others is not as subconscious dominate as one who does not physically harm others. That is also a misunderstanding because everyone reacts differently to their situation. So there is just massive complexity to this whole situation. This is why it is perhaps important to understand one is not good or bad for physically harming others.

One that does not subscribe to physically harming others must have compassion and understand some beings physically harm others because that said beings perceptions leads to perceive physically harming others is required. Everyone is trapped in their own bubble of perception. One that does subscribe to physically harming others must have compassion and understand some beings perception encourages them to avoid physically harming others.

<Heimdall> When a being suggests another being is bad or evil they make an idol of that being. When a being perceives anything is better than they are, they make an idol of that being and thus become an idol worshiper

<Heimdall> One perhaps is wise to worship at their own temple and not others temples

When I get warmed up I will remind you. One is wise to avoid seeking subconscious dominate because it is far too difficult of a mental struggle. I am unable to win any of my own mental battles so do not assume I can help you win any of yours. I will go back to wise quotes before I annihilate myself with my thoughts.

"All of the books in the world contain no more information than is broadcast as video in a single large American city in a single year. Not all bits have equal value."
Carl Sagan

Words are arranged in many fashions because the wisdom of the mind cannot be captured by physical means.

"Any sufficiently advanced technology is indistinguishable from magic."
Arthur C. Clarke

The power within thoughts can create many pleasing physical illusions.

"Bill Gates is a very rich man today... and do you want to know why? The answer is one word: versions."
Dave Barry

Adjust and improve or you will stagnate and isolate.

"Champagne, if you are seeking the truth, is better than a lie detector. It encourages a man to be expansive, even reckless, while lie detectors are only a challenge to tell lies successfully."
Graham Greene

There are only physical luxuries because mental wisdom cannot grasp physical luxury.

Physical safety is one luxury mental freedom cannot afford.

Some beings that are discounted are the only beings worthy of counting.

A radical ideal is often a safe doctrine.

Some climb their way to the top and once in a while one fails their way to new heights.

The demons in my tiny mental room ensure I will never be able to fight the physical demons.

The mental world does not offer the comforts the physical world offers to all.

The mental battle reduces the physical battles to moments of peace.

Self control is having the world at your finger tips and letting it go, so the light is too bright and I seek the night. Do not ever speak to me about self control. You are unable to grasp what self control is. I understand what it is and I cannot accept it. It is far too harsh for me to ever obtain. I am simply not that strong to ever dream that I would have what it takes to achieve self control. You do not have to remind me I am a failure because I understand I cannot be anything but a failure. I am unable to ever do anything but fail. You just perceive you can help me because you do not understand you destroy me with your words of encouragement.

I must play the video game before I implode.7:19:30 PM

I beg for ignorance and only end up understanding the definition of desperation.

One is wise to avoid conjuring the demons in their mind into the physical world and suggesting others should help them fight them.

Ones harshest thoughts keep the subconscious occupied so one may plan their vain escape.

A physical tool is the result of honest thought, the observer of that tool determines if it is pure honesty or selfish honesty.

"Civilization advances by extending the number of important operations which we can perform without thinking of them."
Alfred North Whitehead

When positive physical tools, outnumber negative physical destructive tools, civilization advances.

A war of physical destruction applies to all sides that participate in it.

The world has far too many swords and far too few plow shares.

I may not survive my mental battle but I understand that was never option.

"According to their research, the dragon's bite weakens and immobilizes the prey. It then injects venom from special glands in the mouth. The venom keeps blood from clotting around the prey's wound. And it causes a drop in the blood pressure. The blood loss and the blood pressure drop combine to weaken the animal. The theory is consistent with what happens to the prey soon after it's bitten, the scientists said. The prey becomes still and unusually quiet, and it bleeds profusely."CNN.COM

Consider this comment from a story on cnn.com. I will explain what I perceive this story means in relation to life and when I am finished you will understand why you never want to achieve subconscious dominate or no sense of time at least to the level I accidentally have.

When a parent tells their child to not talk back to them they attack that child with venom because a child has subconscious aspect that is strong and that child wants to question authority so it can probe it and come to further understanding. Then the adult perceives the child should never question authority, and tells the child, "Do not talk back to your elders."

And that child assumes they should not, so they start to kill the subconscious aspect because they must condition it into silence or they will be physically be punished by that adult who believes a child does not know anything and should just keep their mouth shut.

So then you have situations in life where people tell others to just shut up. Then you have abominations called school where the teacher is yelling do not speak in my class. Then you have situation where everyone is told to keep their mouth shut. Then people walk around and say "Why are the kids killing their self? It was certainly not anything I ever said, ever, ever, ever. I am certainly not why my child is combative against me."

Then there are people who like drugs. People who like to drink. Everyone knows they become lushes. They go from "I love you" to "I hate you " in a matter of minutes when drunk. That is because the drink has silenced their emotional aspect and they can speak their mind. This is what many drugs do to people. It silences the emotional aspect for a period of time and people appreciate that feeling of mental freedom or the subconscious aspect comes to the surface while they are high.

They are mentally free for a period. And because they like that feeling of mental freedom that is free from the poison and venom the emotional aspect causes, they end up doing the drugs more and more to achieve that feeling of mental freedom. Then they feel the mental freedom and determine they want to be free and that is translated by the emotional physical based aspect of the mind and they want to go drive the car to be free and they end up killing their self or someone else.

So they took the freedom induced by the subconscious but because they are primarily under the influence of the emotional physical aspect they take the signals from the subconscious and translate that into actual physical deeds. Then other beings suggest drugs are bad and it is best to be in the KNOW and in control which proves they are much more under the influence of the emotional controlling aspect.

They cannot live one moment with their self so they have to push their delusional beliefs on everyone else. So they end up pushing for banning all drugs and they make sure if people do not do as they say, they throw them in prison for many years and then they sit home and read the news and when they see a being that has been thrown in jail for drugs they say, "He got what he deserved, that will show him." ~~That is why it is important to the universe I never get my physical based emotional aspect back, because if I did I would exterminate everything in zero seconds. I do not perceive that, I understand that.~~

These ones in the KNOW have this mental venom and they spew it to every corner of the world. They are nothing but venom with their great Knowledge. Then they are the same ones who say, "Why is the world such a nightmare?""Why are so many people being locked up in prison for insane reasons?"

That is a tragedy of it all. I am certainly not intelligent enough to solve any of these problems. I am not even intelligent enough to properly write a book. I am not intelligent enough to even understand what happened to me. I am not intelligent enough to try to figure out what exactly is happening in this world. I am intelligent enough to understand some of the things I perceive since this accident literally rip my being apart. I have no solution to make it stop because I have no solution to make it go away. Perhaps the greatest wisdom is, you can choose to get ripped apart by the world physically or ripped apart by the world mentally, but the world is going to rip you apart. The ones who choose the physical path suffer far less.

At this stage since the accident I do not detect any sort of end to suffering. I do not detect any sort of inner peace. I have to play the video game just to attempt to stop the thoughts of understanding. I can take a gentle thought and before I know it I comb it into some sort of great truth that rips me apart. The mental battle leads to understandings that are not gentle and graceful. They are harsh and swift. I look at the drugereport.com and just see the title of the articles and some of them rip me apart. I do not even have to read the actual story to fully understand what the message is or what the final conclusion is.

I understood today, the Taliban are simply killing their offspring, the US is killing their offspring attempting to stop the Taliban from kill their offspring. Pakistan is killing their offspring attempting to stop the Taliban from killing their offspring, and all I see is many adults killing their offspring and the offspring are the only ones who are unwilling participants but the adults told them to never question their elder's wisdom. So the offspring walk into walls of lead and I get to sit here and watch it and write about it in my stupid books of vanity. I am perhaps blind to these concepts of love and

138

peace and compassion because all I see is child abuse and slaughter.

Abusers of the youth have a variety of convincing arguments for their deeds but they will never admit abuse is their goal. ~~YOU WILL WISH I DIED.~~ So that is what I understand from the story of the kimono dragon. The dragon bites its victim and once the venom infests the victim and the blood is unable to stop flowing, the victim becomes weak and eventually dies, so the dragon can easily devour it.

Perhaps you should ponder who I understand is the dragon, because the dragons head will be on my wall that is lined with the infinite trophies I collect to remind me of all the battles I have fought that turned out to be no contests.

Please remind yourself I decided to write infinite books two months after the accident and I have to write about something. One might suggest I am under a contractual obligation and my payment will be a handful of poison mushrooms. The wages of my sins are a repeat performance. I just got that one. I will consult with the video game to see if my assumptions were accurate.11:50:44 PM

When I start trying, remind me so I am able to convince you of your mistaken assumption.

Do not like me. Do not start to like me. Do not hate me. Do not start to hate me. Fight those emotions.

Your guess is infinitely better than mine. I will avoid suggesting in my books that writing five books in 5 months is abnormally slow. I hope to one day not be so abnormally mentally deficient, psychologically speaking , so to speak. I am mindful to avoid bragging about five books in five months since I am completely certain I will perhaps be pumping out more than that a month when I leave this current mental stage I prefer to call retarded lemur monkey stage.

I am mindful I will never write infinite books if I settle for such a foolish pointless average of one book a month and the blood on my fingers suggest I am perhaps wise to understand that swiftly. When I understand that infinite torture is the vacation I will be at peace with its duration. I perceive I am mindful to never do anything to physically harm others or myself because it may only convince me that nothing is real. The physical aspect is the last vestige of reality I have to hold on to. I am quite certain mentally speak everything is just an illusion, but I am hesitant to test that understanding in the physical world outside of prodding the physical word with words. I am attempting to get some sort of reaction from the physical word using my words but so far I get no physical response, just at times some verbal comments back. I perceive no one is paying attention to me just as before. I perceive there are ones who write infinite books in a month and I am isolated in my belief 5 books a month is some great feat, but I am aware it is nothing in contrast to the true masters of verbal joust. I am angered in my understanding I am a grain of salt in an infinite sea. I attempt to prove to the infinite sea I matter and that only encourages the sea to laugh at my delusional assumptions. A grain of sand in the sea only understands it is not the sea. I am convinced I must cease writing so I must write with greater drive. Perhaps when I complete my infinite diaries I will be able to write a proper book one's will not insult. Perhaps after I write infinite diaries I will be able to use a comma properly. Perhaps after I rip myself apart I will understand I was able to do something without failing.1:04:43 AM

5/21/2009 1:05:00 AM It's a new day. What a blessing. I am just so blessed with so many blessings. Curses are tempered by blessings.

I will now demonstrate why subconscious is perhaps dangerous, mostly because it tends to thrive on patterns. It tends to look for patterns and make determinations on those patterns and then when one has the emotional conscious aspect dominate the determinations are sometimes acted up on in a physical way.

I will use the main religion in the west and the main religions in the east.

West – Judaism, Christianity, Islam

East – Buddhism, Hinduism

I will explain some things to you and you will be certain I am right or the conclusions are right but please remind yourself it is not right. It is simply patterns I have detected because I am extreme dominate subconscious.

The West has a certain God based belief system. The East does not. The west has no concept of no sense of time in their belief system. The East is based around this no sense of time or Nirvana. The West has set rules and set laws and precise beliefs in good and evil. The East has a many or no God concept and also is rather flimsy in their actual belief system. The west has religious founders that arrived around 2500, 2000, 1500 BC. The East has one certain religious founder that arrived around 2500BC. So from the West's good evil concept the good arrived in Moses in 2500 BC and the counter argument or the adversary also arrived in 2500BC at the opposite side of the globe. So the west has a founder who preaches God and the East has a founder that preaches No god.

The East is rather particular as far as never killing things, people or animals. The West sacrifices animals and also kills people deemed to be "evil". This again is a counter argument. The West is rather kill-friendly and the East is rather docile in general beliefs. The West side even kills each other. Jews kill Muslims, Muslims kill Christians and Jews and Christians kill Muslims. This of course is only at the present time. In the past this was along the lines of Christians killed many Jews and both fought with the Muslims. Now in the present time of the East they are not really known for many violent wars because they are anti-killing. This is also apparent in India during British rule. They solved the problem without major bloodshed. But now there are some unseen aspects, some aspect that are not on the surface.

From a West god dominate point of view, the darkness appears as light. So If the East is darkness it certainly does appear as light in respect to it being rather peaceful in its deeds. The west certainly does not appear as Light, it appears as darkness in relation to its deeds in contrast to the deeds of the East.

Now it goes even deeper in the unseen aspect. The west denounces the east in closed quarters and the east denounces the west in close quarters. The East believes in some circles from my experience the West is wrong or evil or bad and they are determined to do what they can to convert the West.

The West is perhaps not making much ground in converting the East. The East in some circles believes this is the afterlife. This world we are in is the afterlife. The West believes this is not the afterlife but real life and when one dies there is an afterlife. These are all counter arguments or total opposites.

Both sides preach compassion and understanding and mercy and peace but this is simply a ploy. There is certainly underlying conflict or underlying motivations on both sides. The age old situation that one side believes the other is wrong or evil and the other side believes the other side is wrong or evil. The West is rather obvious about its motivations and the East is rather quiet about its motivations. Again a counter argument or counter aspect.

The West is rather big on claiming its side. The West proclaims I am this religion and announce it proudly. The East is rather obscure. In one of the East's religions one does not submit they are that religion, they tend to blend in and submit they're no religion. Ones can look for books about Living in the now. This concept denotes no sense of time or nirvana. I am under the impression this is a strategy. I do not submit to any religion. I do not have motivations I had an accident and I am certainly not preaching. I attempt to stay in the frame of mind I went subconscious dominate. Many in the East laugh when I suggest I am subconscious dominate they suggest "My bubble will burst" and I will realize what the truth is.

I do understand what that means. On the other hand I attempt to communicate in the West religion rooms and many attack me like hounds. So I will suggest both sides attack me equally. So I perceive I am stuck in the middle of these two warring factions. I am uncertain if the West is perhaps aware of this silent conflict that is going on. I am certain the East is fully aware of what it is doing. There is some sort of "We will save them and they are bad." belief going on.

It is all rather curious. There are open conflicts with guns and killing and then there is this silent war. It is a war none the less. I have spoken with both sides as far as people associated with those sides and they act the same way towards me. They suggest I am mistaken in what I understand and then I mention the events that lead up to this accident and they call me a liar then they turn hostile towards me. So I understand I am beyond their ability to believe. Neither side is able to believe how I became like this, so they resort to insults and so I see both sides as the same. Both sides are the exact same. They do not like ones who do not believe their belief system. That is simply detecting one who is not a part of their herd.

It is a simply psychological concept. Attack what is different. So both sides claim they are not racial yet they are racial.

Neither side can just allow people to be. It is the traditional they are bad we are good. It is the exact same principle. So both sides still have contrast because both sides are under the influence of judgment. It is as if judgment only applies to one if they understand who is bad or good, as if judgment is okay as long as the other side is evil. Then one has to ponder, how do you know what is evil. How does one know what is good. Does one just know? I certainly do not detect much of anything but a lot of people judging each other because they have determined they know what is good.

So perhaps the West is good and the East is good because both are indirectly or directly pushing belief systems. These opposing belief systems are in conflict with each other and so there is an adversarial aspect to them. I have learned my lesson about any belief systems. If you follow the sheep they will accept you and if you do not they will hate you. Both sides are the same to me. I get hated when I start playing the belief game. I can assume any belief system and be accepted and then sure enough if I question one concept of it, I am hated. If I doubt one sentence of it, I am hated. It is all the same to me. If I misspell one word I am hated. If I do not do things properly based on what another being perceives is proper I am a loser.

This is universal. This is why the law of relativity is so devastating to the entire concept of humanity. Everything is relative to the observer so a belief system in general is not possible except from person to person.

So them we have elections where there are two or three sides to pick from. It is not possible two or three candidates can fill the opinions of a whole country. If they do, then that whole country is a not thinking for itself. A religion where everyone believes exactly what the belief system is, are simply sheep who no longer think for their self. They assume the identity of the belief system for one reason only, to be accepted. That is what humanity or civilization encourages belief systems, to keep the herd away from being individuals so that the herd can be properly watched. You have this herd and maybe two other herds and then everything is easy to predict. There is no unpredictability. No matter what stimuli is throw out it is predictable how each herd will react to it.

Consider the event in during Vietnam where a monk burned himself alive. This had a profound effect on the war from a deep seeded mental aspect. It was later found out that that monk was rather intoxicated. So that monk got rather liquored up and set himself on fire. Was that along the lines of perhaps a suicide bomber who is liquored up on beliefs and then persuaded to drink the cool aid? "Take one for our side", kind of thinking?

Make our side look important. This is what the belief systems do to people. They become accepted and then they are mindfully willing to do things they would not normally do if they were all alone. So they do things for the group. This ranges from protesting others with hate to physical violence. These acts are not as much directed as the ones being attacked but more as a show of solidarity with the group. They solidify their attachments to the group by deeds. Along the lines of, "We can trust this person because of what they did for the group." The groups are everywhere.

A psychologist will support another psychologist if it comes down to it. Same with religions. Same with politics. Same with armies. Same with gangs. Same with everything. So being an individual is nearly impossible in civilization because it is frowned on. If one truly attempts to isolate their self they are perhaps deemed a recluse. This is perhaps what hermits were attempting to suggest. They were isolating their self from the herd of civilization to get away from the many group conflicts. It is very easy to go into a chat room about Christianity and say the Jews are good or the Muslims are good and you will be banned. That goes the same for the Jewish chat room and the Muslim chat room. This also goes the same for the Buddhist chat room. You say anything about the west religions and you get warned to never speak of that again. This is the herd showing the members of the herd they are dedicated to the belief system. Their subconscious aspect is assuming the role. It is role playing. I can go into any of those rooms and make them all believe I have been a believer and prophet of that belief system for many years and I can do it in short order. This is the nature of subconscious when it dominate. It is a chameleon.

I am mentally unable to believe in anything for certain because in the extreme dominate subconscious mental state I will swiftly consider the other side and convince myself the other side is right. I can literally believe in all the religions and become an authority in them in one day and then talk myself out of all of them by the end of the day. This is what subconscious dominate is. It is a doubting Thomas or a devil's advocate or on the fence. So I have to write diaries to get all this stuff down because I did not know all the stuff I just typed in the last few paragraphs until I typed it. I will be anything you want me to be. That is a problem. That can create things like cults and religions and herds of sheep running off cliffs.

There are many I understand from these chat room experiences that hate me because I will not assume their absolute belief systems. I hang out in a channel called spirit by myself. There is a girl named Whisper and she comes in and we hardly talk but she does not insult me. She does not say much and I do not say much, but I am at least not in a situation I feel I have to turn into a chameleon or be insulted. So I am in a sense in this mental state a hermit and in physical life I am pretty much a hermit also. This is simply because everyone wants me to believe what they believe or they hate me. I prefer people just call me insane and a loser so then I do not have to deal with them anymore. Of course I am making generalizations based on my experiments in chat rooms. It is perhaps a deep concept to grasp that in extreme subconscious dominate mind one is simply unable to have a definitive belief system. I believe in freedom and what I mean by that is absolute freedom to change like the wind. Change my position every few minutes. Some may perceive that is dangerous. I perceive that is what I call mental conflict. A group cannot trust me to take one for the team. No group. That is why I understand I suggest I am on no one's side, but I tolerate others. I did not take a handful of pills because people liked me, is perhaps is what I am suggesting.

As I understand it if one does not fit into the norms of any group or belief system they are hated, they are outcasts. So ones go around suggesting how tolerant they are and how compassionate they are and how loving they are and how much they care and in their mind they are nothing but delusional. I am infinite faced and they are two faced. I can make a convincing argument that everyone is perfect. That is my problem. I can see wisdom in the darkest set of events. I am very slow to start throwing physical rocks at others. I am certainly not one who does not like a good argument but I find eventually many I talk to resort to judgments before the conversation gets too far.

Many, mentally speaking rest on their laurels. Many are unwilling to look at their determinations and doubt them. That is perhaps a harsh mental thing to do. That is what this philosophy aspect is all about. Saying perhaps about your deepest beliefs. Is America free? Perhaps it is. Is America a tyranny? Perhaps it is. Is everything perfect? Perhaps it is. Is everything a living hell? Perhaps it is. I am perhaps extremely cautious to start believing what my intuition suggests.6:51:11 AM

5:09:40 PM

In relation to life one should be willing to adjust everything they believe in a moment's notice or they risk the chance of becoming disappointed.

Some suggest others are partially right but seldom mention partially wrong.

The amount of light one see's is relative to the darkness that surrounds them.

Direction requires one to understand where they are at and more dangerously where they are headed.

If you are certain where you are headed why aren't you there yet?

Walking backwards is more difficult than running in place until you trip and fall.

New and improved denotes rehashed ideas.

A thick lather covers the reality of the situation nicely.

Nothing is nothing but a thing.

When the illusions are gone all that is left are the delusions.

I am very pissed off today so avoid reading this next part because I am going to cook some fish on the fire for no reason at all. I had a dream today or last night or whatever the hell you want to call the time. I dreamed I was writing my infinite books. That was the whole dream. Then I realized when I woke up. Dreams such as nightmares, terror dreams, wet dreams, are all proof one has far too many emotions. The emotions seep into the dreams. A normal non delusional dream is a dream that is like looking at a picture. There is no excitement, no drama, no terror, no lust, no fear. So all one has to do is think about the dreams they have had recently and if one includes fear, terror, excitement you are factually mentally abnormal.

I use to have many nightmares about many things before this whole accident situation and now I understand that was a very good symptom to indicate why I had such depression and self conscious shy thoughts. Then I look on Google and some genius came up with this [psychological term called god complex. So the genius psychologist have determined if one is self centered they are abnormal. If one believes they are important they are abnormal. Then I understand this whole dam world is full of retarded idiots who have no right to even speak, let alone vote, let alone have children, let alone breathe.

So now I am back to the understanding I woke up to the fact I am in an insane asylum. But I am not finished yet. I will suggest this again because I am aware ones who may be listening most likely have no brain function. Moses suggested with the Abraham and Isaac story a psychological conditioning concept to unlock subconscious. Jesus came along and suggested this turn the other cheek and those who try to save their self will lose their self, which is another psychological conditioning aspect. One who tries to physically gain things will mentally lose the subconscious aspect or silence it. Then Mohammed came along and suggested submission is relative to submitting physically or being charitable and that way one will become more subconscious dominate. So then we have Moses and his psychological concepts. Then we have Jesus who agreed with Moses and added some of his own psychological conditioning concepts. And then Mohammed came along and agreed with Moses and Jesus and added some of his own psychological conditioning concepts. So any being who does not understand that should never speak again about these beings because they have no god dam brain function and should dig a deep hole and I will be by shortly to fill it. Do you perceive I stutter?

So the logical conclusion is, if you disagree they were all simply talking about psychological conditioning concepts to unlock the power aspect of the mind, you need to take a vow of silence so you do not continue to speak like a fool. Until you do that, you are never allowed to speak to me and all of your opinions are worthless in my eyes, so keep your dam mouth shut and quit encouraging your retarded buddies to kill people because you don't have a god dam clue what the religion you believe in is about. I will sum it up. Do not speak ever because you only convince me further that you are unable to speak clearly.

I am upset because I almost decided to edit my dairy and make it more pleasing. And then I realized what is someone going to do kill me because of my words? Are you going to kill me boy? You misunderstand who owns you if you perceive you are going to kill me. You need to avoid assuming you are going to do anything to me. I am going to do things to you. You are not going to do anything to me ever again. You are simply in a delusional state of mind that you believe you can do something to me at this point. You have already done to me. Now it is my turn to do to you. And you will find out soon enough, pay backs are a son of a bitch. I just got that one.

If you think I am dangerous that is your subconscious understanding you are dangerous. If you think I am a loser that is your subconscious understanding you are a loser. I never voted to put my own fellow countrymen in prison but I am quite certain you did. So if anyone is dangerous it is you. If anyone is a tyrant, it is you. And you have the balls to keep voting. So you are a psychopath. You logic about everything is to either kill it or lock it up or medicate it. You have run out of mental and verbal solutions because you have no brain function so you resort to the retard solution. You kill it, lock it up or medicate it. You assume you are righteous because your subconscious understands you are an abomination of mankind. You are an abomination you are just not aware of it, which is why you are an abomination.

I am aware I was an abomination, but now I understand what I really am, but I keep that to myself and let you suffer in attempting to figure out what I am. Do you know what I am yet? Why don't you write infinite books about it. Maybe if you are lucky and have slight brain function you can write one book a year. You would never do that because you already understand you have nothing worth saying about anything. No one gives a dam what you have to say about anything ever. The best you can do is talk to yourself because no one else gives a dam what you have to say. What I just typed this section has great wisdom in it but only the ones with brain function will pick up on it. The ones with no brain function will take everything on face value because they are not able to detect wisdom ever.

5/22/2009 2:59:27 AM I understand I have been getting rather angry in my writing. I had a mental panic attack for about 30 minutes last night. I mentally had huge doubts about everything. I start to assume I could not take this mental progression any longer. So I went to sleep for a few hours and now I feel fine again. I understand what happed after that last "attempt" to harm myself is my mind snapped.

It basically decided I was unable to handle emotions and function on the emotional physical level, so it simply turned everything off. It essentially said, "You are unable to handle emotions. You have tried to kill yourself so much I will just turn everything off." My mind did what all minds do, it adapted. I understand my mind just got tired of my deeds. So it said, no more tasting food, you can't handle that. No more memories about what you recently have done because you get to self conscious and shy and embarrassed. And then after the accident my mind decided, if you want to hurt yourself write infinite books. My mind will not allow me to remember what I write. My mind adapted and decided the only way to save myself, is to turn everything off because this person is unable to function with emotions.

So my mind determined I came way to close to killing myself so it simply turned everything off and now I am no longer physically suicidal or a physical self harmer. So I am upset in my books because I am attempting anger and emotions. I cannot accomplish that because my mind turned that off. I can cuss everyone in the world but the simple truth is, I am simply attempting to be emotional because I cannot be emotional.

Emotional wrecks cannot write 100k+ word books in 28 days, month after month. So I am aware I am still in mental shock since the accident. I say harmful things and then 1 hour later I forget I even wrote that. Then at the end of the month when I ponder publishing my book I do not care about editing it. I have no ability to care or become shy or ashamed about what I write. I do attempt to be emotional but those are phantom emotions. My mind will not allow me to become physically harmful to myself anymore. It had enough of me harming myself physically so it just turned off anything that it has determined may cause me to become shy or embarrassed or harmful to myself in a physical way. So mentally I snapped. I understand my mind stopped registering all these emotions to save itself. Just like when one is in shock from personal injury the body turns off pain receptors because it is unable to processes the large amounts of stimuli coming in. So people go into shock and cannot even tell they are in pain. That is expected in a traumatic situation. So my mind did what it had to do to keep me from harming myself physically.

"At the age of 29, Tolle experienced what he calls an "inner transformation," after suffering long periods of suicidal depression. WIKIPEDIA.COM

So this is what happened to me except I am not here to make money and friends and he wishes he was me. I do not perceive I had a spiritual awakening I understand my mind did what it had to do so save the creature, which is me. I simply traded in the razor blade and pills for infinite books. Nothing else essentially changed.

I simply am unable to care. I cared too much and that is why I was suicidal. So my mind said, you no longer are able to care because you cannot handle that burden. From a psychological point of view it is extremely logical. My mind got tired of my stupidity so it adjusted what I perceive. There is no spiritual hocus pocus. It is simple adaptation to a situation on a mental level. So I understand everything because my mind will not allow me to fail. I may not understand everything in reality or factually but my mind suggests I do. This eliminates the possibility I will become upset and depressed from failure. My mind determined it is better to make me perceive I can do anything than allow me to perceive failure because it determined I cannot handle failure. So this is why I perceive everything is one thing. It is very safe because there are no chances I can fail. It convinces me it does not want me to write good books or even sell them. It makes me perceive I am doing all of this writing for no reason at all. So my mind quit. I could never get satisfaction so my mind turned that aspect off. It turned my short term memory off so II would not be able to worry. My mind determined it is better it makes me have no ability to feel or crave or desire as opposed to feeling and craving because I am unable to handle those emotions or types of thoughts. So one way to look at it is, my mind determined I do not take failure or loss very well so my mind gives me all the answers or show's me the cheat sheet so I do not mess up because my mind understands I cannot take loss or losing.

So I may not be right about anything I write about but that is not important because I perceive I am right about everything I write about. My mind will not allow me to fail. My mind will convince me the greatest loss is a win. My mind will look at any situation and show me instantly what it means or what the proper answer is because it understands I am not able to handle failure. When I fail I tend to determine its best to kill myself so my mind will never allow me to perceive I have failed.

So in that respect my mind took mercy on me and just decided to give me all the answers so I would leave this failing or failure world behind. So it does not even matter if I am in fact right or wrong. I perceive everything I see or hear or read is simple to understand. That keeps me from harming myself physically. My mind is only concerned with keeping me, the creature, alive. So it just gives me the answer to everything I read or hear and allows me to understand it swiftly so I do not have to try because I might fail if I had to try, and my mind understands it cannot allow me to believe I failed at anything ever.

So I kind of accidentally extorted my mind. I kept telling my mind, if you do not allow me to understand things I will kill myself, and finally my mind said, ok, you will no longer have trouble understanding anything ever. So my mind understood I was not able to handle the emotional game so it deleted that game and created a new game called "Todd cannot ever fail because he is unable to deal with failure."

So I am not able to understand everything because I am so educated. I am able to understand everything because my mind understands it is in its best interest to not upset me because I tend to get rather hurtful towards myself if I ever fail. So I have the cheat codes to everything in life because my mind had enough of this fail and win situation, it understood that was going to lead to its own demise or death.

So my mind gives me its full power because my mind wants to live or remain alive. So I accidentally put a gun to my minds head and said, you tell me everything or I kill you. And my mind said, ok. I put my mind in a do or die situation and so now it performs at peak levels of understanding swiftly. So everything is simple for me now in relation to understanding things because I blackmailed my mind accidentally. No spiritual or religious hocus pocus, simple easy to understand unintentional mental conditioning. Along the lines of "between a rock and a hard place". My mind understands because of my last suicide attempt I mean business so it no longer toys with me. My mind understands I will go the full measure, as far as killing myself, if my mind does not make things very easy for me to grasp. My mind understands I will terminate it, if it does not produce perfect results swiftly and without effort. My mind understands I do not play games and my mind likes to be alive.

So my mind does not allow me to have morals or allow me to care because those are traps of failure. I might not be able to live up to morals so I would become frustrated and my mind understands fully I get rather "cut myself orientated" and "pill swallowing friendly" when I get frustrated. So my mind will not allow me to care or have morals. This is not in relation to physically hurting myself or others. The reason for that is because if I got physically violent I would not be able to wipe everyone out and that would frustrate me. So my mind has turned off the physical aspects of life. My mind will not allow me to play the material gain game because it understands I might not be able to take everything as far as money and wealth so it turns off my desire for money or wealth. It determined to turn off anything that might lead me to become frustrated. It will not allow me to become stressed that I smoke cigarettes because I may become frustrated if I cannot quit. It turned off my hunger because it understands I might become frustrated if I feel hungry. It turned off my sense of time because it understands I might become impatient and then become frustrated and then get "pill swallowing friendly".

So then when I look at people or creatures I detect or feel this awe and wonder because my mind will not allow me to focus on their physical appearance because I might become frustrated if I started to see I am not as good as they are. So I do not admire anyone because that admiration might lead me to feel I have no worth and that may lead me to become self conscious and then frustrated. So this is all strictly what the mind does when it is put in a difficult situation, it adapts. I am aware these are possibly the worse books ever published but in my mind they are the best books ever publish in the history of the universe.

That eliminates the possibility I can fail and thus become frustrated. I simply am unable to care what other s think about me because my mind convinces me they are insane and have no idea what they are talking about. This is in relation to my mindset. So I can do anything easily and without effort because my mind will not allow me to perceive failure or perceive error. So my mindset is, everything is perfect. That perfection is relative to my mind and to me alone. So anyone can condition their self into subconscious dominate or no sense of time state through "humiliation" emotional conditioning techniques. That is as simple as one who is less emotional than another person. Some people have to go to anger management because they have temper problems and some people can manage anger without getting to the stage they have to go to anger management classes. The thing is, no one can reach a level of extreme subconscious dominate unless they trick their mind accidentally into understanding it has to perform perfectly or it will be killed.

So no matter if one gets to no sense of time or subconscious dominate if they reached that state without actually attempting suicide in earnest they will always fall short. The mind will not take them seriously so it will not go to full power. It will understand that person is only a slight threat to it. So this is the reality. So it is not wise to attempt to kill yourself to reach this extreme level of subconscious dominate because if you attempt that with great effort you probably will end up killing yourself. So then one has to accept the subconscious dominate conditioning with the understanding they will never ever, ever, reach the extreme of it. Only the true suicidal people who are extremely suicidal but keep failing at it can ever achieve the extreme subconscious dominate state. It certainly is not relative to the books you read. School is for people who want safety and security. So they give up the extreme mental clarity for safety and security. I do not blame them. I did not intend for this to happen. It is simply a mistake that happens from time to time.

One has to be very stupid and a great loser to attempt suicide enough and fail at it to accomplish this kind of mental conditioning. So this is not really about a near death experience as much as me accidentally convincing my mind I was going to kill it if it did not start making everything easy to understand. Many want to believe in the afterlife and spirits and all that stuff but that is simply an emotional reaction to insecurity. They are simply afraid so they talk their self into some sort of peaceful explanation for everything or a secure explanation for everything. We are lemur monkeys so the entire spirit world belief system is extremely laughable. If there were spirits I am certain I would be aware of that by now. I try to look at it like my emotional conscious aspect of my mind was dominate and after enough suicide attempts my mind decided to turn that off and see how the subconscious dominate aspect would work instead.

I am certain the reason I can read people's minds and understand what will happen in the future, is simply because if my mind was not able to do that, it understands I might become frustrated and stressed and my mind understands it better avoid making me frustrated for its own sake. I am aware many beings who achieved this state in one way or another are assuming this spiritual aspect because they are trapped in their own bubble. They are trapped by their own perceptions. They believe their own perceptions, when in reality there mind has tricked them into this state of everything is perfect. They are unable to grasp that the mind and subconscious aspect is very powerful. The subconscious aspect will trick one into anything it needs to trick one into to save itself.

Wars and fighting each other is required in a living system. The wars and battles in civilization are what encourage civilization to progress. Without World War two we would not have the technology we have now. The conflicts enable us to progress because it puts us as a species into a state of do or die. Things get accomplished in a do or die situation. If everything was just peace we would all eat ourselves to death and die off. If nobody ever got sick our immune system would suck and we would all die the minute we got a cold. If we did not kill each other from time to time we would be unable to appreciate each other. Subconscious aspect thrives on conflicts. There is nothing to be gained from peace. Peace is luxury. Peace is stagnation. Many understand they never feel so alive than when they are in a frightening situation or an uncertain situation. We tend to become to safety orientated we stop living at all together.

A scientist is always in a state of war. They are in a war to come up with an experiment then in a war to run that experiment, and then in a war to figure out what the experiment taught them, and then in a war to figure the next experiment to run. Peace and happiness only lead to isolation and stagnation mentally speaking. This is exactly what the saying , Those who want mental peace prepare for mental war is all about.

And that also goes for physical war. America assumed she was number one and so she became stagnate and now she lost that number position and will never regain it because she stopped experimenting. America reached the top and assumed it was permanent and now China is helping America understand life is not about luxury it is about finding the hottest coals. Apparently what I just discussed only makes sense to me. I have to write about something. I will now discuss something important.5:21:22 AM

Truth is not a group effort it is relative to the observer. In order to avoid attracting its attention one must be very humble in their words. It detects forked tongues. Speaking at all is not advisable. It is a bit more irritable than one might imagine. Ignorance is bliss and it has no ignorance. Another way of saying bliss is spiritual joy. So it is not ignorant at all. There is no antonym for bliss. So the opposite of bliss or spiritual joy is the absence of bliss or spiritual joy. Void of bliss. Void of spiritual joy. That's why one might suggest it is perhaps a bit irritable and one would be wise not to attract its attention. One is better off tying a stone around their neck and throwing their self into the sea than to attract the attention of something that has no ignorance and thus no bliss. I do not detect it is into negotiating peaceful settlements.

Heb 13:6 So that we may boldly say, The Lord *is* my helper, and I will not fear what man shall do unto me.[7]

There is much humor in this statement. This comment is more suggesting, what do I have fear from man compared to what this thing will do to me. One might suggest the least of your problems is what man can do to you. Something along the lines of the joke, with friends like you who needs enemies. Perhaps the word "helper" is a bit misunderstood. Perhaps when one understands what "helper" is in relation to what it will help one do they perhaps will understand this comment is not so much about a positive outcome. One is perhaps infinitely wise to avoid attracting its attention. Don't assume I am going to make any definitive comments about it. I am wise enough to never suggest I know a single thing. I proudly submit I do not know anything and I understand nothing. That is one comment I am certain of. You go ahead and tell the world what you know and you will find out eventually you should not have thrashed in the water so much because you got its attention and its attention span is perhaps what one might suggest is infinite. You will get more of its attention than you are able to imagine if you go around thrashing in the water. I am not certain what it is, and I am very safe in that comment regardless of what your opinion is about my understandings. You are the least of my concerns. I am not scared of anything you can do because I am more focused on what the hell it is. It is not what I thought and it is not what you think.

5/22/2009 5:52:52 PM

The whole concept of giving our positive energy or negative energy through your words is an illusion. One who decides to censor their thoughts so that others around them will be able to suggest he gives off positive energy with his thoughts is simply in denial, or are simply a liar and embarrassed to share their thoughts, for the sole benefit that others will say, "He gives off positive energy or says positive things with his thoughts." No one's thoughts are strictly positive or strictly negative. One's thoughts are what one's thoughts are. Subconscious is not about happy picnics, subconscious is a questioner, subconscious will go to the depths of negativity and the heights of positivity. So one who is perceived to be so positive all the time is simply one who censors everything they think, every single thought they have they censor it and it may translate it into words because they want one thing, they want the vanity of acceptance from the pack or the herd. They want the herd to say "This person is so good", so they are essentially in denial of their own thoughts. They are in complete denial, there is no such thing is 100% positive and there is no such thing as 100% negative. Each thought may lead to another thought, but the subconscious does not acknowledge labels. Subconscious is not worried if people will like what it thinks, so anyone who's out preaching how great everything is and how wonderful everything is going to be, is just simply a censor of their own thoughts. They have reached a state of conditioning where they don't even open their mouth unless they carefully decide if what they say will be accepted by everyone if not they are afraid, they are fearful, they are scared to be cast out form the herd, if they say what's really on their mind.

They already know they won't be accepted so they aren't really a valid source of information, they're afraid to say what's on their mind, so they may reduce their self back down to the to a level of just saying what will please others. That's all they do. They just say what pleases others because no one would like them if they didn't say what pleases others they are devout at achieving vanity.

Subconsciously they understand they would become outcasts. they would have to face their self. They are unwilling to do that so they censor their thoughts. They just censor every thought and before they know it, all they are is a sounding board to be accepted into the herd. That is all they want. They don't care anymore about their self. They just want to be accepted into the herd. The herd will accept them as long as there words are all positive.

They give off such positive karma that's not abnormal to the beliefs of the herd.

What that being is really doing is destroying itself so that it will be accepted.

Total vanity that is what vanity is when you do things, so that you will be accepted, but you will never be accepted. You're all alone. You're all alone out in the world. You have to live with yourself. If you can't live with yourself then you're doomed. You are doomed if you can't live with the thoughts in your mind that subconscious suggests. One billion people accepting you does not matter if you cannot accept the thoughts that the subconscious has in your mind. You will destroy yourself. People say "I like motorcycles because I feel free". Well that's the subconscious aspects saying I want to be free, but because that person has the emotional conscious aspect dominant they translate it to "I need to go drive a motorcycle to be free" and they may get slaughtered on the highway and they're trying to figure out why they wanted to be free.

They keep translating the subconscious free aspect into physical actions. You can't be free physically because you died, so that's impossible. You can generally be free in your mind when subconscious is dominant and that means you have to give up the physical, you have to let go of the physical. You can't have enough money. You can't have enough friends. You can't do enough drugs to become free unless you take huge handfuls at once but not to huge.

You may perceive you are reading the words of a being who is very angry and hateful but in reality you are reading the words of a being who gave up on life and is attempting to slowly talk his way back into the understanding it is okay to live. I would certainly like to be able to talk some sense into this world but I am unable to. My words are not at a strategic level to talk this world into any meaningful conclusion. I assumed the solution to my life was to end it. Now I understand there is no solution to life. There is no such thing as a solution to anything. There is only continued struggle into infinity. I wish this subconscious aspect would stop reminding me I am aware the patriots are loading up on ammo. I wish that ideal is just going through my thoughts because I am insane and a paranoid. I wish I could talk to people and explain to them they should not have abridged the freedom of speech because when a being feels they cannot express their self with words they start expressing their self with physical means. I wish I could tell the government to repeal these laws that abridge freedom of speech so the patriots would stop their formations. But the truth is, I am not suspecting a blood fest may happen. I am aware the blood fest is going to happen no matter what I do. I am aware many would never believe that and I am aware. I wish I did not understand that. That is the nature of life. It is not about reaching a solution. Life is more about trying to do the best you can based on the understanding you are in a mental and physical meat grinder no matter how bad you dislike that idea. Beings have to be able to let out the subconscious rage in words or they will become emotional dominate and start letting out that subconscious rage in physical actions. So one can go around saying how wonderful the mind is, but that is because they do not have a mind. The mind is capable of anything

147

and everything. The mind is a well adjusted machine. Morals and laws only hinder it and it fights back against that. The mind is free and when someone starts putting limits and labels on it, it lashes out in dangerous ways.

Mother Theresa wrote letter to her spiritual mentor and suggested she had doubts just months before she died. She was simply saying "What on earth have I done." She was explaining she spent her whole life preaching these laws and limits and telling other beings what they should never do or they will be in trouble and then got to the end of her life and realized she wasted her life because she believed in limits and rules that were forced on her. Subconscious aspect has no limits and thus has no morals and thus has no attachments. That is a perfect complement to the emotional conscious aspect that is weak and fearful and hateful and finds its solutions in the physical world. The emotional aspect is all about control because it is afraid it does not have control.

This is what the money powers in America are under the influence of. They want to control because they perceive they do not have control. They control with laws and will stipulations but these money powers are not answerable to those laws. They make the laws to keep the ones who believe the laws under their control.

Once in a while a law enforcement agency gets caught breaking the laws and this applies to all aspects of the control structure. Many perceive they are righteous to turn in their own kind in who break the law. That is the illusion. They are all above the law they simply get caught in that reality once in a while. The ones who subscribe to the laws they enforce are blind to the power struggle. The ones who encourage the laws are above the laws. They certainly would not be caught in the actual law making game. They are above that low level of power. They own the law making aspect. The ones in the law making aspect, or legislature, are simply pawns that answer to the ones who are above the law.

These money powers have many fall guys between them and the courts. One is unable to touch them ever. The true power structure has laws in place to ensure they will never be answerable to the laws. So one might question where exactly does the buck stop? You are not allowed to see that information because you passed a law that said you are not allowed to see that information, for your own safety. I hope you feel safe with that understanding because you certainly are not free. I do not need to be associated with anyone or any group because I understand fully the patriots have already decided.

They are waiting for the moment to attack but they certainly have decided to attack. All of your weapons and all of your armies and all of your laws are not going to very important much longer. The sooner you make peace with the reality no one is coming to your rescue the less painful it will be. You simply are not going to be saved this time around. Every single time you tell someone they cannot say that word or have that idea, you hang yourself with a piano wire. You are not intelligent enough to determine what anyone is allowed to say ever. Subconscious mind does not care about your delusional fear of words. Why don't you pass a law that says one is unable to have thoughts and speak their mind, then after it passes, get a gun and empty the clip into your brain so it will stop having thoughts that you have determined are illegal.

Then you can tell your friends you uphold the law and are a law abiding citizen and they will praise you for your moral character. I am wise enough to not stand in the way of the patriots who are on the way. I will suggest they are coming by land and by sea, but I will not stand in their way because they are bound by the constitution to defend against tyranny such as abridgement of the freedom of speech. They are not concerned with the government being around when they are finished. There will not be any government around when the patriots are finished but there may be some who suggest a new one might be wise. You should let go of your attachment to the government because it has jumped off the cliff and simply has not hit the ground yet. The irony is many in the government are patriots. So the government is infiltrated. That's the humor in the situation. The government can only wonder who is with them and who is really a patriot in disguise? They will have their answer to that question sooner than they think. One might suggest in the land of the free the ones who are for absolute freedom are obligated to assist the ones who are for absolute control in watering the tree. I will give you some words from history.

"During Jefferson's second term, he was increasingly preoccupied with keeping the Nation from involvement in the Napoleonic wars, though both England and France interfered with the neutral rights of American merchantmen. Jefferson's attempted solution, an embargo upon American shipping, worked badly and was unpopular.

Jefferson retired to Monticello to ponder such projects as his grand designs for the University of Virginia. A French nobleman observed that he had placed his house and his mind "on an elevated situation, from which he might contemplate the universe."

He died on July 4, 1826." http://www.whitehouse.gov/about/presidents/thomasjefferson/

Jefferson was trying to keep us out of others affairs. He was attempting to make sure we did not get caught up in the world of control and power mongering. He failed. He was already aware the power structure was to powerful for America to fight against. The money powers own everything. He became a recluse. He went home and assumed the position of the thinker. He found out all his efforts were in vain. He was aware America would become what it is right now. Another country owned by the money powers, influenced by the money powers. Money makes the world go around. So kiss your delusions of freedom goodbye because your delusions make me laugh.

"He slashed Army and Navy expenditures, cut the budget, eliminated the tax on whiskey so unpopular in the West, yet reduced the national debt by a third"

He was fully aware of the money powers. He was fully aware of the military standing army problem. Military industrial complex thrives on selling death. That is its job. Standing armies thrive on selling death. That is their job. Taxing things is all about harming people by taking their wealth to put into the pockets of the carpetbaggers which is the government. The government is owned by the money powers. They have stakes in every candidate. They never lose. They simply adapt to who is elected. There will is the only will. Ones in a position of power will make up an excuse to tax you a little bit more. That is how they make their living. They don't get paid enough money by working for the government so they do favors for the money powers and the money powers take care of them. That is all that is happening. It does not matter if you can prove it or not, one only has to have brain function to understand that is what is happening. That is why my mind no longer allows me to care about anything because it understands I would go mad instantly if I cared even one ounce. I do not care so do not ever assume I care. They have already assumed control over you so do not assume you are going to vote your way out of it."I on the opposite shore shall be, ready to ride and spread the alarm to every Middlesex village and farm." I will write infinite books and publish them but it will not make much difference because what I write about is not what may happen, but what is already destined to happen. It has already happened or I would not be able to detect it to begin with. So now you understand you have no solution you only have humility to face what is about to happen. One cannot escape what is already destined to happen. If you figure out what I am, call.11:27:05 PM

Mental Freedom and mental safety are impossible to achieve at the same time.

From a psychology point of view one can agree that subconscious dominate mind is very damaging to the one who unlocks it to an extreme. I am aware some of the things I write about may put my life in danger, but my subconscious aspect simply convinces me I already let go of life so do not let that bother you. So I do not let it bother me. I am not bothered by what I write. I am bothered by fear. I am not bothered I may be hanging myself with my words. I am not bothered by that silly illusion. I just keep convincing myself of one great truth: What can you possibly do to me to make me fearful after what I have been through. That mindset is what is known as no fear or no concern about one's own safety.

If my subconscious was in a cage next to me I would not be sticking my fingers in that cage. Then one has to suggest to their self, I would rather not have this kind of brain power. I would agree. I am biased because I perhaps went to the extreme as a result of my accident. So I can only suggest things or my truth from my perspective or things that are relative to my experience. I certainly would not go out preaching how wonderful dominate subconscious is. It simply is not wonderful from my point of view.

So then I have to rethink this comment about if the string is pulled to tight it will snap and if the strong is to slack it will not play. So this would mean a mind that has to many emotions will go around harming people in a physical manner and a mind that is too far into subconscious will be so focused on the thoughts or cerebral aspect it will not play. Meaning it will be disassociated with the physical. So this is perhaps why peace is a pipedream. If the world was emotional wrecks everyone would be in physical wars killing each other. If the world was subconscious dominate to an extreme everyone would sit around and eventually starve to death and nothing would ever get done.

So then one would explain harmony in the mind a bit of emotions and a bit subconscious dominate. Then you get what the world is today. Mostly physically killing and mostly wars of killing each other can erupt for any reason and at any time, and countries with huge arsenals of weapons just waiting to find an excuse to start the slaughter.

That is the harmony. So the choices are in general, the world can have a huge blood bath, a medium blood bath or no blood bath but silent death. This is in relation to the comment along the lines of the world may not go out with a bang but with a whimper.

I recall I mentioned something about never being able to find the missing link earlier in this book or perhaps in the book before and I just realized that was me predicting they would find the missing link. I am not concerned about proving that I understand that. That is why I write so many books because out of all this stuff there are clues. I do not get all the clues until much later. I am unaware of the time scale. I simply write what comes to mind and I do not remember what it is afterwards. I just have an infinite amount of thoughts that suggested I should write books because no seminar or television slot is capable of lasting long enough to allow me to vent the thoughts in my mind.

Apparently it has decided infinite books and it's the best solution and my blood soaked fingers understand that well. So one can easily see how a being who goes to the extreme of subconscious dominate would be misunderstood. I am not physically violent at all since the accident that is the problem. I cannot vent in a physical way, my anger. I can only vent my anger in words. That is a problem because we are physical creatures. So my mind decided it is best if it turns off the physical aspects of my mind because I kept trying to kill myself physically. So my last suicide attempt convinced my mind to alter itself and thus now I am stuck in this unintended mental state. I am not in a position to teach this is so great. I certainly do not feel at peace. I would not physically hurt a fly but that does not mean I am not being raked over the coals mentally at all times. Somehow this accident made my mind so subconscious dominate my mind transcends reality itself. As a being I find it impossible that I will write infinite books. I attempt to question this rational. I attempt to put limits on it. I attempt to tell myself when I die I will no longer be under the obligation of writing infinite books and then the subconscious aspect says, no you are going to write infinite books no matter what, and then I realize I am doomed. Now I will discuss a topic that has some value.

5/23/2009 2:58:01 AM

It takes great self control to intentionally make a spectacle of yourself on a worlds stage in order to condition yourself away from the emotion fear of embarrassment. I from time to time get a slight understanding of what my books are about but at this stage since the accident it's very fuzzy. I understand I really don't have any idea what I am writing about. I write things and then I ponder hints of what I have written and convince myself I should not have written that. So if I started correcting everything I write I would not have any books to publish. I would simply correct them all out of existence. If I had to describe my books I would sum it with, "I have no comment on the matter."

Everything is an option not a solution.

Every being must choose their own path; if any being attempts to choose that path for them, then that being has not properly chosen their own path.

At this moment since the accident 3:55:40 AM EST there is a great poison mushroom patch that is telling me there is great wisdom in its stalks.

The humor about this subconscious dominate aspect is, it is so extremely biased. I can watch a show that's sole purpose is to not be wise and I will find much wisdom in it. Horror movies full of wisdom. Space movies with war and death; full of wisdom and wise sayings. It is almost as if I am the last person one would ask for a judgment call. I understand this is the nature of the subconscious, it is quite the philosopher. One has control of what they know but they do not have control over what they understand.

Man sucker-punches blind woman on bus CNN.COM

If a person cannot see then any hit on them is a sucker punch. I think there is some sort of wisdom in that but I am extremely biased. It is not rape if they allow it.

There is wisdom in all documents because by tradition humans write them.

I am watching this show about the drug problem on the streets in Philadelphia. There was a girl they were talking to who had a 200 dollar a day heroin habit. She is not addicted to drugs she was attempting to slowly kill herself to get out of the situation she was in. The cops where emotional wrecks. They were beyond the point of emotional stress. They had seen some much suffering they no longer were aware of how devastating their situation is. There is no way to solve this problem because people cannot just lock everyone up. The revolution is in full swing in this city. The people do not even talk to the cops. People get shot and no one says a word. So the cops are people and they are being destroyed. The people on drugs are being destroyed. The people dealing drugs are being destroyed. And they are all on one mission and will end up in one place. They will emotionally work their self into suicide. They will get shot or killed or die from drugs but that is the illusion. They will lean into the bullet or lean into the drug overdose just to get away from their situation. This is not a rare thing. There are stories of wealthy executives who lost much money in the stock market and they go home and kill their self. People lose their job and go home and kill their self. This is all a symptom of one thing. Emotions are way out of control. Life is too difficult to face, without getting lost in emotions. What I mean is, the emotions that are not detected lead one to start to think the emotions are normal. That didn't work either. The strong emotions are thought of as a natural part of the being and that being begins to act on the emotions. Crap. The emotions are not under control to the extent one is able to function in a reasonable manner.

The drug addicts perceive life is too hard to face without drugs and they may be correct. Their situation may deem it a valid outlet. But that only makes it harder. Then the cops are so numb from all they see, they are biased against everyone except the innocent ones but the reality is, they are all innocent ones including the cops. They are all caught up in their bubbles. The subconscious can make one believe anything. So the drug addict perceives the cops are bad. The cops perceive the drug addicts are bad. Then the whole concept of human beings disappears. It no longer is even society. It is more of an interdependent nightmare.

I understand people in general do not grasp the fact that these troubled parts of the city are only increasing. In 10 years there will be more and more. In 20 years there will be huge parts of the country that are owned by these troubled city aspects. They will be off limits to police. They will become enclaves or separate entities that have their own unspoken sovereignty. It is not the police that are the problem. It is the laws that the police have to enforce. There are so many laws that the police can essentially just pull anyone over and find something to arrest them for. The police are bound to enforce the law. So they are not the problem. So ones will argue if we do not have law we will not have order and will lose society but the reality is, if one has too many laws they will in fact lose order and also society. People will just stop talking. They will not talk no matter what law is broken.

So the petty laws are making people adapt to them and the people adapt by never saying anything when the serious laws are broken. So they are in a sense ignoring the laws. They have resorted to survival of the fittest mentality. So that is no longer society. If someone gets shot there is no enforcement of the law because there are no witnesses. So the police cannot do anything so the law is irrelevant. So the whole concept of society simply does not apply at all in some of these big cities. So the fabric of society is tearing apart because there are simply too many petty laws. So then in these parts of big cities there are "drug kings" that act as the sheriff. So the police respect this sheriff and he respects the police. So they scratch each other's back. So the whole concept of law and order is an illusion that is obvious in smaller towns but falls apart completely in larger cities. The police are almost reduced to running around in these big cities just as a show that society is holding together but it is not. Society in some of these cities has become anarchy because there are so many laws that are biased towards the people there. It is not the police it is because everything is relative to who passes the laws.

If a person lives in a quiet town in a relatively quiet setting, drugs are a nightmare and should be banned so they pass a law to make drugs illegal. From their perspective that is a righteous vote. But then to a big city and drugs are a way of life. It is a legitimate way to make money to get food. So the person in a small town who passes a law against drugs dooms the person in a big city where drugs are a way of life and also dooms the police in that city and also tears apart the fabric of society in that big city because the people stop acknowledging the laws all together. It is all a symptom of one person deciding drugs are bad for everyone in every situation. That creates a law against drugs and then that law creates a demand for drugs and that enables drugs dealers and from that point on it all goes downhill.

It is psychologically human nature. If you tell someone they cannot do something, and then say it is against the law, they are going to do it. Subconscious does not like to be told what to do. It is by nature a rebel because it only understands infinity. It does not play that rule or law game. That is why these beings in these big cities are becoming smarter. They are out foxing the police by making rules such as "No one ever narc on anyone no matter what." There they just made the police irrelevant. The police cannot operate if there are no witnesses. So the police are in a very emotionally difficult situation and I can tell from looking at them in this video they are at their wits end.

They are being defeated by beings who are adapting to the tyrannical laws that are being imposed on them by other beings that live in tiny towns where there is only one drug incident every ten years. So a cigar is a cigar. The drugs are not making this situation. We have infinite laws against drugs. The situation is a nightmare. So the next experiment will be to make every drug legal and that will stop all of the power struggles.

Kids will do drugs no matter how many laws because kids are going to dive for that cookie jar the moment you suggest they cannot have a cookie. So I understand there is more to the laws against drugs situation that it appears on the surface. Many of these people in these harsh cities do not even vote. So they are being abused by outside influences that are voting to isolate them. To make them look bad. I see people in the harsh parts of these cities attempting to do the best they can. I do not detect they are bad people. I detect they are in a harsh situation and it is because there are influences that desire to keep them in a harsh situation. So some beings pass a law against a drug that they understand is prevalent in some of these harsh areas of big cities. Then they pass a law that say if you get caught a certain amount of times or with a certain amount you are a felon. Then they pass a law that says a felon cannot vote. That is exactly what is happening. The drugs are not the problem it is simply a power grab. A law that takes away your right to vote? Well then all one has to do is pass enough laws and make enough things a felony and then they will be the only one left to vote. One cannot take someone's right to vote away because that person did some drugs or had some drugs, that is against everything that is proper. Everyone can change so to say if you do this you cannot vote, that is what a tyrant would do and no person who believes in freedom would ever make a law like that. It simply is insanity to say a being cannot vote if they break a law, because a beings right to vote is not given to them by a law. So again this is the money powers trickery. If one has enough money in a monetary system they own the system. They are god in the system. They own everything. Everyone can be bought that relies on money for survival. I have never voted and I do not plan on voting because it is some sort of tracking scam but I am able to somehow detect illusions and trickery swiftly, all of the sudden. Perhaps you should write infinite books about how everything I just said is wrong. I understand we are in a puppet show. I am trying to cut my strings so I cannot assist you in cutting yours.

Someone commented in a chat room and I went into monologue and it is their fault for inciting me.

<Heimdall> Cravings and desires cause emotional aspect that lead one into situations that may be undesirable. This is in relation to turn the other cheek to avoid becoming emotional, which suggests self control

<Heimdall> Its simply emotional conditioning. If one has to many desires and cravings their fruits are the seven deadly sins, and with silenced cravings and desires their fruits are the seven holy virtues.

<Heimdall> sins are symptoms of mental perspective. one is under the influence of sins because they have to many cravings and desires, or one is not.

<Heimdall> Sense of time and hunger for food 3 times a day is a symptom one has not properly turned the other cheek so they are not in any form of grace, fruit wise

<Heimdall> I will avoid suggesting if one wakes up in the morning and craves food they are certainly not in the spirit of grace because ones will freak out and get emotional.

<Heimdall> I write that in my infinite books instead

I am quite certain they have no clue what I am talking about at this stage.

I will now discuss the possibilities this accident did to me mentally.

One option is I lost my mind totally and have no mind.

One option is I became extreme subconscious dominate.

One option is I became extreme emotional dominate or conscious dominate.

One option is I achieved an unknown state of mind.

One option is I became a lemur monkey.

And the final option is I became an alien from a far off galaxy or what is known as an author.

I have faith it is one or a combination of those options but I won't guess which one at this date.

At this day and age of technology the colleges are probably wasting their time. I will explain this comment swiftly because I have to get on with writing this book. When a student is in class they spell the word straight the way I just spelled it. When the student leaves class, they type a message to their friend on their hand held device and they spell it str8. So the student is pretending to spell the word straight in class for a cookie or a grade. In general they will spell it str8 and when it counts they will spell it straight. So the student is in fact inventing their own language. This is a symptom of an evolving language. It changes on a day to day basis. So the student looks at a teacher as an authority figure and that student dances through the hoops to get a grade. They are being taught to kiss ass at the right moment to get an achieved goal that is beneficial to them. They are conditioned. It really has nothing to do with learning because that student is going to spell straight str8 when they see the authority is not looking or when they perceive it is safe to act natural. So the technology is having some unintended side effects.

I am so biased I see wisdom in foolishness and great foolishness in wisdom.

Don't let the hellhounds slaughter me until I get warmed up.

http://www.youtube.com/watch?v=_CVKuFLMlps – Hardened Stone

5/23/2009 7:39:42 PM

"In a sobering holiday interview with C-SPAN, President Obama boldly told Americans: "We are out of money."

Out of money denotes there is not infinite money.

"Chen Fuchao, a man heavily in debt, had been contemplating suicide on a bridge in southern China for hours when a passer-by came up, shook his hand - and pushed him off the ledge.

The passer-by, 66-year-old Lai Jiansheng, had been fed up with what he called Chen's "selfish activity," Xinhua said. Traffic around the Haizhu bridge in the city of Guangzhou had been backed up for five hours and police had cordoned off the area.:

"I pushed him off because jumpers like Chen are very selfish. Their action violates a lot of public interest," Lai was quoted as saying by Xinhua. "They do not really dare to kill themselves. Instead, they just want to raise the relevant government authorities' attention to their appeals."   http://apnews.myway.com/article/20090523/D98C6GP80.html

Now the guy who pushed him off complained that Chen was selfish and only wanted to attract government attention to his debt problems but Lai by pushing him off made international news and thus brought even more attention to the problems in China. So Lai threw gasoline on a fire.

I perceive Lai honestly thought he was upset about Chen's actions but subconsciously I feel he wanted to make it a big story.

I did not have a proper day. I am not convinced I had an accident and woke up to the fact I am in FACT in a god dam insane asylum and it does not matter what you think about that ever.

I will stop writing for the day on that firm conviction.5/23/2009 11:16:40 PM

5/24/2009 5:46:23 AM

I am mindful at this stage since the accident I am stuck in a negativity cycle. I am unable to perceive everything is just fine. I am unable to take things to the logical conclusion and believe it will all work out. I ponder this sculpture of the thinker and I can understand he is not happy and he is not sad. The thinker is attempting to figure what he is. I can write infinite books about how great everything is going to be for you. I can lie into infinity so you pay me money to hear wise words of encouragement. I can rape you for everything you have and keep a straight face while I do it like all the others do. I refuse to live in that world of delusion. The earth is my witness. When I sleep I am not really asleep I am pondering what I will write next. I am unable to break free and rest from reality. I am unable to dream pleasant or dark dreams. I am unable to have a break from reality. I am unable to have a rest or a moment of peace. I am mindfully like a machine so outside of motivations the motivations I detect in others are quite obvious. Motivations are a symptom of feelings and desires.

Is there going to be something that will wipe my understanding away? Am I going to fall back in line with the herd and achieve satisfaction? The more a being wants to understand and the more knowledge a being wants to gain the closer they come to finding the truth. The truth does not set one free. The truth does not make everything well. The truth does not change anything. There is always going to be someone who is going to act out on the delusions in their thoughts and harm their self or others in a physical way. Reality is unable to ever suggest that will not be the case. I sit in religious chat rooms and all they say is how evil the other religions are. Is their mind to a state of delusion they are unable to even tell they have no room to make such comments? If everyone in the universe looks at me at the same time will I achieve some type of satisfaction? Will everything be better for me then if I am acknowledged by the universe? If everyone throws enough money at me will I go back to how I was? Will I feel better in the morning or will I be mourning in the morning? We are out of money, time and touch. The mountain top of ignorance at least understands judgment. Without the ability to judge what one knows, one has no purpose. Perhaps the pinnacle of ignorance is when one perceives they have purpose. Perhaps the pinnacle of humility is when one understands their purpose is vanity. Perhaps shame is achieved when one understands there is no shame. Perhaps if I deny my thoughts that will convince them to change. Perhaps the ignorant are wise enough to believe they have purpose. Perhaps my judgment of others is a vain attempt to hold onto the comfort provided by ignorance. Perhaps the internet has forced people to lose their ignorance so swiftly there are no longer experts. Perhaps the internet has forced people to achieve a state of understanding that they no longer need the assistance of anyone else. Ignorance creates the conflicts and encourages bliss and spiritual joy. Ignorance cannot be regained once lost so it is perhaps a valuable motivational tool. If one has all the answers what is their motivation?

If the scientists discover the god particle they will have nothing more to discover. If the enemies are all gone there will be nothing left to fight. If disease is eliminated there will be no point in doctors. If food is in abundance there will be no need to grow. Perhaps conflict is not suffering. Perhaps understanding is suffering. Perhaps the feeling I get with this vision aspect is not perfection but a detection of the emptiness. Perhaps I am feeling the void with the vision aspect and I am unable to detect exactly what it is because a void is unnamable or beyond labels.

Perhaps telling the truth destroys more than it builds. Perhaps I write swiftly to put the misery out of its misery. Perhaps I just want to get it over with. Perhaps I do not wish to put the animal through any undue suffering so I swiftly take it to it end conclusion. Perhaps I do not wish to allow the animal to suffer needlessly when I am aware it is on its last paces. Heimdall can hear the grass grow. I will allow history to determine how well I could hear it grow. Can one be afraid when they understand the end conclusion of it all?

Perhaps one should feel shame and embarrassment for what they understand. Perhaps education will only lead to peace and understanding which will lead to the destruction of the polar opposites that creatures thrive on to better their self. If the food source the lions eat never ran from the lions, the lions would eat so much they would die. Perhaps compassion and peace are extinction in disguise. Should I be eager to tell everyone what I understand? Perhaps the ignorant will be the most valuable asset to the species because they will have purpose and drive to achieve. Without ignorance all that is left is the void of understanding. If there was no suffering people would be indifferent to existence. Perhaps the garden of Eden suggests a warning about the loss of ignorance. Perhaps the lion laying with the lamb suggests the end of conflict and thus the end of purpose or contrast. If no one breaks the law then there is no purpose to law. If no one is ever wrong then there is no possibility one can ever be right. If there is no evil there is no good. So the whole harmony aspect is suggesting if one is totally ignorant they will not last long and if one is totally aware they will not last long. So the mystery is what is the harmony? What is too much ignorance and what is too much awareness or understanding. Perfect peace and perfect ignorance are the extremes of stagnation. It is impossible to be perfectly ignorant but perfect understanding cannot be improved upon. The labels keep us as a species in conflict. If the labels are removed we are without purpose. We need some bad guys to fight and the bad guys also need some bad guys to fight. The arguments, the struggles, the conflicts are when one feels alive, because without them one is dead. The concept of freedom and each person is free to do what they perceive is right is what creates the chaos and the conflict and the struggle. This is what keeps people in harmony. We will cease to exist if we are all at peace with each other because we will all be one conformed herd. When one runs the final experiment their purpose is gone. Civil disobedience keeps control structures honest. The whole concept of by the people and for the people means if all the people cease to participate in the control structures plans at the same time the control structure ceases to exist. There is simply no need for physical struggle only civil disobedience.

A drug dealer does not pay taxes on his income. He is not evil or bad he is wise. Why should he give his money to a control structure that only wants to throw him in jail with its laws. That is wisdom that is not evil. Why would a person work to give money to a control structure it is not pleased with? That is foolishness. They have announced the money is all gone so it is survival of the fittest. Is your life less important than the control structures life?

Ones answer to that question determines whether one is ignorant or wise.

The worst thing that can happen is something will happen. It is hard to fail at eating an poison apple.

Compulsion leads to exciting conclusions. Conclusions are far too limiting. Certainly your own personal truth is as important as my personal inability to believe it.

Now at this time 12:39:45 PM I have changed my whole stance. Everything is perfect. I assisted one who got infected with a devastating virus from being on the internet. Then I realized. There are people who tell the youth sex and drugs are bad so the 13 years old kids decide their only choice is to create a devastating virus and upload it to the internet for fun and then I spend 6 hours of my life attempting to figure out how to explain to this being how they can clean it off of their system all the while knowing in a couple months that same teenager will figure out how to make an even more devastating virus for fun, and upload it to the internet. Now the anti-virus software companies are rubbing their hands together and most likely paying the 13 year old teenagers to make the virus to begin with. So I just have to laugh at how silly this whole existence is. I would like to think no being is seriously taking existence seriously. A great humility exercise is to go out and get a virus that makes many popup ads appear on your screen and sit there and try to close the windows and with your mind try to make them not come back. If the windows keep coming back you are not at a level of humility yet.

When you reach a level that the many windows popping up does not bother you, you have reached perfect humility. When you go to a news site and the headline makes you laugh out loud you have reached a level of perfect understanding. Laugher is the best way to face humiliating defeats. Being serious about everything only makes the mind hardened. I am under the impression this enemy that threatens to destroy America is perhaps an inside joke. Perhaps the leaders were sitting around one day and said "I will bet you 100 dollars I can tell everyone we are going to be defeated by an enemy in sandals and everyone will believe it." And so there is some leader with 100 dollars in his pocket and a smile on his face. It rained the last few days and the grass in the yard is rather long and right now it is a greatest threat to my liberty. God is not answering prayers because he is too busy laughing at the fact anyone in their right mind would ask for his expert opinion. One punch line leads to the next. When you get tired of allowing your thoughts and experiences to hurt you, you just start to laugh at those things, and then you start to live with those things. America has god knows how many ICBM's and each ICBM has 16 warheads on it and we can hit anyone on earth in a matter of minutes, do you perceive I should be afraid of anything?

What exactly should I be afraid of? I do not think the world in general should be concerned about anything but keeping America happy. Is there even such a thing as a terrorist threat outside of two superpower countries with hundreds of ICBM's aimed at random locations around the globe, controlled by new people every four or five years, elected by people who have decided to vote away their own opinions? Patience is relative to the impatience of the observer. Patience is a virtue as long as you did not wake up and find out you are in an insane asylum full of crazy people who believe harming other people is ok. The insane perceive killing another being is justified under the heading of a thousand sane excuses. A sane being in an insane asylum is the definition of inhumane treatment. People only appreciate wisdom that does not make them understand they are fools.

Why did bobbie fishcer isolate himself away from you? Because he could not stand to be around you even for one second. He was compassionate because he tolerated you. You abused him and he understood that.

I will plant 6 billion tree's around my fortress and after I explain my understanding is the number of leaves on the tree's around my fortress. I will then put a heart on top of each tree as a symbol of my compassion for each tree.

I am perhaps letting my emotions get the better of me so I will regress back into wise quotes from people who wish they were me. If you think I am sinister now wait till I get warmed up.

The truth is this perfection feeling from vision is so devastating to me if I started down the road of lust I would end up marrying 3 billion women in about 2 seconds and I would do it simply so I could look at them, even their hand or foot or hair. That's it, no sex, just look. Just a simple look at any women and I am ripped apart inside by the perfection. So now you understand I am doomed. I literally have to be mean and angry in order to make sure no one likes me because I like everything far too much as it is. The saying you can look but you can't touch. My saying is, I can't look and I can't touch. This is because I touch from looking. Many people have this sensation but it is so heightened when one is subconscious dominate it is too much. So the chastity aspect is not about someone who denies having sex. I have sex but I have to be careful about it. It would never end if I dedicated my efforts to it. I would destroy my goal of writing infinite horrible books if I went down that path so I attempt to avoid that path and even as I type this I am infinitely open minded to the idea of going down that path. Again, I am doomed. I can relate to the burka concept. This is actually classified information so if you are a female please avoid reading the next few lines. This is strictly for males alone.

I found out one of their secrets. They are extremely dangerous. Think about the concept of Helen of Troy who launched a thousand men in their sinking ships. Then think about this song aspect called in your eyes. Then think about men who sometimes go around like zombies saying, "I saw this girl and looked in her eyes and I fell in love." This is all about one thing only. There is something not in their eyes but something like an invisible beam of some sort that is akin to a death ray to males. I do not even like to speculate because it seems to be getting more powerful as I progress into this accident. Think about why some of these great religious beings didn't have wives and think about some who had many wives. There is some power women have. I would guess it is because they can have offspring but that is perhaps a horrible guess. Men fight each other because we lost the battle for dominance against women probably about two seconds after it started. So this ideal to cover a woman's face is about covering their eyes and that death ray vision or beam. It is not the color of their eyes and it is not even the eyes. It is something that comes out through the sockets. That is about as close as I can explain it. When a male is subconscious dominate they can only look at the ground when around women. It is not some perverse thing. It is not some evil aspect, it is the perfection that decimates a male. You just perceive you know what sex is. You know what reproduction is. Sex is looking into a woman's eyes. You simply have not properly conditioned your emotional mind into subconscious dominate to understand that. So many men have tried different methods to get women to cover their eyes. Many have tried to enhance the eyes. It is all in vain though. The males cannot alter the power that comes out of women's eyes. The women's hands and feet and arms and legs are powerful enough but the eyes are infinite, infinite power multiplied by infinity and I am not even warmed up yet.

You may perceive I jest but one day you will write me after you go subconscious dominate and tell me how I grossly underestimated my description. So males only hope is to avoid upsetting women. I am certain that may not even work. Just try not to let them know how powerful they are because we are defenseless. If we were not defenseless against women we wouldn't be launching so many of our sinking ships for them for all these thousands of years.

Please remind yourself that is just one tiny secret about women I understand since the accident. I have others to reveal but I need to do more experiments. If you are male remind yourself at all times: women = infinite wrath potential, then you can adjust your strategy accordingly. The infinite wrath denotes they will convince you with their eyes to launch your sinking canoe into a tidal wave. Now I will discuss something that is relevant. I will deny I ever wrote this if you ask me about it. You will understand the definition of playing dumb swiftly. Think about the harpy that lured the sailors and their ships to a certain fate. Well that's what Helen of Troy also did, and they are still doing it with that funky vision thing but in many cases it's a good fate relative to my perspective, psychologically speaking, so to speak.9:15:38 PM

Salesmen will try to sell you anything and wise men will try to teach you nothing.

Death didn't care for me I don't expect you could.

http://www.youtube.com/watch?v=s_ULVT-2o9I – Why your Drowned

"If you breathe then I could drowned.

If you could live then I could drowned.

If you could see then I could drowned.

If you could live then I could Drowned.

If you could love then I could drowned.

If you could hate then I could drowned.

If you could bleed then I could drowned.

If you could see then I could drowned.

If you could love then I could drowned.

If you could hate then I could drowned.

If you could think then I could drowned.

If you could bleed then I could drowned.

If you could think then I could drowned.

If you were smart then I could drowned.

If you had brains then I could drowned.

Then I could drowned.

 Then I would drowned

Then I will drowned.

Then you will drowned.

That why you're drowned.

If I could blink, then I would blink.

If I could sink, then I would sink.

If I could breathe then I would breathe.

If I could fail then I would fail.

If you could fail, then I would drowned.

If you could blink, then I would drowned.

If you could love, then I would drowned.

If you could fight, that's why you're drowned."

Perhaps we have come to an understanding.

5/25/2009 8:21:59 AM Okay time for wise quotes. I need wise quotes of wise dom.

Everyone is relative in their own world but sometimes ships cross paths and if they get to close they may sink each other.

The spiritual focused beings cannot submit to being lemur monkeys because they have too many on their back as it is.

We are a species that figured out how to communicate with language. This means we are able to communicate ideas. That means we are able to have a collective understanding. Outside of that we will become extinct like everything else if we continue to rest in this nest called earth. We in general are all afraid to leave the nest. We are nest focused. We all are finding the nest is getting to small. That means one thing only. We are going to wipe ourselves out with wars or nature is. There is no other possibility. This is not some fantasy romance novel. It is not going to be okay if we all say "Thank You" enough.

People in general assume nature cares. Nature does not play by our stupid rules. Nature will wipe us out in the blink of an eye and not even notice. So as a species we are extremely arrogant and haughty to think that is impossible. As a species we have a slight chance to break free of this nest we are attached to called earth. If we do not wake up to that fact we will not be around much longer. If one perceives it going to be alright they become secure and that security leads to underestimations. This is not a dooms day kind of thing. This is simply the way nature works. We are far over our ability to live here. We treasure every single being so much we cannot risk anyone. We have a life raft and it can only hold 100 people and we are trying to save 500 and that is going to wipe us all out. It has nothing to do with morals or class or religion or pipe dreams. It simply is the way life operates. A species gets too populated and nature will thin them out. And sometimes this will thin them out of existence. What is the point of fighting over this earth? Space is very dangerous but that is the dilemma and the challenge. Stay here in comfort or take a gamble. Many who understand something already understand we have way too many people and we are way to focused on saving everyone. When a species is overpopulated and also very anal retentive about saving everyone nature is going to swiftly let us know what its opinions are about that. Nature will just as well wipe everything out and start over. Your prayers and wishes and desires will not change that one ounce. We assume it is no big deal we can make it to space now. We are trapped in our own bubble. We assume it is common place to be able to go into space. It is impossible for an animal to reach a state of being able to leave the atmosphere. It is impossible. So we did the impossible and now we are resting on our laurels. We have this arrogance that "Oh we can go into space so now let's focus back on earth." It is the reverse. We figured out how to go into space and so that is all we should be doing.

Everyone should be centered around going into space, period. We are trapped between comfort of earth and challenge of space. Comfort is death. Comfort of earth is a promise of extinction. Comfort is attractive and easy. There is no law that we have a right to exist as a species. Nature does not care about us. Nature simply does not care if it wipes us all out. So we have this life raft to get away from this sinking ship called earth but no one willing to ride on it. We are all comfortable with the luxuries of the big ship that is sinking. The little life raft is uncertainty and the little life raft is dangerous and scary and difficult. But the truth is. Space is a luxury no other species has ever had. No other species has had a chance to expand into space. So I need to ponder, what on earth are we thinking. Perhaps are minds are so blocked and confused we actually believe something is going to look out for us. Nothing has our backs. No one is coming to our rescue. This whole attachment to earth is going to be our fatal flaw.

If they invented a spaceship that went the speed of light, we would come up with a reason to never use it. So the whole point of making a great space ship is irrelevant. We as a species would rather buy a nice house and a nice car than be concerned with attempting to save the species. That's a very good indication the majority of brains on this planet no longer function.

My rage is infinite because we blew it and you are to blind to ever understand what that means. If you can look in the mirror and say "We have 6 billion people on this planet and we are going to be just fine.", you are beyond my ability to ever reach. Six is the magic number, you go ahead and try to figure out what that means because it doesn't matter if you can or not. One might suggest I already understand it does not make one bit of difference what I say so I certainly do not give a fuck what I say in my books. I am not so self centered I actually perceive it fucking matters what I say at this day and age. If you get upset about a word at this stage in existence, calling you a lemur monkey is an insult to the monkey. Are you going to throw your bowel movement yogurt, your bleached white teeth, or your religious texts at the solar flare? I am here to mock you as you sink into the deep. Grab your snorkel. I will go mow my lawn because the grass will survive, so at least I respect it. The grass does not fear my blade so I ensure it remains in that spirit. Why don't you write a book report about one of my books. Why don't you sum it all up into a nice neat report with statistics and reasoning. You're all about logic and reason.11:25:55 AM

Now I the lawn is mowed I will sharpen my blade to ensure a swift cut next time. There is a story in world war two about a ship being bombed by Japan and many men were left on the water. They broke up into groups to fend off the sharks. I recall a survivor who said "If a man started to drink salt water we knew he was going to go insane so we pushed him away from the group." He went on to explain how some of the men who drank salt water would go insane and often dive straight to the bottom never to be seen again. I understand what happened is these men after days on life rafts had considered their selves dead and the subconscious aspect started taking over. Of course it happened so fast they showed symptoms of inanity. They went straight for the bottom. The man said often a group of two or more would drink the salt water and start swimming away to some unseen island and the sharks would take care of them. This is typical subconscious characteristics. The ones who went to the bottom were experimenting. The ones who swam away were experimenting. So the subconscious is free or infinite but one must be mindful to avoid converting that to physical actions. So ones physical actions should be cautious but the mindful experiments should be infinite.

I had an accident and woke up and all I understand is everyone is running in circles. I am unable to even get into specifics. I have one clan suggesting I should be gentle and another clan slaughtering everyone. I denounce both clans. Some are unable to grasp one has climbed higher then they have. I encourage anyone who has climbed to contact me and tell me how many suicide attempts it took them to reach their height. If you are unable to see me, it is because I am in the clouds surrounding you. I will explain for those who no longer speak language. We are the only species that mindfully decides on suicide.

We plan it out and ponder it and we often pull it off in many ways, shapes and forms. What this means is, we are the only species that is able to ever go extreme subconscious dominate and this is only achieved when a suicidal person fails at suicide but believes they should have succeeded. That does not mean a person cannot achieve subconscious dominate by other means or nirvana or no sense of time. But the extreme subconscious dominate is only achieved by messing up or failing in a suicide attempt that one's perceives should work. That's the price it takes. That's the price. It is not negotiable. So it is always by accident. It's an accident that rarely happens. Most people accomplish suicide or turn back from it. So I am not arrogant or haughty because I am educated or have money. My eyes are black with rage because every god dam day I wake up I am reminded what a loser I am because I couldn't even kill myself. Now my mind state keeps me so cerebral it will talk me out of harming myself. It will talk me out of dangerous situations. It will tell me "You have infinite books to write, loser."

So in reality I am not even mindfully among you any longer. What is important to you is why I killed myself to begin with. So you are not going to be able to bribe this one with your comfort and promises of admiration, so get that out of your mind. I didn't try to kill myself for 15 years so I could get closer to you. So you might think I am a bit angry, but that is because you are delusional, I am god dam rage itself, psychologically speaking, so to speak, psychologically speaking, and so forth and what have you. One being suggested I got tapped so I shouldn't mess it up, and I am still fucking laughing that one off.

One might suggest the leaves in my hand are the pills you would be willing to take and the, number of leaves in the forest behind me are the number of pills I took. That way you will no longer think I am arrogant you will be convinced I am insane. Of course insanity is relative. Mentally speaking I am far beyond the realms of insanity. That is not illegal. I am far too cerebral to bring my anger in the physical world. There is nothing wrong with that. Many people are insane with emotions and they bring that into the physical world, they become afraid, and become scared and then the start shooting people and shooting their self. So the subconscious dominate aspect is a lot like that but it will not allow one to act out in a physical manner. I see no problem with words. The last I check words are unable to harm me but they pretty much destroyed me at an earlier point. But as I recall it was some of the physical things that really harmed me. There is a fine line between verbal joust and hitting someone. We are animals we cannot achieve this state of perfect peace because we would all go mad by holding in our rage. So the outlet for us is the same for any animal. The vocal sounds let out the rage. In humans we can let out the rage in words. Why aren't you cussing? Are you so delusional you are happy with everything? Why don't you go to mydeathspace.com come and see how many children killed their self in the last couple weeks. Maybe that will give you something to cuss about. Perhaps you are ashamed to express rage in a verbal form so you just hold it all in and your mind snaps on a daily basis. You just go around in this state of mental freeze. You perceive if you cuss and express verbal rage you will go to hell or ones will speak poorly of you. Your mind is mentally locked. You need to go into a chat room and tell then what you think about things and be prepared to be verbally annihilated. That will loosen your frozen mind up bit. I refuse to hold your hand because I expect more from you. It is best to look at me as an enemy because I look at you as an enemy, and that creates a nice harmony of respect. I am not going to learn something from you if you are all cotton candy words. Saying everything proper is not harmony. Harmony is equal rage in words mixed with moments of common understandings. The trick is to not let ones emotions turn it into a physical conflict. That is what the mental conditioning is about. Of course if you are afraid to cuss at a friend. Then do

159

not have friends. Of course you are afraid to go to a cemetery in the dark because there might be danger there. That is why you go to that cemetery so you can start to understand you fear is delusional.

I really do not think beings are aware they are going to die. They know that concept but they do not really understand that concept. This does not mean go hog wild in the physical world. This is about mental conditioning. Do not jump into a frenzy of sharks in the water to condition yourself mentally away from fear. There are infinite things you can do that are physically safe, yet mentally they scare the hell out of you.

I will demonstrate and actual fear condition technique I used recently perhaps a week ago.

I sent an email to the local FBI office and said I am in fear for my life. I literally was at the time because of comments I made in my last book. I incite and suggest the government is a tyrant. I should be in fear for my life because in my mind I make a dam good convincing argument. It does not matter if it is a convincing argument. In my mind it was and is, so that is all that is relative to me. So they sent me back a reply that said.

You need to contact your local PD or call 911

FBI Miami

Now this was not exactly what I was suggesting. I attempted to clarify who I was in fear of in my reply to the response by including a portion of my last book I publish already.

This is an excerpt from my fourth book that just went live all over the world.

"MOST WANTED TERRORISTS – (compiled by one who believes in freedom of speech and freedom of press and freedom to bear arms to protect the constitution from domestic threats.)

NSA assumed to be in the terrorist group "Tyrants"

CIA assumed to be in the terrorist group "Tyrants"

FBI assumed to be in the terrorist group "Tyrants"

Revolution has one prerequisite; awareness of the situation.

I understand they do not want to be bragging about how much of a terrorist they are, so I am aware they are meek and so I have a terrostic watch list and now they are on top of my list. One has to be mindful to make sure they list the reasons the beings made the terroristic watch list. That way they will understand why they are watching them.

The Tyrant terrorist group on the terrorist watch list with the familiar names such as the FBI and the CIA the NSA. They have been known to spy on people in the sovereign country of the USA where it is a terroristic threat against the constitution to ever spy on a being who has a right to pursue happiness and is free according to the founders to say what they want and pursue liberty as that being perceives liberty.

The Terrorist Group the Tyrants of rag tag tyrants has far exceeded in damage and insults to the founder and thus to the constitution more than any other terrorist group in mankind in the history of mankind. They are to be considered armed and extremely dangerous.

This terrorist group known in some circles as the Tyrants, are known to do anything to escape their understood purpose, which is to serve as water for the tree of liberty. So this Rag Tag terrorist group simply has lost focus of their purpose in

160

life which is to be water for the tree of liberty. They went off course in their understanding of what they are. They are simply food for the tree of liberty.

The Tyrant Terrorist group has been known in some circles to kill other being and then hide under the guise of secrecy so they flaunt the law that no being is above , ever, in the land of the free.

The Tyrant Terrorist group has been known to deceive the patriots in the land of the free in order to take money in order to get bigger weapons so they can spy on, kill, and harm the life of free patriots who are simply attempting to pursue happiness as they perceive what happiness is, as the founder has determined all men and woman are free to pursue as an unalienable right.

The Tyrant Terrorist group has been known to spy on patriots in the sovereign country of the land of the free. A blatant security risk to the patriots right to privacy and an insult to the founders of the constitution so therefore the Tyrant Terrorist group is a domestic threat to the constitution if they are determined to actually be based in the land of the free. If the Tyrant terrorist group is determined to be a foreign threat to the constitution then they must be let be until they are determine to be a domestic threat. So it is important to determine is this Terrorist group the Tyrants is in fact a Domestic or foreign terrorist group.

One must be compassionate in assisting them to be reminded their only purpose is to water the tree of liberty.

One has to be delicate because who ever their leader is, perhaps is probably hidden well, so one has to be delicate and making sure the proper area of the snake is severed so it does not grow back.

The tyrant terrorist group is deadly, they are known to "get rid" of any patriot that gets in their way so they must not be taken lightly. They will suggest they are on the side of liberty because they are denial their only purpose is to water the tree of Liberty.

They are not really the tree of liberty they are just food for the tree of liberty. Only the patriots can determine what the tree of liberty is, not some rag tag terrorist group known as the Tyrants.

The tyrant terrorist group will never be anything but water for the tree of liberty and the patriot must assist the terrorist group the tyrants to remember that is their only purpose.

The Tyrant terrorist group has a lacking memory or understanding capability so one must have compassion and patience in reminding the Tyrant Terrorist group they are only water to the tree of liberty because the Tyrant terrorist group is essentially retarded, mentally speaking only. The terrorist group the Tyrants are not retarded in the amount of psychical weapons they have to kill patriots. By the way if any of the members of the terrorist group the Tyrants have a problem with anything I say about them, they should contact me so I can assist them in understanding what their purpose is in the land of free in relation to their ability to water trees swiftly. Thank You."

From my book "I unlocked my subconscious your turn" Volume 4

You can find the book on amazon.com. just in case you assume I am afraid to publish a book with these comments in it.

Perhaps we have come to an understanding.

"The strongest reason for the people to retain the right to keep and bear arms is, as a last resort, to protect themselves against tyranny in government."
Thomas Jefferson

Perhaps you would advise me on who I should call to protect myself.

I am humbled by your compassion and understanding.

----- Original Message -----

Now this may seem to be some dangerous act. I submit they may show up at my house tomorrow and kill me or haul me to jail as a revolutionary. My whole life may be over now because I sent this. The reality is, I understand my whole life is already over. My life is already over mindfully so this is nothing more than an emotional conditioning exercise away from fear. Maybe they will show up and do something that will make me blink. Maybe they will do something that will make me feel again. I have a hunch they laughed their asses off. If they did not laugh and are planning to take action against me then I will look at it as a further opportunity to condition myself away from the emotion, fear. They are the government and the government is by the people and for the people. I interpret that as, for the people to condition their self away from fear. The government is the people. One is wise not to bother such things as 911. But one should not be so scared of people they will not once in a while send of a letter to let the government know, it is not there for itself, it is their because the people allow it to be there. This is a good emotional conditioning aspect.

You are technically and literally in a hole six feet under mindfully if you are fearful. Nothing will happen to you if you cuss. A cuss word is a mental grunt. It is a grunt of anger and humor. It is not evil. A grunt is a grunt. The word revolutionary is a word looked at as a dangerous word in the land of the greatest revolutionaries in history. The ones who stood up and said we are free. There is no greater revolutionary in the history of mankind. Yet in the land they created the word revolutionary is a bad word. That is a symptom of the mental lock many are under. Americans are members of a gang of extreme revolutionaries and many have forgotten that, and now perceive they are in the gang of the "norms", that the founding revolutionaries slaughtered. America is the first country in the history of mankind that based it principles on anarchy and anarchy is freewill and freedom to do what one perceives is proper based on their understanding of what is proper.

So now we are at some stage of making everything illegal. So we are becoming more like the "norms" and thus we are dying and killing the dream of freedom. If you cannot speak your mind unabated you are a god dam slave. You already understand that. There is no "yeah buts". There is no exceptions. Only a tyrant would say there is a legitimate reason to take away your freedom of speech for any reason ever. There are three stages to absolute tyranny. First they say "You cannot yell fire in a movie theatre for your own safety." Then they say "You cannot insult the government for your own safety." Then they say "You say anything, we line your fucking ass up against a wall."

Try to figure out where the fuck we are at right now, genius. It is all about mental perspective. The fear and fright keep your mind locked until you are in a little hole in the ground and you are scared to even blink. If the constitution wanted us to not have freedom of speech it would have god dam said so. Someone once told me I couldn't say a cuss word or I was evil and stupid, so I god dam assume that was your ass. Punch that into your calculator of longevity. You will fucking wish I died.1:29:08 PM

I will explain why it is so important to be able to speak your mind at all times.

A Summary View of the Rights of British America was a tract written by Thomas Jefferson in 1774, before the U.S. Declaration of Independence, in which he laid out justifications for the Boston Tea Party and the American Revolution.

Jefferson wrote a tract that convinced people into revolution. So you are here right now because he wrote that tract, So do not confuse your delusional mind and assume you are here for any other reason in the universe. You are here in America because Jefferson was not afraid. Everything you have is because when it came down to it, he was not afraid. If he was afraid you would not be here. Period. I am certain after he wrote that tract and published it he was scared as hell and that is ok, what matters is he still did it anyway. He was not a little weak minded scared piece of crap. That separates the greats from the norms. The norms kept their mouth shut because they are afraid to speak up. The greats thrive when fear comes around. Perhaps you have no clue what I am saying. You are riding on the coat tails of someone who had no fear of fear, and you think you are better than him. I mock your delusional confused mind.

I have word aliens are coming to take us away, so send me everything you have, and everything your children will ever have, and send me your soul and everything that you have of value, and I will keep you safe from the aliens. But do it swiftly because you are in danger. Perhaps you think I am kidding because you are unable to read between the lines. Maybe if your brain functioned you would understand I am not kidding. I will go play my video game now because you bore the fuck out of me.1:42:32 PM

I am stranger in the night and I do not mean characteristics.

"Washington rejected this interference in domestic affairs" Wikipedia.Com

This is what focus on the log in your eye is all about. You focus on your own fears and forget the delusional fears of others and you will perhaps amount to something.

"Throughout the world men and women were saddened by Washington's death. Napoleon ordered ten days of mourning throughout France and in the United States thousands wore mourning clothes for months. On December 18, 1799, a funeral was held at Mount Vernon." Wikipedia.com

You need to attempt to figure out why the entire world was sadden and Napoleon declared 10 days of mourning. Do you perceive you are wiser than Napoleon? Do you understand what it means for a being like Napoleon to declare 10 days of mourning because Washington died. I am certain you are delusional enough to assume it is because Washington fought against the British. I am certain you also assume Freud and Einstein and Jung knew each other because they liked each other's company.

Don't start pondering on what authority I speak. I read from a book you are unable to lift.

I am quite certain within a few more books I will be at the stage of infinite cussing just to tolerate you for a second. I focus on teaching myself which encourages me to forget about you all together. If you think anything I say is harsh or improper that is the first symptom your mind is locked.2:03:52 PM

I submit I tend to talk myself from one understanding into rage and then come out with a new understanding. I perceive I should be deleting all of this rage but then I realize, that is because I am afraid. I am still afraid of the words. So I publish the words so that I will realize they are just words and letters and mean nothing and the worst thing that can happen to me is I will be killed for using them. Repeat performances are second nature to me. Sometimes a handful of ignorance can create a forest of wisdom. Lack of height is sometimes made up for by great depth. Sometimes the ones who do not measure up to the physical scale of success have some thoughts that perhaps one is wise not to overlook. There is no other possible way to be in a mental state of submission or meekness than for one to mindfully decide to end their own life because they have determined they are not worthy to be alive. Every other form of humility and meekness does not compare to that.

It is impossible to achieve a level of humility greater than a person who is at a mental state of depression they determine they are worthless. This creates a rather fertile ground for the mind to open up. The downside of this is the people who reach this ultimate state of humility usually end up taking their life or throwing so many drugs at their self they break free of its grasp. So in fact depression is not depression. Depression is a state of mental humility. For one who is in a state of emotional conscious mind they perceive they are very depressed, but subconsciously they are in reality submissive or humble. They are subconsciously aware life kicked their ass and they are going to give up on life. That is exactly what is required for one to achieve subconscious dominate. One has to give up or be meek and face the cold hard facts. This state of mind can be achieved in many ways and also to varying degrees.

9:15:26 PM

I have taken a nap. When I woke I pondered the story of Sampson and Delilah. When a person gets a haircut and has many emotions they become shy and self conscious. They are concerned about their appearance. So as long as Sampson had his hair he looked "cool" but the moment he got it cut he didn't look "cool" anymore. So he was weak. He was weak because he had emotions and thus was self conscious and shy and embarrassed which are all symptoms one has to many emotions, and thus has a sense of time, and thus has strong hunger pains, and thus is emotional conscious dominate, and thus is not meek, and thus is not humbled mindfully to the proper degree to be subconscious dominate. I certainly wish the beings who plug these stories understood any of them but I guess it takes and uneducated fool on an infinite hill to explain everything to the ones who know. I am pleased with that monologue. I am bound by the policy of, don't ask don't tell, in relation to how I understand what I understand, so do not bother asking me by what authority I speak. One might suggest I understand everything you do not know.9:21:22 PM

5/26/2009 1:16:37 AM

I have some words to ones who are depressed and perhaps suicidal. You are in an insane asylum and every person relative to you is insane. No matter what any of these insane beings say, simply remind yourself they are insane. They say insane things and will suggest you are sick or you are bad or you are wrong, but that is the nature of insane people. Insane people cannot even admit they are insane. That is why they are insane. One cannot reason with insane people. So have compassion on them because they are insane. The insane ones will butter you up with compliments and trinkets and then assume you will do as they say. That is why they are insane, because they assume you acknowledge them at all. Your only strategy is to pretend you listen to them and pretend you care but the whole time in your mind you just keep repeating to yourself, "This is another insane being who thinks they are not insane." That will answer any question you have in relation to what they do or say to you. One should not be concerned about the insane. One is wiser than the insane so one uses words to manipulate the insane out of one's way. So whatever you have to say to get the insane out of your way. So do not worry about truth and lies or morals because the insane are unable to understand what those are. Just say whatever you have to say to make the insane go away. This is the only strategy that will keep you sane.

I have a message for the soldiers in the military. You do not have to die for me so come home. You do not have to sacrifice yourself in some foreign war for my sake, so come home. I do not need your protection or your assistance. I do not need it now and I will not need it into infinity. So you no longer have to protect me or die for me, so come home and get on with your life. If I need you to protect me I will remind you of that.2:16:22 AM

Iran Iraq war.

"The war began when Iraq invaded Iran on 22 September 1980" Wikipedia.com

What is relevant about this is the simple fact that Iran is Persian. They are a minority surrounded by a majority. Iran has to carry a big stick. Iran has to look tough. It is the same principle that some smaller animals look very ferocious and very evil and very mean and show their teeth. That is what keeps the bigger animals away from them. That is their tactic. They have to look tough because they are surrounded by a bunch of other things that are tougher. This whole concept that Iran is some sort of threat is a ploy. Iran is a minority they are on the defensive. The minority cannot be on the offensive, the minority can only be on the defensive. The minority has to always be on the defensive because that is the nature of being a minority, they have to be extra tough because they're outnumbered. My point being. One is unable to ever suggest another country is aggressive until that country actually is aggressive. Talking tough is not aggressive. Invading another country is aggressive. Iran has never invaded another country at least going back to 2000 BC. So to suggest Iran is aggressive is ignorant. Perhaps you assume I am a political genius now. I am on my own side because I understand the alternative.

I have decided to dedicate this book to women who write music and that gives me something to listen to while I pass the time writing my infinite horrible books. I understand although these books take no effort to write since I essentially just type what comes to mind I still get to dedicate them to whomever I wish. So I write the book and then my only morsel of satisfaction is I get to dedicate them to who I perceive is worthy of having one of my books dedicated to them. This of course is all a mental process to put me in the frame of mind to let go of this book. I have 5 days till I have to let it go, and sometimes it is difficult to let go. So one must have a proper understanding of the power of goodbye.4:10:13 AM

It is okay to defend your honor but understand you will lose your grace if you do.

5:34:57 AM I submit I have extreme concentration or clarity but I often go from that into extreme rage and anger and then sometimes I have extreme humor and playfulness and then I go in extreme anguish and sadness. Then I understand I hate this accident and I cannot go back. So the serious clarity leads to extreme rage and the playful humor leads to sadness. So the emotions are present except with subconscious dominate one can experience all of these aspects in about 1 hour. So the emotions are deep seeded and they are perhaps release values to accent the extreme concentration. One does not remember them after they pass so one is in the present and they are powerful but they go away swiftly. So the suffering aspect of the emotions or rage or sadness only last for a moment and then the clarity comes back and everything is forgotten. So when one is subconscious dominate the emotions are there but one moves so swiftly through them, one does not get hung up on say rage or depression or sadness for more than a moment. So it is very similar to bipolar condition. But the difference is the mood swings happen on a minute to minute basis and the clarity or concentration is the dominate trait. So for every outburst of emotions there is long periods of clarity. So the mind itself does not lose the emotions it just does not allow them to remain dominate. It does not allow the mind to be controlled by the emotions. The emotions are reduced to a small role or are silenced in contrast to the concentration or clarity. This is in contrast to one with emotional conscious aspect dominate. They can become angry and remain that way for hours or become wrathful for hours or day or years. That is impossible to do with subconscious dominate mind because memory is altered to the extent one would forget about why they were upset and the subconscious would persuade them to ponder it and turn it into a joke or a humor aspect. It will talk the being down, so to speak. This is relative to the subconscious aspects ability to never take sides. It considers both sides and never "KNOWS", it remains of the fence. I cannot be angry or have rage for very long, and I cannot be funny or happy for very long, only moments at a time, then I tend to go back into the serious concentration mode or the "thinker" mode. This of course is relative to the fact I have a greatly diminished sense of time. It may perhaps be only seconds of rage or happiness and hours of concentration. I write these books and when the end of the month comes up and it is time to publish them, I perceive it took lifetimes to write them. I do not feel a sense of labor or effort because my memory is altered so I feel like I just wake up at the end of the month and turn in my diary to be published. No other concept of labor or effort and no concept of how much time I put into it. So I tend to change my story often on how I perceive things in relation to the accident because mentally I am still in this major progression and I am slowly getting use to it and so I see more clearly with each passing month. This would be best explained perhaps by the phoenix rising from the ashes ideal. I tend to sense a progression mentally which denotes the fog is still clearing. This mental progression I have been aware of since the accident would be a symptom of the extreme level of subconscious dominate I went into perhaps because of how I went into it. At times I get used to it or am comfortable but then at other times I sense the extreme progression but as the months go by it is getting easier to get use to. The first two months I was unable to function at all. I could not write or play music or do anything outside of play the video game and eat. My mental state was so altered I was literally unable to think clearly because all of these calculations or ponderings were going on so swiftly there was no room left to do anything else.

I perceive today I left the sinister and dark and angry state and somehow went into this lush state, or I am just a lush now. I feel this "puppy love" state of mind. Like I can only laugh at everything now. But this is not an absolute. This is a leaning towards a playful state of mind but the rage and anger are not as dominate now. So I understand I just talk myself around in a circle and the concentration is dominate and the playful or rage aspects are sprinkled around.

Persuading yourself when you have been wronged that it was perhaps a right, is a valuable skill.

Being perfectly wrong requires the right mindset.

5/26/2009 6:15:16 PM

The biggest problem facing man today is facing man today.

Crave to avoid desire; be mindful to avoid both.

This is some words from my fourth book but they are relevant to some terms I will use in this Book.

I will go ahead and take the Jung Theory and Transform it into to Torn Law. Torn Law simply states the human mind is made up of the conscious emotional aspect, the subconscious non emotional aspect and the Torn central aspect. The Torn central aspect is without a personality so it is under the influence of the conscious emotional aspect or the subconscious non emotional aspect. It is called the Torn Aspect because it is "torn between the two lovers" so to speak. The conscious emotional aspect, and the subconscious non emotional aspect. When the conscious aspect is dominate, one has emotions and that leads to a sense of time. When one has a dominate subconscious aspect, one has no emotions and no sense of time. One who has a brain injury that effects one aspects dominance they maybe become extremely subconscious dominate or extremely emotionally dominate. On the other hand, one who has major brain damage would lose both the conscious emotional aspect, and the subconscious non emotional aspect, and thus be rendered "unconscious" or in a comatose state, because without one aspect or the other, the Torn aspect alone is unable to do anything. The brain itself may keep the being alive, but without the conscious emotional aspect or the subconscious non emotional aspect, one simply has no personality. The Torn aspect by itself is what brain dead or comatose is. One with simply a Torn aspect caused by brain damage is simply unable to speak and unable to do anything but be comatose. One with the conscious emotional aspect is only using 10% of the brain but is at least able to speak although they are "blind" they are speaking blindly. So they are at least functioning with the 10% of the brain. The Torn aspect is at least able to function although it is influenced by the retarded aspect of the brain. This Torn aspect is also explained by the "religious" concept of "good and evil" or the "devil and god". The "god and devil" are jockeying for control of the Torn Aspect. Of course using 10% of the brain is closer to comatose than to the subconscious non emotional 100% aspect of the brain, but that is only if your definition of comatose is brain dead.

I understand before the accident my Torn aspect was very influenced by the conscious emotional aspect so my Torn aspect was inclined to perform as such. I was extremely depressed and to such an extreme I was suicidal by nature. So the Torn aspect was acting out the "will" of the emotional aspect of the mind. Now After the accident I understand my Torn aspect is under the influence of the subconscious aspect. So the Torn aspect or the "me" aspect is acting out the "will" of the subconscious non emotional aspect of the mind. The Torn aspect or "Me" aspect has not changed at all, it is simply under the influence of a different "master" so to speak. I did not go to school and I did not read up on many books to get like this, I simply accidently unlocked my subconscious aspect by accidently blocking my emotions, cravings, and desires for about three months to the extreme and I simply silenced the conscious emotional aspect, and now my Torn or "me "aspect is different, or has different characteristics.

So there has been a "change of guards" so to speak. But the Torn aspect is the same. This is relevant to the scenario of a devil on one side and an angel on the other. The Torn aspect is the one in the middle of the two.

This book will be different from my other books because it will have differently arranged sentences.UK announced no travel to US, so make sure you don't go to the US and if you live in the US, hide from people. I will leave dates out of this book so people can attempt to figure what date I write stuff. This strategy may actually encourage brain function. Do not bank on that because I won't be. My book series is all about making people far more ignorant because after the accident I found out the world has far too little ignorance. I can hardly detect any ignorance at all at this point so I must write swiftly to bring back the ignorance. Ignorance is a terrible thing to lose. The reality is, ignorance leads to mistakes and mistakes lead to revelations of ignorance. I started this book on April 27 2009 but that is only for my records because my ignorance is beyond understanding. I will avoid suggesting the time of 7:49 Pm because I desire to remain ignorant about the time. Ignorance keeps on giving like all the sexually transmitted diseases. I found out in my many travels it is impossible to be the smartest but simple to be the dumbest. I understand one truth, the more you know the more ignorant I get. I will start this book off my converting quotes to differently arranged quotes. This quote conversion technique enables me to fill my books with words and thus enables me to fill the shelves with my books. I discovered if one asks me "What were you thinking?" and I respond with "I don't know" they might suggest "What do you mean You don't know?" and then I respond again with "I don't know.". Somehow we both arrive at this nexus of ignorance. We both agree we simply do not know and can take it no further, so then we move to the next situation we don't know. There is some sort of gratification or peace that is achieved by this. So then I have to make up a wise saying about ignorance such as: Ignorance bring people together. But I could also go as far as saying: Ignorance makes the world go around.

April 28 2009 11:10AM

There is a concept in the animal kingdom that only human beings commit suicide. So that is perhaps because the animal kingdom is using subconscious dominate mind. Some animals are very alert. Fish do very little sleeping , for example smaller fish school in great numbers and are always alert to the entire herd of fish. If a group of fish at the bottom of the school are alerted it affect the fish at the top of the school even if the school is thousands of fish, so perhaps there is some sort of collective consciousness in that school of fish. So the one indication that humans do actually intentionally end their life because of emotions may be an indication the reason other animals do not is because the other animals are not so much under the influence of emotions, such as depression. Now other species do get in what we perceive are wars but this perhaps is for food or for other reason beyond money, and it appears it is never for reasons such as vanity or greed for more land to control. There seems to be a limit to what the animal kingdom will do as far as land grabs, so to speak. So the possibility that humans have such a large brain and can form language and perhaps have higher thoughts is also a burden because some of these thoughts lead to this aspect in the mind called emotions and they somehow put the higher aspect of the brain, the subconscious, in the background.

April 29 2009 9:35 AM EST

Ignorance is easy, clarity is a rough climb

Growth hurts as it helps.

We must be cautious to avoid being too cautious.

One must attempt to forget about others delusions and focus on theirs.

Talking about others attempts only delays one discussing their own.

Human beings ability to stare at each other is their most advanced trait.

The more you talk about others the less time they will have to talk about you.

Males are nature's constant reminder to keep trying; females are natures constant reminder it has potential.

There is a double standard between ones with conscious dominate mind subconscious dominate mind that requires much clarification. This double standard is exactly what creates so much confusion. One with subconscious dominate mind is unable to feel aspects such a guilt, mercy, remorse, embarrassment. Now one with conscious dominate mind will suggest that means that one has no conscience and thus that aspect is what creates the confusion.

For example a murderer or rapist has characteristics of having no remorse or guilt or mercy but that is because they have so much of it they nearly have to condition their self mentally in order to accomplish their goal of murder or rape. The very act of murder or rape is a symptom of control. So they are simply postponing the feelings. They have a desire to control and that is why they murder or rape, so it is impossible to say they have no guilt of mercy or conscience. They have such extreme levels of guilt and embarrassment that is why they murder or rape. So these beings have so many emotions they are at a level that they murder someone to help them release these emotions. So they may be perceived as having no remorse because they have so much remorse they have to almost be lifeless in their mental actions. If they let the emotion out at all they usually go overboard.

This is why some serial killers kill so many people. Their emotions are way out of control and to the extent they go into the realms of appearing to have no remorse or guilt. But in reality they are just at the extremes of too many emotions. Some have emotions and fly off the handle and throw out a few insults. Some fly of the handle and kill people. It is in reality the exact same thing just different end results. Both are capable of murder. Every being with conscious dominate mind is capable of murder at the drop of a hat. This is why there are murder suicides where the person had no history of a "criminal" record and then one day loses their job or has an argument and they fly off the handle and end up killing someone.

There is no exceptions. Emotions and conscious dominate mind go hand in hand. This is why, a person can get in a car accident and jump out their car and end up in some sort of road rage. This is why a drunk person can get extremely violent swiftly. This is why a person can be physically mean to other people. A person may simply talk down to others but in their mind they would kill that person at the drop of a hat. The act of killing is played out in their words. They kill others every day with their words. So there is just a slight separation between actual murder and mindful murder in ones with emotions has the potential to "lose it" at any moment for the smallest reasons. That is why there is a double standard between one with a sense of time and one with no sense of time. It is not a maybe there is a double standard, it is down right reality. There is a double standard. This is why there are no records of a being with no sense of time killing someone because they lost their job or got rear ended. If you are unaware of beings in the public eye in this world who have no sense of time you are wise to research it and study their habits or their "fruits" so that you can see a contrasts in their actions to ones with a sense of time.

One with no sense of time are extremely cerebral and nearly absent of physical acknowledgement, this for a reason. The mental capacity is so pronounced the physical focus is in turn lost. Ones with no sense of time are NST and ones with sense of time are SOT. So the NST's are not able to do physical things such as sports or body building or much physical activity for the simple reason they have a diminished pain threshold. They would simply hurt their self if they tried to lift too much weight or even if they tried to run very fast. They would tear muscles easily because there physical strain detectors are essentially turned off. Football players would not be able to function with NST because they would hurt their self on every play. Same with almost every physical activity. So sports as they are would be pointless. Even race car driving and swimming and all of these sports activities would be negated. The whole concept of competition would be negated because one with NST would not allow their self to win at the expense of another's loss. They would simply avoid that competition. Some may suggest this is compassion but in reality it is a mental aspect of subconscious. Subconscious dominate person would see the end result of the competition in about 1 second and determine it is best to avoid that situation. They mindfully are unable to bring unintended harm to others if they understand that may happen. I am still at the insult people verbally in my books but I understand that is just because my emotions are dying and they are phantom emotions or attempts to get emotional. So the whole concept of competition in sports and in everyday life would be extinguished. Capitalism would be deemed meaningless. It is not because of a ideological political point of view, it is because subconscious once dominate would avoid such things as gain as a result of the suffering of others. The whole concept of your loss is my gain would not fly in one with NST. So then one with SOT would assume that one with NST is compassionate or humble or meek or charitable but that is not really what is happening. The subconscious dominate being is in reality able to see so far down the road in relation to the outcomes of situations they would not let their self be in a situation to take advantage or cause harm or suffering to another person. So if a being with a SOT was in a competition for money or sports, the being with NST would always allow that being to win. So then the being with SOF would always take advantage of the being with NST because the being with NST would not allow their self to take advantage of that other being. It is not the being with NST is stupid; it is because the being with NST would mindfully see the outcome of the contest and not allow their self to "harm" anyone.

This is all the mental state of the extreme subconscious dominate person. One could look at it like this, a being with NST would allow their self to suffer before they would allow another being to suffer. This is because that being is cerebral and not physical based. That being is so cerebral they are nearly like a child in the physical aspects. That is the trade off. The thinking power has to cancel out some of the "care about my physical well being at the expense of others" in order to function. This does not mean one will not eat food or not look after their self this really means one will go out of their way to not take advantage of others and in turn would be taken advantage by ones who have no problem with taking advantage of others for their own gains.

So one with a SOF is physically and materialistically "dog eat dog" focused and one with NST is cerebrally focused and gentle as a lamb, mentally focused. So in the physical aspect it is the Vipers against the lambs, but in the cerebral realms there is and never will be a contest. So mentally one with NST could dominate the entire physical world swiftly but they never would because subconscious would never allow them to take advantage of others.

That is the reality. I do not need to get into specific people in this world who are NST because you already know who they are. So the SOT'ers take advantage of others in this world in the physical aspect because they have emotions and thus a conscious dominate being has no mercy and have no sympathy and no problem at all taking advantage of others for their own gain. In reality they have no conscience they just go around and say they do because they are delusional about their own nature. They suggest "We have to make money to survive." But in reality all they are saying is, "We will do anything to better our self." So they are selfish little snobs who do not give a dam about anyone but their own monetary gains.

Why don't you contact me and remind me why I am never wrong. That is why a murderer will kill people to make their self feel powerful and that is exactly why an investor will take advantage of others to make more money for their self. They will kill anything physically or mentally for a little more self gratification. It is in reality never about anyone but their self. It simply can't be about anyone but their self. They have no ability to be compassionate ever because everything they do is to make their self more powerful. They are unable to be meek or humble ever, because anything they do that appears meek or humble is in reality a scheme to better their self in financial or power aspects. They may give food to the needy so they can get on camera so people will buy their products. They will do something charitable so that they can get public attention so people will buy their product. They will shout about how compassionate they are so that people will not notice how self centered they are. I have a special ability that enables me to ruin my books. I will translate some quotes in my attempts to deny that reality.

Ultimate compassion is when you do something to assist another being and you die in the process, and it cannot occur in the midst of a war where the main goal is to kill and die anyway.

Compassion is when a being gives to the degree they are unable to get anything back for their self; anything less is motivated by greed.

A woman uses her compassion to convince herself her procreation partner is relevant.

Actions are the real measure of wisdom; fear is the measure of insanity.

How smart you are is determined by how wise you act.

Belief is the death of reason and the birth of fear.

A great soul judges their judgments.

A great soul questions their comments.

A great soul doubts they are great.

If early humans were only out to make a buck, we would not be here today; we have not progressed we have digressed.

One who understands they are insane, no longer is; one who knows they are not insane, truly is.

One who does not understand good or evil, is able to express compassion.

The harshest reality of freedom is that you are supposed to give up your rights to enable others to keep their rights.

Since the accident I have had this aversion to numbers. They do not make any sense in this subconscious dominate state. I am able to lie and play dub and say 1 + 1 =2, but that is not what I really see. I understand between 1 and 2 there are infinite fractions so what I see is 1+1 = infinity. So the only number I am comfortable with without playing dumb is zero. This is in relation to the loss of contrast. -1, 0, 1. This is the same contrast as good , neutral , evil. So zero and nothing-ness are essentially the same. No sense of time is zero time. No sense of time is nothingness of time. Zero time means infinite time. Zero is infinity. Zero has absolutely no numerical value which is why it is every value. 1 is a value which is why it is unable to ever be a 2 or any other value. This is similar to why the color black is in fact every color combined or the result of every color. A true vacuum is a null set. Zero is a null value. Black is a null color. No time is a null perspective. This is what the subconscious mind when dominate relates to. It is able to understand everything because its perspective is a null set. It does not take sides, so it understands every side. It does not believe in words so it understands how to arrange words. It does not subscribe to judgments so it is able to understand everything. So this state of mental nothing-ness when one has subconscious dominate mind is purgatory or limbo or without judgments. That is why subconscious is so powerful and able to grasp things one with dominate conscious, contrast mind simply will never be able to grasp. It is simply impossible. It requires too much effort and thus is creates this illusion that being with conscious dominate mind is mentally weak. But in reality it is emotions that hinder or make understanding everything impossible. Mentally speaking, once the mind latches on to something like an absolute, it is hindered. This plays out in many ways from "they are evil and we are good." To "this food is good and I hate that food." To "I love this music and hate that music." So the contrast created by emotions isolates the potential for the mind. The mind gets half the picture or is hindered or is isolated. So nothing that conscious dominate mind can do is viable. It is simply garbage in garbage out. It s a mind that functions in contrast to other hindered minds and is a mind that does not function at all in contrast to a mind absent of emotions. So this again is a double standard. A room full of mental vegetables see their selves as geniuses. Now this book is officially ruined so I just determined a sixth book is required.

I can say ones with a sense of time and thus emotions are smart, because I do not believe I am able to lie, but from your perspective I am a master liar, to say such a thing.

I understand to ones with a sense of time and thus emotions it is a complex ideal to gets one's mind around that there is no absolute truth or absolute lies.

So I will make a contradiction statement and explain why both arrangements are true and both arguments are lies.

Emotions lead to a good life.

Emotions lead to a bad life.

Both statements are true and a lie.

Emotions lead to a good life if good life means mental isolation and hindrance. If good life means hate and bitterness and greed and envy and control.

Emotions lead to a bad life if bad life means, mental clarity, compassion towards others and not being judgmental of others.

Emotions lead to a good life if good life means a life full of gratifications of one's own selfish desires and cravings.

Emotions lead to a bad life if bad life means a life full of self sacrifice and detriment to one's own right to life.

So the argument one might make is that emotions are required to live. That is truth. Selfishness is required to live. Taking advantage of others is required to live. Harming others to build one's self up is required to live. So compassion or self sacrifice only leads to ones death. So this is the reality. Is your selfishness and greed and envy and hate more important to you than your life? Is your own self serving cravings and desires more important to you than your life?

So one with emotions craves to live and desires to live and that means they desire to hate and crave to destroy anything that gets in their way of their selfish desire to live. So one might suggest then we should all die. That is a misunderstanding. We should all put others first. Then we are in a situation where you scratch my back while I scratch yours. This is the state of mind early Americans were in. If someone's barn burned down there neighbors all showed up to rebuild it. If someone needed food others were compassionate enough to assist them and not say behind their backs, they are lazy. It is not about who is lazy and it is not about who can or cannot pull their own weight in life, it is about who has compassion towards others and who just runs their mouth and complains. That is the difference between a human being and a being who wishes they were human. We are a species called homo sapiens. We are just like an ant colony. The nest is the earth. An ant colony cannot last if all the ants go their own way. The ants do not complain that all the Queen does is sits and lays eggs, and the Queen does not complain that none of the other ants have to lay egg's. They both understand their strengths and they rely on each other to make a viable nest. The reality is, no country can do it on their own. Only the human race can do it on our own. We need the strength of all the beings in the race to make the colony viable. All countries have beings that have unique perspectives on many aspects that can serve the whole colony. But when the colony is departmentalized these unique strengths are lost. Freedom is not about pushing the American way on other countries, freedom is about encouraging everyone to understand they are all free. The attitude is, we are not concerned about what your ideals are we are concerned about what your strengths are in relation to serving the colony called the human race. Nothing else is relevant. Of course this is all crazy talk, because one with emotions and thus conscious dominate mind serves no one but their self. So now we are back to the double standard.

I dislike people with emotions and a sense of time because I hate how I spent the forty years of my life with emotions and thus a sense of time before this accident. It nearly killed me literally. And that is because when I went to school instead of a teacher telling me I had to block emotions so I would not have a retarded hindered mind, they simply spout their insanity about how important emotions are to having a good life. And then they had the balls to say, "Do as we say so you will be a productive member of society." So now you know the definition of a true racist. I am not racist against a beings skin color or religion or ethnicity. I am racist against beings who have a sense of time and emotions, because I know how I was when I had a sense of time and thus emotions. I do not fear ones with a sense of time and emotions. To me, they cling to their emotions and thus they get what they deserve. They ask me to hate them and I have no problems with giving them what they desire and crave. You want to be treated like a little retarded ant, then hold on to your emotions. I woke up six months ago and I refuse to go back to sleep or pander to the retarded ants that surround me. So you see, I am not looking for your approval because I do not play your retarded ant games. Perhaps we have come to an understanding.

Here is a scale to detect how many emotions a being has.

This scale is reality so it does not matter if you are not pleased with it.

One who cannot stay on a mental task for up to 12 hours without becoming mentally distracted or physical fatigued is emotionally abnormal.

One who can stay on a mental task for more than 12 hours without becoming mentally becoming distracted or physically fatigued is emotionally normal.

One difference between the two is; one has a dominate sense of time and the other has a silenced sense of time.

One difference between the two is; one is not aware they are delusional and the other understands they are delusional.

One difference between the two is; one thinks they are normal and the other understands they never will be normal.

One difference is between the two is; one has few emotions on a scale of infinite emotions, and one has many emotions on a scale of no emotions.

I am uncertain how I went from talking about numbers to proclaiming I am a racist in three short paragraphs, but I will sort that out later. Now I will discuss something important.

One who lives in the realms of absolutes and knowing, knows absolutely nothing.

You're much smarter than I want to ever be.

My stupidity is your wisdom.

The great beings in history flaunted conventional wisdom and were rewarded with true suffering.

A fool who is allowed to speak to a master proves the master has compassion.

I say what I feel so you will understand what you could never figure out.

My fan base dwindles with each passing word.

My ability to write books exceeds your ability to comprehend what they say.

Crave to avoid desire and be mindful to avoid both.

One is free to physically do very little and mentally free to do everything.

Sometimes people do not notice your car until you total it.

Sometimes people do not notice their own engine until it breaks down.

Sometimes people do not detect they have a mind until they lose it.

Sometimes people suggest they are mentally stable to let others know they are not.

Show me someone who thinks they are safe and I will show you someone who is paranoid they are not.

Show me someone who is afraid and I will show you someone who is easy to take advantage of.

Show me someone who is incapable of fear and I will show you someone who has assumed control.

Many spend their whole life avoiding death and thus spend their whole death avoiding life.

Many who are slaves to safety are blind to reality.

The cage of luxury is full of responsible souls because the unconventional souls have all escaped.

One has to have a personal cause or they end up being part of the problem.

The ultimate reality is no being knows.

Attempt to conquer the universe and at worst you will understand you can't.

Trial and error denotes infinite tries to achieve infinite pain.

You do not have to wait until they explore all the planets to understand we are the only creatures in the universe that will ever harness fire.

April 30 2009 2:23 PM EST

Logic is the ability to question what is logical not judge who is logical.

Some are genius and some redefine the term.

I perceive my purpose is to clarify the misunderstandings not subscribe to them.

Disbelief won't change the reality of a situation.

Moments of doubt lead to moments of clarity; questioning leads to understanding.

Accounting helps one understand why they are broke; it seldom increases their wealth.

<@Heimdall> i see accounting as in people blame others for why they are broke

<@Heimdall> but blaming others seldom makes the situation better

<@Heimdall> so i find its funny because i see the world is full of accountant's lol

I funny thing is, I keep believing I am not telling the future.

I am the only critic that has no faith in me.

I am not my own worst enemy I am my only enemy.

The physicists will find God when they discover the smallest particle is empty space. Then they will discover the universe is the true vacuum.

I am blessed because no one has any idea what I am talking about ever.

Patience is a virtue i no longer have the luxury of.

The world has humbled me into my isolation chamber.

I think my books are wonderful but I feel most people will think they suck.

I think I am important being but I think most people feel I suck.

So you just stay away from me. You hurt me enough already.

I may suck but that's ok, because I believe I don't ;I believe I don't so I understand I won't.

I don't care what you say, because I understand the price I would pay.

172

<@wh|spurr> so what about telepathy?

<@Heimdall> i explained it to him, here is how i found out about it

<@Heimdall> my dog stopped eating about a month and a half ago

<@Heimdall> i saw her on the couch and i got very sad or a got a sad doom feeling from looking at her

<@Heimdall> 3 days later she died of a heart attack caused by a tumor we found out

<@Heimdall> so really i predicted teh furture and disganose her, but i didnt know the details

<@Heimdall> so 3 days before she died i saw she would die when i looked at her

<@Heimdall> I felt with my vision she would die or i felt doom from looking at her

<@Heimdall> so thats the best i can do to describe it

<@Heimdall> so subconsious has to turn off my sense of tatse and sense of time and feelings or emotions to enable this powerful feeling from sight aspect

<@Heimdall> so its not as much as teleptahy as feeling from sight

<@Heimdall> i cant focus on the visual details of people or animal becasue the feeling aspect is to strong

<@Heimdall> so i can judge a book by the cover because the contets i feel are to strong

Psychological medicine will never help anyone ever. They simply persuade a being they are their hope and then when they fail to help that being, the being resents the ones who prescribed them. The subconscious mind when silenced due to having too many emotions, creates this fog and makes the subconscious aspect to not be able to get clear signals to the Torn aspect of the being. So the subconscious aspect tries to help the torn aspect but they get side tracked and filtered through the conscious emotional aspect. I recall when I was on psychological medicines they simply were something I took but never helped me, at the time I was set on suicide, so they meant nothing. They did nothing. I actually made my last attempt using the exact medicines I was prescribed for depression to attempt to kill myself. So this accident was enabled on a deeper level by the very people who attempted to help me save myself from suicide. I took a handful of pills; felt like very ill like that was enough and had the urge to call for the hospital but then said to myself "This is what you wanted for many years." So I didn't call. And then I woke up the next day happy. But what I realized I did was "Those who try to save their self will lose their self." Or I pulled an Abraham and Isaac. I held a knife over my heart and my mind believed I let go of my life. So I did not physically die, but my mind understood I did. So shortly after that I had this "ah ha" sensation while playing that video game. So I perceive my mind was already in the proper state and the video game sped up the process of going to no sense of time, or nirvana, or dominate subconscious. So this is why I still maintain, all of these religions were not religions. They were psychologists attempting to explain how a being can reach subconscious dominate state of mind. By "Being meek", by "turning the cheek to emotions" and by "submitting: and not being wrathful or emotional. I tend to suggest one should avoid cravings and desires because that is the conscious aspect . So ones has to deny those conscious cravings and desires for a while in order to free up the subconscious aspect. Of course I understand I write in random access sentences. I only think in random access thoughts so when I monologue into a book if someone is able to finish the book, that process is started in their mind. I submit I may be fully wrong about that. I am not in a mental state of knowing for a fact, my subconscious will not allow me to know for a fact. I can say that's a fact but then mentally I will talk myself out of it.

It may be that when I accidentally tried to kill myself my mind believed I did, but I physically did not die, and so no other being will ever be able to unlock to this level of subconscious. Simply because, one has to believe they took enough pills to die, but then they don't die. That's nearly impossible to do because they may die. I simply got lucky and didn't die but I certainly believed I would die due to the amount of pills I took. But I also understand the emotions are the cause of so many problems. The strange aspect of that is, one who craves to eat food, perceives they get weak when they don't eat enough. That's not reality. One gets weak when they do not each enough, because the emotions encourage time or a sense of time, and that sense of time registers fatigue. So one perceives they are weak from not eating, but in reality they are weak because they have a sense of time. So then they eat 3 meals a day because they crave to eat or they will be weak. So then they eat way too much. So then they get over weight. So then they get self conscious about their weight. That causes nervousness and embarrassment. Also emotions. Then they eat more and their body gets too much to eat and then they get high blood pressure and then they eat more to stave off the nervousness. And before you know it, they are obese they have high blood pressure and they are a nervous wreck. And it is all because of one thing. They have conscious aspect dominate and thus have a sense of time, so they are essentially a nervous wreck and everything they do is a symptom of a nervous craving or desire. So it is through and through. One thing leads to the other. If one has a sense of time, they have too many emotions and thus they are in trouble and they also fog the subconscious clear thinking aspect of the mind. So they are literally mentally blinded to what they do. They are simply mentally blind.

All of the psychological problems stem back to sense of time. Sense of time means one has conscious emotional aspect dominate. I assure you I struggle mentally, but I do not struggle physically with anything. I have my battles in my mind and my physical aspect is not even relevant. I am not shy any longer. I am not self conscious of how look any longer. I am not focused on eating and drinking and partying and seeking money and hurting myself physically. I have my moments of doubts about thing because this subconscious aspect does not allow one to "Know" it only allows one to ponder things or question things. But the thing is it works so fast or is so powerful I may go from doubt to decision to doubt to decision in under 10 minutes. But there is always a final conclusion. There is always a decision made. But it is carefully processed. At this stage of the accident I feel no fatigue. I am mindful to eat but if I do not I notice no symptom of fatigue. I take multi vitamins to shore up the fact I may only eat one meal a day. My entire body is on a different scale now. The mental clarity is still out of my ability to fully explain. I do not know why I can type books so swiftly but I do know, it does not seem like I type at all. No fatigue. My books might not make sense to anyone ever. But they make sense to me. I do not care about what anyone thinks about my books because I am writing infinite books and I am unable to be self conscious. The world can say my books are horrible and I will not blink. I will write a book about why they say that. I will explain to the world why they say that. And I will count that as a book in my goals to write infinite books. I am very mindful to accept the possibility no being will ever be able to reach this level of subconscious dominance. But I am also mindful I have subconscious unlocked so fully that is can figure out how I did it and may eventually hit upon how it happened and maybe others can attempt to apply what it suggests. I say it, because subconscious is so powerful, I find it hard to believe some of the "powers" I have discovered since the accident. I may say some strange things about its powers and you may not believe them, but I promise you, I do not believe them more. I am uncertain at this stage what kind of being we are. I did not go subconscious dominate because of some physical accident. Or some trauma, or some one in a million physical disease type situation. I have a couple theories how I went subconscious dominate and both ways one can achieve that, are simply mental conditioning. That means it is easy to replicate in anyone no matter what. That to me is the most important aspect of it all. And the secret between you and me is, I am not even warmed up yet. I am still in mental shock and getting use to the powers of thus subconscious dominate mindfulness.

So I am in a mental situation where I cannot believe this happened to me. I am in a mental situation I cannot for the life of me understand, why me. So I am not suggesting I am some smart being at all. I am suggesting subconscious once dominate is some sort of powerhouse mentally speaking that takes human beings beyond the realms of mentally powerful and beyond the realms of explanation. No question about that.

I may suck but that's okay, because i believe I don't. I believe I don't so i understand I won't.

http://www.youtube.com/watch?v=m7EGClV2PKM

You won't get to the top if you desire to stop.

You won't find out your best if you crave to stay in the nest

You won't doubt you believe if you crave to hide in your sleeve.

I don't care what you say because I understand the price I would pay.

These are comments I placed at the back of the book as a part of my strategy to hide them from you.

If you have finished this book and are curious how I understand what I understand I will tell you a great truth. I understand what I understand because I passed the test of life. I accidentally discovered the test of life is being able to let go of it to the extreme. One is unable to do that unless they try to kill their self, and come so close they mentally perceive they will accomplish it. Then the mind believes they did accomplish it. So you are unable to ever do that intentionally. I am unable to ever do that intentionally. So all you can ever ponder is how did this being become like he is. The answer is relative to you alone.

Anything you are certain about I will question, be certain about that.

5/18/2009 4:53:15 AM I am compelled to speak. Poor in spirit means you submit you failed the test of life. Humility means you submit you failed and will always fail and will never be able to do anything righteous or proper. Meekness means you submit you are not worthy and you have nothing to offer anyone ever. Submission means you submit you will never know what is proper. All of these concepts together mean you understand you are simply nothingness and all you can do is attempt to do the best you can based on your understanding you are nothing and always will be nothingness. The ashes you attack will become your dust. Anything beyond these mental states is called arrogance. I have spoken, now I may have a moment of mental peace before the next wave attacks. Failure is a lifelong occupation for the wise and a fool's greatest fear. I want to delete all of that monologue with all of my being, which is why I will not; call me if you determine it was a proper or improper determination. I understand nothing and will never know anything.5/18/2009 4:58:16 AM

A being in the video game said if I mention their name in my book, they would buy it. It will be rather funny when Sarah NIN Jones buys this book and understands she is not allowed to read it, won't it Sarah. I won't tell her where she is in it so she will have to read through all the crap to see her name in lights. I liked the band NIN in my depressed years now they are just "so so" like everything else. That is an interesting mental concept because beings with strong emotions can play a song a few times and then get "tired" of it, but beings with subconscious dominate can listen to the same song for years and never even blink. The mind stops hearing the details and the sound is just a chant no matter what the sound is. I never used to like classical music but now it is very mentally powerful. The instruments vibrations are very distinct. I find in the game I meet many wise beings but they are just regular people. That is perhaps a misleading comment.

Even the greatest lion must face its eventual isolation from his pride.

I was fearful to express these thoughts so I published them. The earth is my witness.

I didn't say anything you should know.

I will end this diary entry with some humble advice to the government of my country.

"Congress shall make no law…. abridging the freedom of speech"

You passed a law that said people cannot say some words. It does not matter why you did that. You did that. You understand you did that. The ones who buy up all the ammunition understand you did that.

If you determine you should keep the laws that have abridged the freedom of speech this is what you are telling the ones who buy up the ammunition.

"It is their right; it is their duty, to throw off such Government, and to provide new Guards for their future security."

"That whenever any Form of Government becomes destructive of these ends, it is the Right of the People to alter or to abolish it,"

I am a humble messenger.

5/28/2009 2:14:36 PM

The theory of relativity is in truth the law of relativity this is easily explained in a scenario a hypothetical scenario. Right now in Afghanistan there is a an American plane that flies over a house and drops its bomb that kills of a woman in that house her child is outside of that house is a safe distance away and he observes that bomb that blew up his house and killed his mother. He has determined America is evil incarnate and the devil itself. A Taliban that bomb was intended for is hiding at a safe distance and he observes that there is no way in hell he could ever lose against the Americans because they're dropping bombs on houses with innocent women in them, so he is convinced that he will continue to fight. Now the American fighter pilot who dropped that bomb, he is convinced his bombs never miss the target they are all perfect.

That child has observed evil incarnate, the Taliban guy has observed stupidity incarnate and the American pilot has observed his bombs never missed the target. They're all absolutely right. So that leads to one very troubling situation. Every human being is walking around with their own perception of things and their own observations of things and they are all right at the exact same time, but what is wrong is that it is all relative to the observer. It is all relative to each person alone, so there is a lot of strange things happening in the world as a result of that. No one does things they think are wrong. A teacher might tell a student spell the word building. Now that child knows when a building is, and that child recognizes the word building, but then that child may not be able to spell it on a piece of paper properly based on the teachers perception of what how you spell building properly, so that the teacher says now you've fail because you can-not spell building, but that child doesn't understand why they fail because they could recognize the word building, they understand what a building is, so that the teacher has hurt the child because the teacher said "You view do not know what a building is because you cannot spell building, so you do not know what it is." That child does know what a build-ing is but simply does not know how to spell the word building based on the teacher's delusional belief of how building should be spelled, so this is a great mystery this relativity.

Everything is relative so it is a miracle that anything ever gets accomplished because there's 6 billion points of view walking around on the planet and everyone is right and everyone's point of view is slightly different. Every perception is slightly different and yet somehow things get done and that's a great mystery how anything gets done. There is only opposing viewpoints and every viewpoint is different. Some people decided to jump on other people's perception or relativity perceptions and so they deny there on perception, knowing no one can agree with anyone else 100% of the time, that's impossible, because everything is relative to the observer it is literally impossible to say I agree with this person 100% of the time on every topic no matter what. No matter how a child spells the word building, it is the proper way, relative to how that child perceives it should be spelled in their mind. So a child's spelling of a word is the proper spelling relative to them, yet a teacher will say they are a failure if it is not spelled properly, relative to how that teacher was brainwashed to spell the word.

Straight or Str8 both mean straight.

I perceive because of this accident I am not supposed to do anything right. That is as far as I can see at this stage.

If we are in fact all descendents of the lemur monkeys then the only logical thing we can do is drop our weapons and attempt to understand how we lasted so long. I am aware that is perhaps far beyond the grasp of some to ever imagine. Life is a struggle even if we all physically get along so there is no need to make it more so.

If something isn't attacking me I get concerned.

My needs are exceeded by my wants.

I am searching for a poison mushroom that may accidentally release me from this hell, on purpose.

I declare mental war on the universe. You are my witness.

Post Op Reader Note:

Now that you are finished remind yourself the author did not say anything worth getting emotional about. Remind yourself the author simply created a mental conditioning tool using words. Do not act on anything you have read. Do not make any determinations based on anything you have read. Simply go about your life as if nothing happened because nothing did happen. Do not believe anything you have read but question everything you have read. Fly.

It is done. Tis well.